Breaking Bad

Breaking Bad

Critical Essays on the Contexts, Politics, Style, and Reception of the Television Series

Edited by David P. Pierson

LEXINGTON BOOKS
Lanham • Boulder • New York • Toronto • Plymouth, UK

Published by Lexington Books
A wholly owned subsidiary of Rowman & Littlefield
4501 Forbes Boulevard, Suite 200, Lanham, Maryland 20706
www.rowman.com

10 Thornbury Road, Plymouth PL6 7PP, United Kingdom

British Library Cataloguing in Publication Information Available

Library of Congress Cataloging-in-Publication Data
Breaking bad : critical essays on the contexts, politics, style, and reception of the television series / edited by David P. Pierson.
pages cm
Includes bibliographical references and index.
ISBN 978-0-7391-7924-6 (cloth) -- ISBN 978-0-7391-7925-3 (electronic)
1. Breaking bad (Television program : 2008-) I. Pierson, David, 1958-
PN1992.77.B74B739 2012
791.45'72--dc23
2013030625

∞™ The paper used in this publication meets the minimum requirements of American National Standard for Information Sciences Permanence of Paper for Printed Library Materials, ANSI/NISO Z39.48-1992.

Printed in the United States of America

Contents

Contents

Acknowledgements

Because researching and writing an edited collection of scholarly essays is always a collaborative effort, I would like to take this opportunity to thank a number of people who provided assistance, advice, and encouragement in the publication of this book. Special thanks goes to Lindsey Porambo at Lexington Books for her steady support, assistance, and guidance through the manuscript revision and publication process. Lindsey was always patient, friendly, and responsive in addressing my numerous inquiries. I would also like to thank the manuscript reviewers who provided invaluable input on revisions and all the editorial and marketing staff at Lexington Books for their due diligence and professionalism. My gratitude further goes out to my unwavering chapter contributors whose work lies at the heart of this collection. It probably goes without saying (but I will still say it) that the true measure of a scholarly edited collection resides with the quality of work of its contributors. The book's persuasive diversity of perspectives and creative scholarship to *Breaking Bad* as a complex television series clearly speaks for itself.

Closer to home, I would like to thank my colleagues in the Department of Communication and Media Studies at the University of Southern Maine for their support of my research and scholarship efforts. Finally, I would like to thank my wife, Carol, who provided extraordinary support and encouragement throughout the book's original conception to its final stage. She served as my first editor reading through copious abstract submissions, then providing editorial comments and advice on the submitted chapter manuscripts. This book collection would not be possible without her steadfast love and support.

David P. Pierson
University of Southern Maine, June 2013

Introduction

A pair of pants floats freely in the air gently landing on a desolate desert road only to be run over by a speeding Winnebago. The RV's driver is a middle-aged man wearing a ventilator mask and dressed in only white underwear briefs. In the passenger seat another man either passed out or dead also wears a ventilator mask. Two bodies slide across the floor of the RV until it come it comes to an abrupt stop in a ditch. The driver jumps out gagging from the fumes, puts on a dress shirt, then re-enters to retrieve a video camera, his wallet, and a gun. He records a brief, farewell message to his family, then stands defiantly facing a barrage of oncoming sirens with a large gun in his hand. *Breaking Bad's* pilot episode begins with this disorientating, surreal sequence. We discover through a narrative flashback three weeks earlier how the man (Walter White) came to be in this strange, perilous situation.

Walter, played by Bryan Cranston, is a fifty-year-old, financially-strapped high school chemistry teacher living in Albuquerque, New Mexico who moonlights as a cashier at a car wash to support his pregnant wife, Skyler (Anna Gunn), and his disabled, teenage son, Walter Junior (R.J. Mitte). After he collapses at the car wash and is taken to the hospital by ambulance, the doctor verifies the worst. The non-smoking Walt has inoperable lung cancer and with chemotherapy treatments, he has only a couple of years to live. When Walt tags along on a drug bust led by brother-in-law DEA agent Hank Schrader (Dean Norris), he not only learns about the highly-profitable nature of the illegal methamphetamine (meth) market, but spots an ex-student Jesse Pinkman (Aaron Paul) escaping the crime scene. Later that same day, he approaches Jesse offering to either become his partner or to he will turn him in. Working in a used Winnebago converted to a mobile lab, Walt cooks a batch of crystal meth that Jesse declares is the purest crystal he has ever seen. In search of a distributor, Jesse takes a sample of the crystal to Krazy-8, a local drug dealer who happens to be his former partner's cousin. Cousin Emilio, out on bail, believes that Jesse informed on him during the drug bust and the three drive out to the desert to meet Walt. Emilio recognizes Walt from the drug bust and Krazy-8 threatens to kill Walt and Jesse. Walt barters for his life by promising to show them his chemical artistry. Instead, Walt produces a deadly smoke, then dashes out of the RV. Walt places a ventilator mask on an unconscious Jesse and then places him in the passenger's seat. The subsequent scenes repeat the same actions

shown at the beginning of the episode. While *Breaking Bad*'s story premise of a middle-aged, chemistry teacher turned drug dealer may sound
implausible or even morally objectionable, the series has proven to be a
huge commercial success for the AMC Network. *Breaking Bad* garners an
audience less than the two-million-plus viewers who watch its critically-
acclaimed, original series *Mad Men*. Cranston, who formerly played the
goofy father on *Malcolm in the Middle* (2000-2006), has been praised by
critics for his intense, volatile performance as Walter White. *Breaking Bad*
has received its share of critical accolades including winning six Emmy
Awards and three consecutive wins for Outstanding Actor in a Lead
Drama Series for Cranston and a Best Supporting Actor award for Aaron
Paul (Kroll 2010).

Despite its commercial and critical success, the series has not been
exempt from public criticism. Jill Sergeant (2009) says that "Walt White's
decision to use his chemistry skills to cook up and sell crystal methamphetamine—one of the most highly addictive drugs—has stirred contro-
versy." Some people have expressed concern that the series may be having a bad influence on certain young viewers. Of course *Breaking Bad*
hardly glamorizes the illegal world of meth dealing because so many of
its participants are victims of brutal, untimely deaths, including being
crushed, decapitated, poisoned, shot, stabbed, and strangled. However,
in this same vein, the series has also been criticized for pushing cable
boundaries with its profanity and violent content, as well as its decision
to portray its violent acts as black comedy. Beyond its controversial content, *Breaking Bad* touches on several salient topics, including the social
vulnerability of middle and working-class Americans in a neoliberal
economy and society; fatalism and the moral universe of *Breaking Bad*; the
social morality of the war on drugs; race, Latino Americans, and border
politics; the global economy and crises of masculinity; and life and myth
in the modern American Southwest. Despite its popularity and its association with a diverse range of relevant topics, there have been sparse
scholarly studies of *Breaking Bad*. One such study is David Koepsell and
Robert Arp's *Breaking Bad and Philosophy* (2012), an edited collection of
essays on how Walt and his crimes relate to major philosophical themes
and the central philosophical dilemmas that comprise everyday life. The
book highlights such philosophical questions as can a person be transformed as the result of a few key life choices, does everyone have the
capacity to become ruthless criminal, how would you respond to the
news that you only have six months to live, and does the Heisenberg
Principle of Uncertainty rule our life destinies? Although Koepsell and
Arp's book explores *Breaking Bad* series from several philosophical
stances, it does not examine the series, its visual and aural style, its narratives, and its main characters and their representations from a broad
range of critical perspectives—critical-cultural, gender studies, narrato-

logical, political-economic, sociological—all in an endeavor to delve deeply into the complex world of *Breaking Bad*.

Breaking Bad was created and produced by Vince Gilligan, who served for seven years as a writer and producer for Chris Carter's *The X-Files* (1993-2002). The idea for *Breaking Bad* was born out of a conversation between Gilligan and his friend Thomas Schnauz, who is now a writer on the series. Schnauz had just read a story about a man cooking meth in an apartment complex that sickened children in the apartment above. Saddam Hussein's alleged mobile chemical weapon labs also came in the conversation. The two men eventually came up with the idea of driving around in a mobile lab used to cook meth. A couple days later, Schnauz said he received a call from Gilligan who wanted permission to use the idea to develop into a possible TV series. Cranston says that the term "breaking bad" is a southern colloquialism and it means when someone who has taken a turn off the path of the straight and narrow, when they've gone wrong. And it could be for that day or for a lifetime. Series creator Gilligan, who grew up in Farmville, Virginia, simply defines the term as "to raise hell." Gilligan pitched the idea for the series to AMC executives in 2007. The network was searching for a second original series to go along with *Mad Men*, which made its debut that year. AMC's goal was to develop a new original series that was set in the present so that the network would not be pigeonholed as the home of period television. Programming executives wanted a series concept that would skew male and complement the network's deep library of contemporary action anti-hero movies featuring such stars as Charles Bronson, Clint Eastwood, and Arnold Schwarzenegger. Walter White and Don Draper of *Mad Men* are both "bad boy" anti-hero protagonists; one, a drug dealer, the other, a serial adulterer. AMC might be following a similar programming strategy as the FX network, which has had success by producing original series, like *The Shield* (2002-2008) and *Rescue Me* (2004-2011), based on productive, but severely flawed male protagonists. However, White's character is different from most dramatic television protagonists because his character gradually transforms throughout the course of the series from a timid, ineffectual chemistry teacher to a street-smart, dangerous drug dealer. Don Draper of *Mad Men*, for example, is still pretty much the same charming rake he has been from the start of the series, despite a few fleeting moments of self-doubt and personal confession (Segal 2011).

AMC'S TRANSFORMATION

For most of its first eighteen years, AMC was a premium cable network showing generally unedited, uncut, and uncolored American feature films, largely pre-1950s, without commercial interruption. Its revenue came from cable operators that offered the channel to cable subscribers. However, by the late 1990s, AMC gradually began to place commercials between its movies and then, also within them (Gomery). On September 30, 2002, AMC changed its programming format from a classic movie channel to a more general movie channel airing movies from all eras, with an emphasis of showing recent films from the 1970s, 80s, and 90s. Under this new format, the majority of pre-1970s films were relegated to late nights, mornings, and early afternoons. Kate McEnroe, then president of AMC Networks, cited the lack of cable operator subsidies as the reason for the addition of advertising, and cited ad agencies who insisted on programming relevant to their products' consumers as the reason for the shift to recent movies instead of early classics (Umstead 2002).

Because differentiation is critical within the crowded multichannel cable programming environment, it is crucial for each cable network to construct a distinct brand image. One of the key branding strategies is for networks to produce original TV series and specials. This strategy is especially important because most cable programming consist of off-network TV series and second-run movies. "If a network wants to grow, it must produce original series, which serve to differentiate networks," says Mike Goodman, analyst with the Yankee Group in Boston. "You can only get so big showing network reruns," he said (Whitney 2002). A successful series performs two critical functions for a network — it differentiates you and it builds strong audience loyalty for your network. Peter Liguori, president and CEO for FX Networks, describes the other benefits of networks producing a successful original series: "A hit series can prove the network's value to cable operators (and) send a message to advertisers that it can deliver and help bolster creativity within the creative community." He adds that while FX's first original series was the short-lived, comedy *Son of the Beach* (2000-2001), the hit series *The Shield* about a renegade cop and his squad marked the coming of age of the network along with helping to build the network's brand image as the place for edgy adult-oriented dramatic series (Whitney 2002).

AMC is not new to the game of producing original TV series. From 1996 to 1998, it aired its first original series, *Remember WENN*, a half-hour situation comedy about a radio station during the peak of radio broadcasting hey-day in the 1930s. The series, which was produced to complement the network's showcase of pre-1950s classic Hollywood movies, was well-received by critics and had a loyal cable viewing audience (Owen 1997). Despite its popularity, the series was cancelled at the end of its fourth season primarily because of a change in network management ("AMC pulls plug"). AMC's next original series, *The Lot* (1999-2001), a half-hour situation comedy about the behind-the-scenes actions of a fictional Hollywood film studio in the 1930s lasted only sixteen episodes (Owen 1999).

AMC's transformation from a classic to a general movie format meant facing increased cable competition from other general movie networks, including the USA Network, Turner Network Television, and Turner Broadcasting System. Within this competitive environment, AMC set out to produce original series and specials that would complement its new movie format. In 2003, the network produced the *Sunday Morning Shootout* (2003-2008), a weekly, half-hour talk and interview program hosted by Peter Bart, a film producer and editor-in-chief of *Variety*, and veteran Hollywood film producer Peter Guber. The show was divided into two segments: one where the two hosts discuss an industry topic and the other where they interview a Hollywood actor, director, or producer ("Shootout - AMC"). In 2005, AMC produced *Movies That Shook the World* (2005), a thirteen-part series examining the societal impact of controversial movies and comments from critics, actors, directors, producers, and film scholars highlighting the content and context of such films as D. . Griffith's *The Birth of a Nation* (1915) and James Bridges' *China Syndrome* (1979) ("Movies").

In 2006, AMC finally plunged into producing high-quality original dramas when it aired *Broken Trail*, an original Western miniseries, directed by Walter Hill and starring Robert Duvall and Thomas Haden Church, about a pair of cowboys who become reluctant guardians of a small group of abused and abandoned Chinese women. *Broken Trail* garnered several Emmy Awards including Outstanding Miniseries, Outstanding Lead Actor in a Miniseries or Movie for Robert Duvall, and Outstanding Lead Actor and Actress Awards for Thomas Haden Church and Greta Scacchi ("Emmy" 2007). The network followed up its impressive foray into television drama with the 2007 debut of *Mad Men* (2007-present), an original hour-long dramatic series about a Madison Avenue advertising agency in the early 1960s. The influential series was almost immediately lauded by critics and has won three consecutive Emmy Awards for Outstanding Drama Series and three Golden Globe Awards for Best Television Drama Series. *Mad Men* was created by Matthew Weiner, a former executive producer and writer on HBO's *The Sopranos* (1999-2007), who serves as the series' executive producer and writer on several of its episodes (Edgerton 2010). The established successes of *Mad Men* and later *Breaking Bad* in 2008 have given AMC a reputation close to those of premium cable networks HBO and Showtime, both of which rejected *Mad Men* before it came to the network. Charlie Collier, vice-president and general manager of AMC, says that the network's vast array of themes in its originals—western, period piece, and modern-day drama—are entirely intentional. "If we just did *Mad Men*, we'd be a period-piece network," Collier said. "Well, we're not. The mission is to make sure we build a breadth of originals that really complement what we do best—present a diverse array of the best movies of all time." He adds that AMC intends to maintain a reputation for high quality, original dramatic series and that one cannot air *The Godfather* movie and follow it with an inexpensive reality TV series like *Are You Smarter than a Fifth Grader?* (Bianculli 2008).

John Caldwell argues that broadcast and cable networks regularly employ a series of industrial textual practices—programming events, network IDs, making-ofs, video press kits, promo tapes, and ancillary digital media—to theorize and pronounce its presence in the American multichannel flow, as well as "insider" knowledge to audiences about their programming. He asserts that a critical part of network branding practices is the construction of a brand name identifier and a visual logo to establish an essential foothold within the multichannel clutter of cable programming (Caldwell 2006). After its format change in 2002, AMC Network decided to deemphasize its full name (American Movie Classics) and replaced it with AMC, primarily because the network was no longer pre-1950s classic movie channel like the Turner Classic Movies. As with many cable channels, the network began placing its AMC moniker or "bug" on the lower right corner of the screen during its programming for ease of channel identification by viewers. AMC also began employing "snipes" or animated advertisements popping up on-screen during its programming to promote up-coming programs and program events. AMC created a new slogan "Story Matters Here" to accompany its new logo and to emphasize its expanding reputation as the place for original dramatic TV series and specials. AMC's original series and specials are accompanied by a series of print and video press kits distributed to cable operators and media outlets. The network also heavily promotes the premiere of its original series and specials as a major programming event. For instance, AMC provided audiences with an on-screen countdown clock in the movies preceding the new season premiere episodes of *Mad Men* and *Breaking Bad*.

Internet websites, electronic bulletin boards, and online chat sessions all serve as venues for broadcast and cable networks to mediate knowledge about themselves to their audiences. These sites provide a wealth of ostensible insider material: interviews with cast and crew, production stills and screen images to download, and cyberchats with program stars and producer-writers. He asserts that many shows like *The X-Files* (1993-2002) and *Xena: Warrior Princess* (1995-1999) have actually acknowledged that they have solicited input from fans on scripts and characters (Caldwell 2006). AMC provides a separate series-oriented web-page for each of its original series and specials. *Breaking Bad*'s web-page includes full episodes, sneak peeks of upcoming episodes, behind-the-scenes videos, information on cast and crew, graphic novel games based on series characters, trivia quizzes, criminal aptitude test, press clippings, downloadable series images, link to sign-up for the series newsletter, and series' merchandise and DVDs. While these promotional and marketing texts may often appear as textual distractions from the primacy of the show's main texts—the episodes, nevertheless, they do function to provide new, distinct avenues for audiences into the series while serving to enrich their viewing experiences. Barbara Klinger (1989), in her seminal work on digressions in cinema spectatorship, argues that promotional and advertising materials serve to extend the social life of a primary text (film, TV series) within the competitive capitalist economy. Although network websites tend to make less money than they cost to develop and maintain, they do reap financial benefits from building and sustaining strong viewer loyalties, as well as intensifying the quality demographics that exist for shows like *Mad Men* and *Breaking Bad*.

ANALYZING *BREAKING BAD*

Situated in the American Southwest, one of the nation's fastest growing regions, *Breaking Bad*, which is shot in and around Albuquerque, New Mexico, captures and expresses both the region's dramatic, geographic beauty and its dark, socio-economic undercurrents. Since the passage of NAFTA, the region's long border with Mexico has been the hub of immense commerce and trade both legal and illegal. The modern southwest is on the cusp of an expanding neoliberal economy promoting global trade, increased corporate profits and entrepreneurial initiatives, along with minimizing the government's role in business and everyday life. With the exception of California, it is a region with low taxes, few labor unions, poor farming conditions, and limited government-supported social programs. As such, it is a place with great disparities of wealth between the rich and the poor. Working and middle-class Americans often must work multiple jobs to support their families. Walter White, for example, is an underpaid public school teacher who must work another job after school and on the weekends to support his pregnant wife and his disabled son. The southwest region also contains the nation's largest concentration of resident and immigrant Latino Americans. It is an area rich in the myths and traditions of the Old West, especially those of the western outlaw figure, while busy building new myths and traditions for its inhabitants. Gilligan sets *Breaking Bad* in the heart of the southwest in New Mexico, the self-described "Land of Enchantment." In order to address the complexity of topics and representations in the series, this critical anthology will be divided into three interrelated sections. Each section features a range of interdisciplinary perspectives focusing on the series.

Section one, "The Contexts of *Breaking Bad*" examines how *Breaking Bad* is located in and addresses several contemporary social contexts, including cultural, historic, institutional, and socio-economic. My chapter argues that, through its characters and narratives, the series exemplifies several core neoliberal discourses and policies, especially in the areas of law enforcement and penal law, drug policy and its enforcement, criminality and entrepreneurism, and public schooling. As a public school teacher, Walter White is part of a public institution that is derided by neoliberal critics as bureaucratically incompetent, ineffective, and a danger to the capitalist market and democracy. Through circumstance and choice, White becomes an exemplar of neoliberal entrepreneurism as he transitions into a free-thinking criminal who carefully weighs the risks and benefits of his criminal actions. I further assert that, through the figure of Hank Schrader, *Breaking Bad* reveals the racial assumptions that underpin America's drug policies and their enforcement.

Dustin Freeley places the series in the oft-harried existence of our modern daily lives, which includes social networks, smartphone technologies, and the growing ease with which we multitask. Exploring our modern cultural obsession with economies of "time," Freeley analyzes the ways in which *Breaking Bad* expresses concerns about recouping wasted time, building a surplus of future time, efficiently utilizing present time, and dividing and constructing present time into multiple, simultaneous realities. In examining the commonly associated effects of crystal meth: euphoria, sustained energy, alertness, and a sense of power, the essay contends that these effects reflect latent social desires in our contemporary society. For Walt, facing his own mortality is a prison sentence wherein part of the punishment is recognizing time spent and time remaining. Freeley asserts that Walt's choice to begin "breaking bad" is a symptom of our culture's obsession with controlling, preserving, making up for, and extending time, as well as a side effect in a late capitalist society where time is often synonymous with commerce and wasted time represents lost time.

Locating *Breaking Bad* in the context of modern science and its practices, Alberto Brodesco examines the particular ways in which science is placed, displaced, and misplaced throughout the series. *Breaking Bad* provides its viewers with various legitimate scientific domains, like the high school classroom and the Gray Matter pharmaceutical company, as well as illegitimate ones: the RV, the domestic and industrial drug laboratories. Unlike the fictional mad doctor or scientist who is led by his insane desire to defy nature's boundaries, Walt's goals are more modest in design: he wants to leave his family wealthy when he dies. Following modern science's principle of instrumental rationality brings him to make controversial decisions not only to cook meth but to watch Jesse's girlfriend die or to poison a child. Walt's alias "Heisenberg" provides an interpretive frame for all of Walt's actions putting all of his rational actions under the guise of Heisenberg's "Uncertainty Principle" which maintains that a scientist or meth chemist can never stand outside of their experiments or productions, and every scientist is confronted with the impossibility of directing his actions and thus, is confronted with unpredictability and chaos.

The second section, "The Politics of *Breaking Bad*" investigates how the popular series represents and intersects with the present-day politics of gender, race and ethnicity, able and disabled bodies, and social class. Brian Faucette maintains that the contemporary struggles and frustrations over American masculinity during a time of great cultural, economic, and social change are embodied in the character of Walter White. Relying on R. W. Connell's concept of "hegemonic masculinity," he asserts that Walt, through his transformation into a drug lord and cold-blooded killer, finds freedom from normal domestic obligations and strictures that allow him to attain and recoup a traditional model of masculinity that celebrates aggression, violence, and ruthless behavior. This reclamation of traditional masculinity, albeit by untraditional means, expresses the inner desire of some men to reify what they perceive as having lost in present-day culture.

The politics of race and ethnicity are explored in Andrew Howe's essay on *Breaking Bad*'s heterogeneous representations of Latin American identity. As a border narrative involving the illegal drug trade, many of the show's villains are Latino. However, there is a wide variability in the portrayal of such characters, from the crazed, drug-addicted Tuco to the suave Chilean businessman Gustavo Fring, and from the axe-wielding Salamanca cousins to their wheelchair-bound uncle, Hector. Despite their villainy, these characters are thus humanized in that they do not conform to typical stereotypes usually on display in American television. Other characters within the series round out the project of broad-based depiction. DEA Agent Steve Gomez is a very nurturing character, not exhibiting any of the machismo typically associated with Latino culture. Interestingly, the macho swagger is supplied by Gomez's partner, the Caucasian Hank Schrader.

Breaking Bad is, at one level, a show about the politics and consequences of unhealthy and unruly bodies, bodies that are undisciplined and disordered. Indeed, as the series progresses, Jami Anderson points out that each of the main characters has a body that is unruly or unreliable and each struggles to maintain control over his or her body while presenting a public pretense of control. Throughout the early seasons, Skyler certainly regards herself as a good wife and mother, especially when she is accusing Walt of deceitful behavior. Yet on several occasions, she seemingly cannot stop herself from smoking while pregnant. Walter Jr., whose cerebral palsy render his physical impairments most visible, voices the frustrations of a son who cannot understand the disappearance and reappearance of his father in the family home, or the cold war taking place between his parents. The stammering speech of Walter Jr. perfectly expresses the slurred rage of a character that wants to, but cannot, fully understand or take control of the situation he is in. Through its main characters and narratives, the series illustrates that human lives are by nature unruly lives.

"The Style and Reception of *Breaking Bad*" is analyzed in the book's final section. The series' aural, narrative, and visual stylistics make *Breaking Bad* a distinctive and even ground-breaking program on cable television. Pierre Barrette and Yves Picard contend that the series distinctive narrative style, which is dominated by non-verbal scenes and rich, stylistic imagery, is part of an emergent second degree style in which images prevail over sound, visuality over orality. The second degree style is demarcated by an enunciative logic wherein meaning is found through the accumulation and dissemination of layers of self-reflexive structures. *Breaking Bad* is a niche market product with content to provide entertain and a message to the public while the form is designed for the critical few who can discern its complex layers of meanings. One of the notable stylistic and narrative features of the series is its enigmatic teaser segments at the beginning of each episode. The teaser not only functions as an opening but also has significance in itself. Rossend Sanchez Baro asserts that the teaser expresses two of the show's main characteristics: genre and style hybridization and the representation of the surreal in everyday life. Baro theorizes that *Breaking Bad*'s teasers not only serve to disorient and confuse audience expectations at the beginning of each episode, but can be seen as a segment that concentrates and expresses the essence of the episode and indeed the series.

Place as phenomenological and rooted in human experience is a stylistic feature in *Breaking Bad*. Ensley Guffey examines the use of place in the series as a central element of the show's narrative demonstrating that the very nature of a human understanding of place allows certain key locations to function as vehicles for character and plot development and integral parts of storytelling in and of themselves. He points out that inanimate spaces are transformed in the series. For seasons one through three, a 1980s era Winnebago becomes a space for revelation, murder, and relationship-building between Walt and Jesse. Whereas in seasons three through four, a red basement filled with stainless steel, industrial equipment becomes the central site of narrative and character contention. Guffey shows that the series' producers tap into the audience's shared sense of place as meaningful space in order to create a depth of intentional emotional realism rarely seen in television. An additional distinctive style feature of *Breaking Bad* is its use of sound, music, and silence. Carlo Nardi analyzes the series' construction of a distinct soundspace with a particular focus on songs and how they serve metadiegetically to comment on the story. He posits that these metadiegetic songs, by drawing attention to themselves and playing with cinematic conventions, possibly prevent any identification with either the narrative, the characters or both, to engage the audience member in what he calls "complicit identification" with the producer or director's perspective, therefore appealing primarily to audience members with a strong critical sense.

Instead of being a mere by-product of the narrative, Deidre Pribram maintains that emotions can be understood as a form of narrative action that is as significant and determining as any physical action. Emotions are mobile and circulate within a narrative producing social relations by enabling cultural meanings to be established and exchanged. Relying on these two concepts, Pribram analyzes two narrative sequences from *Breaking Bad* in order to understand how they function as emotional, dramatic acts conveyed in the narrative, how they concern the circulation and exchange of emotions between characters, and how they serve to establish cultural meanings and emotional significance for audiences.

Because *Breaking Bad* is a richly textured, television drama, this edited collection can only proffer a critical glimpse into the cultural, economic, and social contexts, representational politics, and aesthetic style of the series. More research is needed on the fictional women of *Breaking Bad* and with the series' reception among a diverse array of audiences, along with how AMC engages with these audiences through its website and a variety of industry-produced paratexts, which include blog and talks, interviews, newsletters, episode previews, games, and podcasts. Of course the fan-based and produced paratexts are also fertile textual resources for investigating the range and character of meanings that audiences construct of the series and its characters. Emerging in the depths of the Great Recession (2007-2009) and in a post-welfare, neoliberal state, *Breaking Bad* expresses many of the social and economic struggles of a middle and working class America where only the ruthless capitalist entrepreneurs, whether legitimate or illegitimate, are handsomely rewarded and the timid often find themselves marginalized or even victimized in a winner-take-all modern society. Walt, in the pilot episode, explains to his students his views about chemistry as the study of change involving complex processes of growth, decay, and change. While he is talking about the subject of chemistry, he could just as well be describing not only his character but the narrative dynamics of *Breaking Bad*. As Quentin Huff (2011) aptly points out, the audience becomes pseudo-scientists observing the physical and psychological changes that occur in *Breaking Bad*'s characters, most notably Walt who shaved his head after chemotherapy, grew a goatee, and becomes more aggressive and assertive in his demeanor. *Breaking Bad*, through its analogizing the series title ("Br" in Breaking, "Ba" in Bad) along with the names of actors and actresses with the first two letters of the periodic elements table, invites its audience to perceive of the series' characters as dramatic elements that combine, like elements in a new compound, in unexpected and unanticipated ways and conditions, like the turbulent, unlikely pairing of Walt and Jesse, or the dissolution, then resolution of Walt and Skyler's marriage into a tense, business partnership. Every change creates a reaction in the series' universe, "the consequences of which might be as minor as a young child finding a gas mask left behind (from) one of Walter and

Jesse's cooking sessions, or as major as an air traffic control worker's pain over his daughter's overdose causing an airplane collision that kills 167 people" (Huff 2011). Throughout the series, the characters repeatedly change and these alterations invariably produce reactions from other characters and thereby, establish distinct dramatic situations. This edited collection provides a range of critical lens and perspectives by which to explore and examine *Breaking Bad's* transformative characters and narrative moments located within a series of intricate social, political, and cultural contexts.

WORKS CITED

"AMC pulls plug on 'Remember WENN.'" *Albany Times Union.* (28 September 1998): C-4.

Bianculli, David. "AMC's Brand-Smart Strategy." Broadcasting and Cable. (29 September 2008): 40.

Caldwell, John T. "Critical Industrial Practice: Branding, Repurposing, and the Migratory Patterns of Industrial Texts." *Television and New Media.* 7:2. (May 2006): 99-134.

Edgerton, Gary R. "Introduction: When Our Parents Became Us," in *Mad Men: Dream Come True TV*, edited by Gary R. Edgerton, xxi-xxxvi. New York: I.B. Tauris, 2010.

"Emmy Winners." *Pittsburgh Post-Gazette.* 17 Sept. 2007: C3.

Gomery, Douglas. "American Movie Classics." The Museum of Broadcast Communications. 2013. http://www.archives.museum.tv/eotvsection.php?entrycode=americanmovi.

Huff, Quentin B. "Characters, Compounds, and the Study of Change in 'Breaking Bad: Season 3.'" *PopMatters.* 8 June 2011. http://www.popmatters.com/pm/column/142497-characters-compounds-the-study-of-change-breaking-bad/.

Koepsell, David R. and Robert Arp, eds. *Breaking Bad and Philosophy.* Chicago: Open Court, 2012.

Klinger, Barbara. "Digressions at the Cinema: Reception and Mass Culture." *Cinema Journal.* 28:4. (Summer 1989): 3-19.

Kroll, Justin. "Aaron Paul's 'Bad' Trip, 'Breaking' Character was Almost Killed Off." *Daily Variety.* 308:40. (30 August 2010): 18.

"Movies That Shook The World." IMDb: Internet Movie Database. 2012. http://www.imdb.com/title/tt0390776/.

Owen, Rob. "AMC Gives Its Quirky Series, 'The Lot,' A Quick Run." *Pittsburgh Post-Gazette.* (19 August 1999): D-1.

———. "AMC's 'Remember WENN' is a Swell Piece of Work." *Albany Times Union.* (6 July 1997): 45.

Segal, David. "Art of Darkness." *The New York Times.* 10, July 2011. 18-23.

Sergeant, Jill. "From Bad to Worse for TV's 'Breaking Bad' Dad." *Reuters.com.* U.S. edition. 3 March 2009. http://www.reuters.com/article/2009/03/03/television-breakingbad- idUSN2628364020090303.

"Shootout - AMC." IMDb: Internet Movie Database. 2012. http://www.imdb.com/title/tt0489613/.

Umstead, Thomas R. "AMC To Move in New Direction." *Multichannel News.* 23:19 (13 May 2002): 90.

Whitney, Daisy. "Original Series Help Cement a Network's Brand." *Electronic Media.* 21:18 (6 May 2002): 28.

I

The Contexts of *Breaking Bad*

Breaking Bad (AMC). Season 1 Episode 1: "Pilot." Airdate: January 20, 2008.
Shown: Bryan Cranston.
AMC/Photofest © AMC. Reprinted by permission of Photofest.

ONE

Breaking Neoliberal? Contemporary Neoliberal Discourses and Policies in AMC's *Breaking Bad*

David P. Pierson

Faced with a terminal illness and a strong desire to take care of his family financially long after his death, Walter White (Brian Cranston), a mild-mannered, put-upon New Mexico high school chemistry teacher, begins producing and selling crystal methamphetamine or meth. He enlists the aid of former student Jesse Pinkman (Aaron Paul) to help him market and distribute his high-end product to large illegal drug operators in the American Southwest. While *Breaking Bad's* story premise may seem particularly unsavory given the dangerously addictive nature of crystal meth, Cranston's intensely intelligent and empathetic performance coupled with a large dose of dark humor have made the show a hit with cable television audiences. The black comedic elements are evident in the episode "The Cat's in the Bag . . ." (1/27/08), where Walt and Jesse are faced with the gruesome tasks of disposing of a dead body and dispatching a drug dealer who tried to kill them. Walt decides that the best way to get rid of the body is to dissolve it in an acid bath. Jesse, however, botches Walt's specific equipment requests which leads to the upstairs bathtub crashing through the second floor and depositing mounds of partially dissolved body parts splattered all over the first floor.

Besides providing viewers with a dramatic and darkly humorous experience, *Breaking Bad* also addresses contemporary discourses about neoliberalism and their effects on society. Before exploring these issues, it is useful to define the core beliefs that underscore neoliberalism, as well as looking at how it has been investigated in television studies. The central idea underscoring the neoliberal ideology is that the market should be the organizing agent for nearly all social, political, economic, and personal decisions. According to Robert McChesney (1999), initiating with the Thatcher and Reagan Administrations, for the past three decades, "neo-liberalism has been the dominant global political economic trend adopted by political parties of the center and much of the traditional left and the right" (McChesney 7). On the political front, neoliberalism is generally characterized as "free market policies that encourage private enterprise and consumer choice, reward personal responsibility and entrepreneurial initiative, and undermine the dead hand of an incompetent, bureaucratic government that is incapable of doing good for its citizenry" (McChesney 7). Increasingly, neoliberal ideology has eroded the powers of democratic institutions to affect public policy that can be shown to have a negative impact on "the market." This chapter argues that the TV series *Breaking Bad* intersects with neoliberal policies and discourses, and exemplifies several of its detrimental social and political effects.

NEOLIBERALISM AND TELEVISION

On network television, neoliberalism has primarily been explored in reality TV programming. Laurie Ouellette (2004), for example, examines how the popular syndicated, daytime courtroom program *Judge Judy* with its reputation of "zero tolerance for nonsense" interconnects with neoliberal policies and discourses in the 1990s. She asserts that *Judge Judy* uses the courtroom as a symbol of state authority to foster the outsourcing of governmental operations and to promote the transition to a neoliberal society. Ouellette claims that court programs like *Judge Judy* make use of the daily trials of everyday working-class women to instruct television viewers on how to function, without state invention, and become a self-enterprising and self-sufficient citizen. Shows like *Judge Judy* do not so much challenge existing democratic ideals as much as they construct new models of neoliberal citizenship "that complement the privatization of public life, the collapse of the welfare state, and the discourse of individual choice and personal responsibility" (Ouellette 232). Ouellette, working in conjunction with James Hay, continued to explore how reality TV constructs "good" neoliberal citizens in their 2008 study *Better Living Through Reality TV*. Reality TV primarily functions as a cultural technology to cultivate good citizenship through self-governance. Reality TV offers instruction and aid in managing lifestyles, health, and finances as well as providing people with ways to improve their homes and personal appearances. Reality TV does not so much promote a neoliberal ideology as it provides accessible models of citizenship for neoliberal social structures. Although reality programming often focuses on individual crises and concerns, it rarely addresses the social inequalities of socioeconomic status, race, and gender that may have contributed to these "individual" problems (Ouellette and Hay, 2-5).

Similarly, Toby Miller (2006) finds that though reality TV and news programming excel as models of commercialized entertainment and consumption, their depoliticized discourse does little to engage audiences with the serious problems confronting our world. Miller draws on examples from news coverage of the war on terror, food and weather coverage programming to reveal that audiences are narrowly viewed as individualistic consumers and denied access to the information they need as citizens. He asks why does the Weather Channel fail to cover the "everyday risks posed by global warming" and why does the Food Network ignore pressing health issues such as childhood obesity, genetically modified crops, and the fast food industry? The model of citizenship promoted by television's news and reality programming is one that focuses on neoliberal individual choices and responsibilities, and is completely devoid of political or social issues. Likewise, Janice Peck (2008) maintains that "neoliberalism's defining political practice is precisely that of de-politicization." Peck examines how Oprah Winfrey's iconic rise and success on daytime television was due, in part, to the neoliberal social climate from which she emerged in the United States. Winfrey rebranded her daytime talk show away from "trash TV" to become the nexus of a positive, self-empowering therapeutic force for her regular TV viewers and devotees. Peck declares that Winfrey's status as a cultural icon helped to construct and promote a neoliberal ideology among her devoted fans and followers.

A few scholars have explored neo-liberalism in fictional dramatic programming. Eric Beck (2011) investigates how the character of Omar Little in HBO's *The Wire* both corresponds to, and departs from, the neoliberal demands of capitalism. Omar as a subject resides in the middle among a plethora of organizing stratum that includes the police, drug gangs, drug addicts, government, labor unions, teachers, and administrators. Beck shows that, with the exception of Omar and his band of renegade thieves, the series' other characters (e.g., cops, criminals, addicts, politicians, teachers) are all circumscribed within the institutional bounds of neoliberal capitalism. Through its characters, *The Wire* illustrates how neoliberal capitalism effaces distinctions between work, life, leisure, love, and politics. Beck finds optimism in Omar's flawed, but defiant character along with the fact that capitalism must rely on a subjectivity outside of itself in order to produce and reproduce its social relations.

Neoliberal discourses concerning social risk are present in the popular *C.S.I.* television franchise. Michele Byers and Val Johnson (2009) claim that *C.S.I.*, with its focus on forensic technologies to solve crimes, reinforces the notion that citizens have been abandoned by the state, especially the police and court system, and that risk is a part of everyday life. In most episodes, crimes are resolved less through litigation and sentencing than through the identification of the elusive 'truth' about the criminal and how he or she did it—which is often a moral lesson in the idiosyncratic nature of risk and the impossibility of protecting oneself from it. If lawyers and the police have failed us, *C.S.I.* reminds us that we still have the truth of the body which can only be made to speak for the victim by forensic science. Byers and Johnson find that *C.S.I.* represents the neoliberal concept of "governing through crime" because it accepts the notion that crime cannot be completely controlled and is the act of rational, calculating social actors (xv). *Breaking Bad* shares a similar conception of crime and criminality. Neo-liberalism, in general, refuses to acknowledge that the social is a realm that informs human action, like crime, and is the necessary domain for resolving social conflicts and finding solutions. This study examines how *Breaking Bad* exemplifies neoliberal discourses and policies in the areas of criminality and law enforcement, drug policy and enforcement, entrepreneurism, and public schooling.

NEOLIBERALISM, PUBLIC SCHOOLS, AND WALTER'S MALADIES

Public schools have always been at the center of neoliberalism's project to create rational individuals who can compete in the marketplace along with refashioning the ways in which Western democracies function. Under Keynesian welfare policies, social injustices and inequalities are reduced through the intervention of government-sponsored social programs and the redistribution of resources and power within society. Under neoliberal post-welfare policies, social injustices and inequalities are the result of individual inadequacies, which cannot be solved by increasing individual dependency on social welfare, but rather by requiring individuals to become fully productive members of the workforce. Since employability and economic productivity are the main goals, there is less of a concern with producing a liberally well-rounded and civic-minded person through the educational system. Education serves the instrumental goal of developing the required skills and knowledge for a person to become an economically productive member of the workforce. David Hursh (2005) maintains that neoliberal governments seek both to reduce the overall public funding of education while at the same time reorganizing it to fit the needs of the economy. Neoliberal critics blame schools for society's injustices and inequalities, while at the same time supporting taxation and reduction in social spending policies that exacerbate these inequalities. One recurring argument among these critics is to blame public schools for not providing enough skilled and well-educated workers for industry and the economy. This claim allows these critics to shift the responsibility for economic inequality away from corporations and politicians, and place it squarely on the educational system. Since public schools are the root cause for most social problems, educational reform efforts seem politically neutral, publically acceptable, and inevitable for the good of society (Hursh).

Hursh says that these educational reforms have been characterized by efforts to standardize the curriculum, to implement standardized testing to hold students, teachers, and schools accountable, to increase school choice and to privatize the public educational funding provision. Many social critics have pointed out the contradiction between these neoliberal reforms that promote competition and innovation between schools while at the same time limiting innovation through standardized curriculum and assessment requirements. Under George W. Bush's No Child Left Behind (NCLB) Act, the state serves as the central regulator of education markets through its increased intervention in state education through curricular standards, testing, and funding. Public schools are no longer controlled at the local level, but rather through local decisions based on requirements of state and federal governments (Hursh).

With the state's persistent intervention into local schools, many teachers feel constrained in their classrooms and wary of introducing any new teaching methods that may interfere with the continual practice of preparing students for standardized tests. These tests have become the instrumental measure of a teacher's performance and a determinant in teacher promotion and retention. Teachers, for the most part, are restricted to teaching the standard curriculum and preparing their students for standardized evaluations. Henry Giroux (2010) points out that when educational reform neglects to connect learning to the public spheres of politics, critical thinking, and democracy, "it loses its hold on preparing young people for a democratic future and condemns them to a world where the only values that matter are individual acquisition, unchecked materialism, economic growth, and a winner-take-all mentality" (368). Under these reforms, the teacher's role as an active, creative thinker is greatly diminished as they find themselves reduced to being mere cogs in a machine driven by an inflexible system of standardized testing and curriculum. It is not surprising that most teachers will feel undervalued and demoralized by these intrusive neoliberal educational reform and accountability efforts.

An early scene of Walter shows him struggling in vain to motivate a class of seemingly disinterested and bored high school students to the wonders of chemistry. Earlier in the same pilot episode (1/20/08), we see the early-rising Walt staring at a plaque on the wall of his home awarded to him in 1985 for his contribution to research that led to the Nobel Prize in chemistry. One can surmise that because he is married and has a son with cerebral palsy, he gave up the lucrative, entreprenuerial field of scientific research in favor of the security of a teaching position. As a school teacher, Walt is part of a public institution probably most derided by neoliberal critics as incompetent, ineffective, and an implicit threat to individual freedom, even democracy. Neoliberal ideologues often scorn the civil servants who work for public institutions. And, while politicians and civic leaders frequently laud the importance of school teachers in our society, at the same time they reduce funding to school districts and favor privately-run charter schools. The reality for most teachers, especially for those living in the American Southwest, is a career marked by low-pay and limited job benefits. Walt has to work a part-time job as a cashier at a car wash after school and on the weekends to support his family. When one of the car wash employees does not show up for his shift, Walt's boss presses him to fill in by washing cars. Walt is humiliated when two of his students laugh, take pictures, and poke fun at the sight of Mr. White washing their car.

Walt is a tired, unhappy, overworked, and emasculated middle-aged man. Skyler (Anna Gunn), his pregnant wife, switches out his breakfast bacon for veggie bacon to lower his cholesterol, repeatedly reminds him to do home chores, tells him to stand up to his boss at the car wash about not working late, and chides him for being late for his surprise fiftieth birthday party. At the party, Walt is further emasculated by his bombastic brother-in-law Hank Schrader (Dean Norris), who is a DEA (Drug Enforcement Agency) agent and supervisor, is showing off his Glock 22 handgun to Walt's son. Hank hands the gun to a hesitant Walt and then comments about the absurdity of the sight with Walt holding a firearm. Hank, who clearly relishes the attention he receives at being a federal agent, interrupts Walt's party to view himself being interviewed on a television news story concerning a DEA bust of a meth lab in which agents seized over seven-hundred thousand dollars in cash. Hank, noting Walt's interest in the bust, offers him a ride-along during their next drug bust. He follows up his offer with a hearty laugh saying that Walt needs to put a little excitement in his stale life. Following the party, Walt's emasculation is culminated in bed when Skyler both sexually satisfies him as a personal birthday present while at the same time attending to her bid on an item from an Internet auction site on her laptop. In the bedroom, Walt is as passive as he is in his life. He appears patient and grateful to receive the sexual attention, even if it is obligatory, from his preoccupied wife. The pilot episode suggests that Walt is suffering from a personal crisis of masculinity and that it is likely linked to his regret in not taking the risks of becoming a research scientist combined with his dependence on the staid security of a low-paying public sector job.

Walt's moral and psychological maladies assume a distinct physical form. Earlier, on the same day as his birthday party, he collapses washing cars at the car wash. On the way to the hospital, Walt asks the ambulance attendant to let him out because he has terrible health insurance. Walt learns that he has inoperable, advanced stage lung cancer. Despite Susan Sontag's (2001) admonition to not perceive of physical illness in metaphoric terms, one cannot help but think that Walt's body is revolving against his systemic passivity and inability to assert his will in his life.

Sontag argues that cancer has become the predominant disease metaphor in our culture. It is considered a disease of repression, or inhibited passion. The cancer sufferer characteristically suppresses emotion, which after many years emerges from the unconscious self as malignant growth (Sontag). Metaphorically, one could say that Walt's body is revolting against his repressive nature and lifestyle, and a last warning to change his life. Cancer, of course, is associated with death and is disturbing to its victims because it reminds them that their death is imminent.

NEOLIBERALISM, CRIMINALITY, AND ENTREPRENEURISM

Classical liberalism and the welfare state era conceived of crime as an aberrant event that can only be resolved through the proper functioning and direct intervention of such social institutions as the family, education, and job opportunities. The criminal was a social deviant who diverged established social norms. The welfare state believed that crime can only be reduced through state intervention and the criminal can be socially rehabilitated to fit back into normal society. In contrast, neoliberal criminology disassociates itself from any social, psychological, and biological explanations of crime and criminal behavior (Lemke 2001). Crime is viewed as a routine event committed by persons who make a particular choice among many choices. Neoliberal criminologists believe the crime can occur anywhere and can never be completely eliminated. The only ways to reduce crime is through individual vigilance, surveillance, penal disincentives, and proper zoning in potential high crime areas (Herbert and Brown 2006).

Under neoliberal criminology, the criminal is not a product of a psychological disorder or a genetic defect but rather is a typical person. The criminal is a rational-economic actor who contemplates and calculates the risks and the rewards of his actions. Crime is no longer a deviant activity outside the mainstream market, but is rather one market among others. Neoliberal penal theory controls and regulates the market for crime by increasing the costs or penalties of committing crime and accepts the fact that crime cannot completely be eliminated from society (Lemke). Examples of neoliberal penal reforms include mandatory imprisonment sentences, such as the "Three Strikes and You're Out" law, to the popular "Zero Tolerance" school policies for students caught with any weapon (Wacquant 2009; Ismaili 2003). Loic Wacquant (2009) asserts that the neoliberal turn in penal theory with its strict penal categories, practices and policies have led to the formation of a "grand penal state" in the United States. For the past twenty-five years, the prison population has increased fivefold and now encompasses seven million Americans which corresponds to one adult male in twenty and one black man in three. Wacquant argues that the rise of a penal state in the United States is not a respond to the rise of crime, which remained constant in the time period, but rather is a response to the social dislocations caused by the decline of the welfare state and the insecurities associated with low wage labor for citizens trapped at the bottom of a polarizing class structure (xiv-xv).

At the center of neo-liberalism's conception of subjectivity is the concept of self-care or the accepted premise that each person is responsible for him or herself. Individuals must assume responsibility for their well-being and personal development in a market-driven society. The individual must take responsibility for his or her well-being and development. Thomas Lemke (2001), examining Foucault's lectures on the discourses of neoliberal governmentality, says that neoliberal forms of government do not necessarily lead to the state assuming a reduced role in social life. In fact, the state devises new strategies for leading and controlling individuals without being responsible for them. Neoliberal governments function to produce self-governing individuals while shifting the responsibility for such social risks as illness, unemployment, crime and poverty, and social life in general into the domain of personal self-care (Lemke).

Under neoliberal subjectivity, labor is not perceived as an abstract element purchased on the market and attached to the production of a specific commodity, but rather as "human capital" that is inextricably tied to the individual worker. For neoliberals, labor is a subjective choice among many other activities for people to choose from in their daily lives. In choosing labor, a person is conceived as an entrepreneur who invests his human capital to produce an income to finance his interest in other activities for his personal development and pleasure. Lemke refers to neo-liberalism's focus on the caring of the self and producing a surplus-value of capital as "entrepreneurism" (197-99) Neo-liberalism seeks to construct practical subjects whose moral quality consists of their ability to rationally assess the costs and benefits of any particular action among alternative acts. Neo-liberalism promotes individuals to conceive of themselves as entrepreneurs in every facet of their lives (Lemke). Within this scenario, crime is just another activity among many to choose from and a criminal entrepreneur can be seen as a person who invests his human capital to produce a surplus-value of capital to partake in his or her personal interests.

The criminal serves as an imaginary figure for revenge fantasies in neo-liberalism. Jodi Dean (2008) theorizes that the criminal stands in for the unpredictable risk and intolerable loss within neo-liberalism's "free trade fantasy" of the market as a place where "everyone wins." Because the criminal is less a person than an image of horrifying loss and deprivation, he must be punished and society must be protected from his presence. I do, however, argue that the neoliberal criminal serves a much more complicated role than representing the horror of losing in the market (Dean). The criminal entrepreneur who builds a criminal empire from the ground up serves as a fantasy figure of American capitalism. The classic Hollywood gangster of the 1930s exemplifies a twisted version of the traditional Horatio Alger American success story. This character is traditionally a newly landed immigrant from "Old Europe" who comes to America to socially advance himself through hard work, perseverance, love of family, and a willingness to break the law and profit from areas outside the legitimate bounds of society. Hollywood's movie gangsters are "neoliberal America's poster-children" because they express the American success myth of self-improvement with minimal state involvement and liberated from the moral prudence and self-restraints associated with American Puritanism (McCalmont). The gangster readily takes what he wants from others, whether through extortion or hostile takeover, exemplifies capital accumulation in its most primitive form. The cinematic gangster reminds us that self-interest and avarice reside in the heart of modern capitalism.

After Walt learns that he has terminal cancer, he decides to become a criminal drug producer by entering the lucrative meth market. Unlike his low-paying teaching position, Walt is able to gainfully profit directly from his chemistry knowledge by producing high quality, potent crystal meth, which becomes the most sought after product in the American Southwest. As a successful gangster, Walt exemplifies the tenets of neoliberal entrepreneurism. He carefully weighs the risks and benefits of all of his strategic business actions. For instance, it is Walt who convinces Jesse that it is worth the physical risks of doing business with the ruthless, vicious Tuco (Raymond Cruz) in order to distribute their product in bulk, rather than selling small bags on the street. And, although Tuco and his men physically assault Jesse, Walt fearlessly demands that Tuco pay for the meth he stole from Jesse plus fifteen thousand for Jesse's pain and suffering. Also, when one of Jesse's street dealers is robbed by a drug-addicted couple, it is Walt who tells him (Jesse) that he must exact street justice for the couple's crime. Walt bluntly makes his point by handing Jesse a gun and telling him to handle it. Walt understands the brutal code of the streets that if they do not punish people who steal from them, then they will be easy targets for every drug addict and felon in Albuquerque.

In the illegal drug economy, dominating a market means controlling territory through physical violence and intimidation. Law enforcement agencies, whether local or federal, function in a pure adversarial role in that they do not want to regulate the illegal market, they want to eliminate it. They want to eradicate it because of the implied moral and social threat the market represents to the dominant capitalist market. However, the illegal drug market and how it is operates has more in common with the vicious nature of modern capitalism than any other system. In a sense, *Breaking Bad*'s criminal market with its constantly changing market territories and wealth, its winner-take-all ethos, and unwanted government intrusion (law enforcement agencies) into its operations represents the brutalities best associated with the global, neoliberal marketplace.

As a successful entrepreneur, Walt's primary concern is maximizing his profits and protecting them from the prying eyes of government officials. Of course, he also has the added incentive that if his massive income is detected by the authorities, then it may lead to an investigation that will reveal his criminal activities. When one of Jesse's street dealers is arrested, Walt meets Saul Goodman (Bob Odenkirk), a local, sleazy criminal attorney, who, referencing *The Godfather*, offers to be Tom Hagen to Walt's Vito Corleone.[1] Saul becomes a business partner and sets up Walt and Jesse with a lucrative transaction with Gustavo "Gus" Fring (Giancarlo Esposito), the owner of a chain of fast food chicken restaurants called Los Pollos, to produce thirty eight pounds of meth for $1.2 million. Saul shows Walt the mechanics of money laundering to provide the appearance that Walt's money derives from legitimate sources. Once Skyler discovers Walt's secret life, she reveals her strong business acumen for hiding their illegal assets by buying a local car wash as a vehicle to launder their monies. Neo-liberalism's liberalization and deregulation of banking and financial laws have led to the increase of money laundering, especially in Latin American countries. While money laundering is an illegal activity, it does share affinities with rapid monetary exchanges and established tax haven countries, which have become common practices of global corporations in neoliberal societies.

The neoliberal entrepreneur par excellence in *Breaking Bad* is the enigmatic Gus Fring. Gus's public image is one of a benevolent, local businessman and community leader. He serves as the main supporter of a local charity race and never hesitates to give his time or money for a worthy social cause. In essence, Gus assumes the appearance of a compassionate businessman, a character type best lauded by welfare era liberalism. However, beneath the surface, lies the cold heart and rational, calculating head of a neoliberal criminal entrepreneur who uses his fleet of Los Pollos trucks to distribute meth across the southwest. Gus runs a multi-million dollar drug empire that has enough capital to build Walt a state-of-the-art manufacturing lab in the sub-level of a large commercial dry cleaning plant. As Hank later learns, Gus's operation is global in scope because the dry cleaning plant is a corporate subsidiary of a German conglomerate. When the circumstances call for it, Gus is capable and willing to commit horrendous acts of physical violence to preserve and strengthen his criminal empire. Gus, in "Box Cutter" (7/17/11), coolly puts on a hazmat suit and severs the carotid arteries of one of men who bleeds to death in front of a tied-up Walt and Jesse. Without fanfare, he coldly sacrifices one of his best men to set an example for Walt and Jesse of the fate that awaits them if they do not follow his orders.

Directly below drug cartels and large-scale operators, like Gus Fring, are the smaller drug entrepreneurs and dealers. In Albuquerque, the criminal drug market is dominated by undereducated, poor Latino Americans and white males who are lured by the quick cash and flashy lifestyle over low-wage employment. The white males usually serve a supporting role to the drug operations and/or act as consumers. Both of these groups are socially marginalized by a mainstream neoliberal global economy that only offers them low-wage jobs with little opportunities for social advancement. The American Southwest, with its sparsely populated rural areas, lack of social services, unproductive farming, weakened labor unions, and close proximity to the Mexican border, is one of the prime regions for the production and distribution of meth (Pine 2007). Latino American males are distinguished by an extreme form of "machismo," which includes toughness, aggressiveness, sexism, and risk-taking behavior (Saez, et al. 2009). The impoverished whites emulate the mannerisms, language, and fashion associated with African American hip hop culture. The media dominated culture that surrounds these young men is filled with images of aggressive drug lords and vicious gangsters,[2] which affects and reflects their self-images and social behaviors. Because of these influences, the criminal drug culture in *Breaking Bad* is coded as hyper-masculine with an emphasis on power, dominance, and aggression.

Methamphetamine or meth has been called a neoliberal drug because it provides low-wage workers with more energy to work longer hours. It enables them to work fourteen-hour days and stay awake for as long as three weeks. Jason Pine (2007) asserts that the illegal meth is part of a much wider range of "performance enhancers" that have become both the fuel and the product of the neoliberal fetish of productivity and achievement within "the market." These chemical boosters include everything from Starbucks double espressos to highly-caffeinated, energy drinks, steroids to Viagra, Xanax, and Adderall. Within this expanding legal narco-capitalism, workplace and everyday pharmacological doping have become normalized, expected, and in the case of students required to take attention deficit disorder medication, even mandatory. And, while increased legal restrictions on the sale of cold medication has made the rural production of meth more difficult, Wall Street brokers and college students are still able to obtain Adderall with few complications (Pine).

"I am awake," declares Walt to Jesse, following his decision to begin cooking meth. Walt's new vocation provides him with the excitement and renewed desire that has been missing from his stultifying middle-class existence.[3] Walt's terminal condition and criminal entrepreneurship, liberate him from his former staid existence and frees him to express his repressed aggression. At the car wash, Walt explodes when his boss asks him to wipe down cars again. Walt assaults the display racks. In another scene, when Walt and his wife Skyler take Walter Jr. (R.J. Mitte) to buy pants, some young guy makes fun of Junior in front of his friends. Walt responds by knocking the guy to the ground. The old Walt would have walked out without saying anything and burned with internal rage. At the end of his first day as a meth cook, Walt is both physically and emotionally shaken, but also invigorated. Back at home, he meets his wife's troubled inquiries with atypical sexual aggression. For Walt, neo-liberal entrepreneurism restores his sense of normative masculinity and provides him with new-found confidence. Over time, as Walt finds himself becoming a full-fledged criminal, his cancer eventually goes into remission and his doctor is impressed with his recovery.

Neo-liberalism's economic-rational individualism is conflated with aggressive, hyper-masculine behavior in the series.[4] Neo-liberalism, with its prime concentration on promoting aggressive individualism and self-interest, does not leave much space for non-aggressive emotions, like compassion and humility, nor for socially-directed actions such as charity, working for social and economic justice, and community-building. Neo-liberalism's focus on the primacy of self-care and entrepreneurship make it easier to attain support for cutting social services and public programs that do not directly support or promote the self-interests of the economic-rational individual.

The Drug Enforcement Agency (DEA) agents are also characterized by their aggressive and hyper-masculine behavior. With their male-bonding and masculine bravado, the DEA agents are social counterparts to the drug kingpins and dealers they are investigating. Similar to Eric Beck's description of the social structures of *The Wire*, both groups are circumscribed within the bounds of neoliberal capitalism (Beck). While the drug dealers are filling a demand within an illegitimate market, the agents are busy protecting the legitimate market economy and society. The DEA agents' aggressive behavior is best epitomized by Walt's gregarious brother-in-law, DEA Supervisor Agent Hank Schrader. At Walt's birthday party, Hank repeatedly berates Walt's masculinity. In the episode "Grilled" (3/15/09), Hank boasts about a drug raid explicitly tying his sexual virility to his actions. During an intervention orchestrated by Skyler to persuade Walt to undergo treatment for his cancer, Hank is only able to relate to Walt's situation through lame sports metaphors about winning and losing.

Beneath Hank's tough, immodest exterior lies a deep undercurrent of emotional vulnerability. When Hank goes on a DEA stakeout in Mexico, he spots a tortoise with Tortuga's, a drug informant, severed head attached to it. The words "HOLA DEA" are painted on the shell. To his colleagues' amusement, Hank edges away in disgust. Seconds later, the tortoise explodes killing several of the DEA El Paso agents. Hank's near-death experience shakes him to the core. Later, when Hank is asked to work again with the El Paso Office as part of a promotion, he begins having anxiety attacks. He makes excuses to his boss about not leaving claiming that he is pursuing new leads on a big drug case. Hank's boss decides to give the promotion to Hank's partner Gomez (Steven Queza-da). Marie, Hank's wife, begs him to share his feelings about Gomez taking the promotion Hank was offered. Marie tells him that after his near-death experience, it is no wonder he does not want to return to El Paso. Refusing to acknowledge any concern about Mexico, Hank ex-claims that he is staying in Albuquerque is to pursue critical leads in the Heisenberg[5] (Walt's strange drug alias) investigation.

NEO-LIBERALISM, THE BORDER, AND RACIALIZED DRUG POLICY

The U.S.-Mexico border has long been the setting for America's longest war—the drug war. The first instance of the border drug wars began in 1969 when the Nixon Administration enacted "Operation Intercept," which led to the shutting down the border with Mexico. The operation did little to decrease the supply of drugs coming across the border and was only successful at exposing the economic interdependence of U.S.-Mexico border communities. In the early 1980s, the Reagan administra-tion launched its massive "War on Drugs." The central goal of the war was to block the tide of cocaine coming into the United States through the Caribbean from Columbia. The Columbians countered by finding an al-ternative route into the United States through the large, open border with Mexico. In Mexico, the Columbians found a willing partner in Miguel Felix Gallardo, a well-known drug smuggler who consolidated many of the small-time drug smugglers in the 1960s and 1970s into a single opera-tion and controlled much of the illegal drug trade on the border. Internal organizational conflicts in Mexico eventually led to the formation of the modern drug cartel. Mexico's four major drug cartels have the financial and technical resources to match and even out-maneuver American and Mexican law enforcement. Tony Payan (2006) maintains that the war on drugs and neo-liberal free trade policies, like NAFTA, have only strengthened the positions of the cartels. NAFTA has allowed the cartels to use the millions of border truck crossings to effectively smuggle and distribute their drugs throughout the continental United States. Almost two decades later, NAFTA's promise to help Mexico build a viable, mid-dle-class never happened. Migration out of Mexico has doubled and be-cause of a tight labor market, wages have been stagnant on both sides of the border (Payan).

The 1980s "War on Drugs" was not justified. Since marijuana and cocaine use actually declined in the late 1970s and the "supply-reduction approach" to drug use had a long history of failure in the United States, there was no rational reason for Reagan's escalated drug war. Reagan's neoliberal drug policies and their enforcement ended up disproportional-ly targeting African Americans living in economically depressed neigh-borhoods in large urban centers. The policies reinforced fears and concerns among Americans about the city's "underclass," who are believed to be socially and morally mired in an endless cycle of drug abuse, poverty, and welfare dependency. Because these areas were already dense in police presence, it was easier to spot drug trafficking and it was easier to make arrests and convictions of young drug suspects who did not have the financial and legal resources to fight their convictions. These areas were deemed easier to patrol and make arrests than the city's high-rise apartments or the outlying suburban communities (Wacquant).

The history and growth of U.S. drug prohibition laws is intimately linked to particular ethnic and racial groups. The first drug prohibition law, the Opium Exclusion Act of 1909, banned the importation of opium for smoking, but not for medicinal uses. Congress, in making the act, argued that the importation of opium for non-medicinal consumption as part of a Chinese plan to weaken America. Later, African Americans were closely identified with cocaine use and cocaine possession was criminalized because southern politicians feared that African American "cocaine users might become oblivious of their prescribed bounds and attack white society" (Schneider 1998, 434). Congress also criminalized marijuana possession based on the fears that it was primarily being used by Mexican immigrants and it served as "a source of crime and deviant behavior." Cathy Schneider (1998) argues that the most passionate support for U.S. drug prohibition laws has been based on the fears associated with a particular drug's effect on a specific minority group. For instance, Latino/a Americans living in the Southwest were believed to be drawn to violent behavior by smoking marijuana (Schneider). *Breaking Bad* reinforces the association between Latino/a Americans, illegal drug use, drug trafficking, and violent behavior. In the episode "A No-Rough-Stuff-Type Deal" (3/9/08), for example, Tuco snorts a sample of Walt's meth to test its potency, and then, without much provocation, viciously beats one of his own men nearly to death. Also, Tuco's Mexican "cousins" are a pair of cold-blooded, cartel assassins who cut off Tortuga's head with a machete and murder a half dozen of their fellow Mexicans who recently crossed the U.S.-Mexico border.

Most neo-liberal drug policies are popular and widely accepted among people because they have the appearance of social neutrality. Todd Gordon (2006), in examining Canada's neo-liberal drug policies, argues that, despite their neutral appearance, these drug policies do affect and are often aimed at minority populations. He adds that racialized drug policies are not driven by overt racism (Gordon). *Breaking Bad*, however, does suggest that some law enforcers may harbor racist attitudes. Hank frequently reveals his deep-seated, racist attitudes toward Latinos and Latina/o culture. In the pilot episode, for instance, Schrader makes a twenty-dollar bet with Gomez, his DEA partner, that the suspect in a meth raid is "a beaner." In the episode ". . . And the Bag's in the River" (2/10/08), when Schrader comes across a hydraulic suspension device in a

Latino drug informant's low-rider car, he laments to Gomez about the precipitous decline in Latino culture.

Neo-liberal drug policies are not predicated on the tacit fear-of-the-Other-syndrome among white citizens. Instead, Gordon (2006) claims that racialized drug policies are rooted in the bourgeois order and its systemic moralistic character, which involves policing and maintaining the dominant, normative moral order through imposing market relations on minority communities. Law enforcement is charged with eradicating any social alternatives, like drug trafficking, which would compete with the capitalist order. Ironically, the Mexican drug cartels and Latino/a American drug smugglers are completely immersed in capitalist relations. Payan (2006) says that the drug cartels follow the "laws of the market." Since drug trafficking is an illegal market, the cartels are unable to use legal remedies to settle market competition and internal disputes. Violence is just one of many options (e.g., negotiation, profit-sharing) available to cartels in their business operations (Payan 868). *Breaking Bad* illustrates how cartels and drug dealers adhere to capitalist relations. Gus asks a Mexican drug cartel to delay their revenge killing of Walt for Tuco's death so that he can complete his business agreement with Walt to pay him three-million-dollars for manufacturing three months' worth of meth. Later, Gus impresses Walt with his ability to masterly out-maneuver and eliminate his chief business rival, a Mexican drug cartel. Despite his efforts to be a successful drug producer and avoid the brutalities of the criminal drug economy, Walt eventually finds himself pitted against Gus whom he believes wants to kill him. As with the characters in *The Wire*, Walt and Jesse's freedom is always illusive and they are invariably circumscribed within the institutional boundaries of a neoliberal society.

CONCLUSION

Following in the tradition of Beck and Byers and Johnson's work on *The Wire* and *C.S.I.*, this study explores the intersections between contemporary neoliberal discourses and policies, and television fictional dramas. As with neo-liberalism, American cable TV programming is dynamic in form and expressive of popular discourses in American society. John Fiske (1984) argues that popular TV programs are popular because there is an "easy fit between the discourses of the text" and the discourses that are drawn on by the audience to express and make sense of their social experiences (168). This study asserts that neo-liberalism is one of the central discourses in *Breaking Bad*. While neo-liberalism can be an abstract, difficult concept to comprehend, the fictional series makes it accessible and manifest through its main characters and their intense narrative situations. *Breaking Bad*'s criminal meth culture not only presents opportunities for Walt to flex his entrepreneurial muscles, it exemplifies the harsh brutalities, risk/benefit calculations, and winner-take-all ethos best associated with neo-liberalism. Walt's transformation from a dying, emasculated public school teacher to a self-confident, aggressive drug lord attests both to the seductive power and the dangers of a neoliberal lifestyle where there can only be winners and losers. Even when Walt's cancer goes into remission and he has amassed plenty of capital, he still wants to continue to cook meth.

NOTES

1. In *The Godfather* (1972), Tom Hagen (Robert Duvall), the Don's adopted son, serves as the *consigliere* or advisor to Don Vito Corleone (Marlon Brando), the head of the Corleone crime family. In *Breaking Bad*, Saul offers to be Walt's personal advisor and counselor for his meth production and distribution business.

2. I'm referring to the popularity of gangsta rap, a subgenre of hip hop music, that focuses on urban crime and the violent lifestyle of inner-city youth and criminals, as well as the violent video games, such as the Grand Theft Auto series.

3. Jodi Dean says that, in the 1997 film *The Game*, the main character is a bored, successfully, but emotionally detached investment banker who only finds excitement and renewed desire through "the game" that is "an unpredictable, high-risk game in which the players don't know the rules, the other players, the conditions, the limits, or even what determines a win or a loss." She asserts that the game represents the brutalities of the neoliberal market and thereby, opens the players up to "the possibilities of desire that their successes had foreclosed" (Dean 58). In a similar manner, I argue that the criminal meth market allows Walt to rekindle his desires to succeed. These desires have laid dormant since Walt gave up the opportunity of pursuing a profitable career in research.

4. I am not arguing that neo-liberalism has specific gendered qualities, but rather that its focus on aggressive individualism and distrust of the social are traits normally associated with western masculinity. The institutional shift the welfare state to the neoliberal state can also be understood in gendered terms. Wacquant, in *Punishing the Poor*, states that, through the retrenchment of the charitable welfare state combined with strict penal laws and unparalleled growth in incarceration, the government's helping hand has been replaced with the iron fist. He asserts that, through neoliberal policies and directives, the government is undergoing a process of re-masculination away from the paternalism associated with postwar liberalism.

5. The "Heisenberg" reference in *Breaking Bad* may refer to Werner Karl Heisenberg, a German theoretical physicist who made a foundational contribution to the founding of quantum mechanics and is best known for the uncertainty principle of quantum theory. In layman's terms, the uncertainty principle asserts that the more precisely one property is measured, the less precisely another property will be to control, limit, and measure. In phenomenological terms, it means that human perception is always limited and incomplete. Walt's choice of alias may serve as a reminder of the mutable and unknowable qualities of his character and actions. As with reality itself, the audience's understanding of Walt's character and motivations are limiting and restrictive by human perception.

WORKS CITED

Beck, Eric. "Respecting the Middle: *The Wire*'s Omar Little as Neoliberal Subjectivity." *Rhizomes*. 19. Summer 2009. 19 September 2011. http://www.rhizomes.net/issue19/beck.html.

Byers, Michele and Val Marie Johnson, eds. *The CSI Effect: Television, Crime, and Governance.* Lanham, MD: Lexington Books, 2009.

Dean, Jodi. "Enjoying Neoliberalism." *Cultural Politics.* 4:1. (2008): 47-72.

Fiske, John. "Popularity and Ideology, A Structuralist Reading of *Dr. Who*," in *Interpreting Television: Current Research Perspectives,* edited by Willard D. Rowland, Jr. and Bruce Watkins. 165-198. Beverly Hills: Sage, 1984.

Giroux, Henry. "Dumbing Down Teachers: Rethinking the Crisis of Public Education and the Demise of the Social State." *The Review of Education, Pedagogy, and Cultural Studies.* 32. (2010): 339-381.

Gordon, Todd. "Neoliberalism, Racism, and the War on Drugs in Canada." *Social Justice.* 33:1. (March 2006): 59-79.

Herbert, Steve and Elizabeth Brown. "Conceptions of Space and Crime in the Punitive Neoliberal City." *Antipode.* 38:4. (September 2006): 755-777.

Hursh, David. "Neo-liberalism, Markets and Accountability: Transforming Education and Undermining Democracy in the United States and England." *Policy Futures in Education.* 3:1. (2005): 3-15.

Ismaili, Karim. "Explaining the Cultural and Symbolic Resonance of Zero Tolerance in Contemporary Criminal Justice." *Contemporary Justice Review.* 6(3). (2003): 255-264.

Lemke, Thomas. "'The birth of bio-politics': Michel Foucault's Lecture at the College de France on Neo-Liberal Governmentality." *Economy and Society.* 30:2. (May 2001): 190-207.

McChesney, Robert W. "Introduction." In *Profit Over People: Neoliberalism and Global Order,* edited by Noam Chomsky and Robert McChesney. New York: Seven Stories Press, 1999.

Miller, Toby. *Cultural Citizenship: Cosmopolitanism, Consumerism, and Television in a Neoliberal Age.* Philadelphia: Temple University Press, 2006.

Ouellette, Laurie. "'Take Responsibility for Yourself': *Judge Judy* and the Neoliberal Citizen." In *Reality TV: Remaking Television Culture,* edited by Susan Murray and Laurie Ouellette. 231-250. New York: New York University Press, 2004. 231-250.

Ouellette, Laurie and James Hay. *Better Living through Reality TV: Television and Post-Welfare Citizenship.* Oxford, UK: Wiley-Blackwell, 2008.

Payan, Tony. "The Drug War and the U.S.-Mexico Border: The State of Affairs." *South Atlantic Quarterly.* 105:4. (Fall 2006): 863-880.

Peck, Janice. *The Age of Oprah, Cultural Icon for the Neoliberal Era.* Boulder, CO: Paradigm, 2008.

Pine, Jason. "Economy of Speed: The New Narco-Capitalism." *Public Culture.* 19:2. (2007): 357-366.

Saez, Pedro A., Adonaid Casado, and Jay C. Wade. "Factors Influencing Masculinity Ideology among Latino Men." *The Journal of Men's Studies.* 17(2). (Spring 2009): 116-128.

Schneider, Cathy L. "Racism, Drug Policy, and AIDS." *Political Science Quarterly.* 113:3. (1998): 427-446.

Sontag, Susan. *Illness as Metaphor and AIDS and its Metaphors.* New York: Picador, 2001.

Wacquant, Loic. *Punishing the Poor: The Neoliberal Government of Social Insecurity.* Durham, NC: Duke University Press, 2009.

TWO

The Economy of Time and Multiple Existences in *Breaking Bad*

Dustin Freeley

We meet Walter White in media res: underwear-clad, gasmask-wearing, maniacally driving an RV; his pants fall in slow motion to the desert road. Two bodies in the back of the RV shift along the floor with each hard corner, and the vehicle skids off the road, coming to a stop in a ditch. After Walt springs from the vehicle, he dons a lime green dress shirt that was hanging from the rearview mirror and picks up a camera to record what he believes will potentially be his last words to his family before he is apprehended by the scrannel of sirens in the distance. Here, his disheveled mismatched body illustrates a broken down and reconstructed amalgam of Walter White: the nakedness of rebirth, the formal dress shirt of his professional life, the gun-in-the waistband that bespeaks danger, death, and renegade. This first scene in the *Breaking Bad* "Pilot" (1/20/08) sets the viewer up for the final scene wherein Walter stares amazed at the flurry of fire trucks that whiz by him on the same desert road without batting an eye at his smoking RV, or his half-nakedness. At this point, he is a changed man, something driven home by his wife Skyler's quizzical response as he climbs in to bed, kisses her lustfully on the mouth and penetrates her from behind as Mick Harvey's "Out of Time Man" plays in the background, providing us with an outline for Walter, a man of whom "time made a fool" and who is at a point in his life where there's "no use in waiting no more."[1] And, it is here that Vince Gilligan begins a narrative that explores our anxieties over time and the multiple existences that thrive within the converging past, present, and future of Walter White in *Breaking Bad*.

It would be an understatement to suggest that a minor anxiety over time permeates our culture. This is most apparent in that "Time squeeze is a phrase often used to describe contemporary concerns about a shortage of time and an acceleration of the pace of everyday life" (Moshe 2012, 69). However, this anxiety over time is not exclusive to our century. In *Gulliver's Travels* (1892), Lilliputians investigate Lemuel's pocket watch, describing it as "the god that he worships" because "he seldom did anything without consulting it" (Swift, loc. 338). Sardonically, Swift offers us a world where each action is obscured by the time in which it happens, leaving each act as merely a marker, but the duration of it as the importance. It seems rather improbable that Louis-Francois Cartier, who made a watch with a wristband for an aviator who needed better use of his hands than to handle a fob, saw his innovation as a symbolic manacle that quite literally fastened us to the awareness of time (Gleick 2000). Our own culture of amalgamated computers and cellphones "encourage[s] a new notion of time because they promise that one can layer more activities onto it. Because you can text while doing something else, texting does not seem to take time, but to give you time" (Turkle 2011, 164). Adding to this effused dialectic is the serialized television series *24*, a unique program in its inception in as much as the show is shot in real time, creates tension through plotted points of action in the narrative and heightens it by running these points simultaneously with a digital clock whose ticks and tocks resemble a bomb's imminent detonation. The show itself blatantly plays on our anxieties. In a sense, this clock becomes as nefarious as the villain that Jack Bauer hunts. Each hour compartmentalizes various plot points, successes, and failures that all count down to an inevitable degeneration of the season and the events within the narrative.

The largest concern over "clock time" is its tendency to obfuscate "temporality as emergence and substitut[e] it with a temporality of orderings" (Leong, et al. 2009, 1278). In other words, past actions, present cognizance, and future possibilities are replaced with an attention to duration, making the blocks of time more important than the events that occupy them. A problem arises when this constructed time meets the unpredictable and unforeseen, thus coercing the subject to look closer at the moments that led to the present. Here, the focus shifts from the ordinance of "clock time" to a more philosophical discussion of time that frames it as a simultaneous existence of the past, present, and future. In *Matter and Memory* (1929), Henri Bergson asserts, "our perceptions are undoubtedly interlaced with memories, and inversely, a memory [. . .] only becomes actual by borrowing the body of some perception into which it slips. These two acts, perception and recollection, always interpenetrate each other" (loc. 1052). Bergson's interpretation of memory requires the subject to reflect on the past as the impetus for the present and the future. Such a theory is further expounded on by Gilles Deleuze

(1994), who believes, "Memory is the fundamental synthesis of time, which constitutes the being of the past (that which causes the present to pass)" and "The past in general is the lament in which each former present is focused upon in particular and as a particular" (80). For both Bergson and Deleuze, this shift of ordinate time to reflections on temporality also offers an additional way in which a subject views his or her *own* time. This philosophical approach to temporality compels the subject to attempt to relive and revise the past in order to alter the present to similarly stretch future time (the time remaining). This convergence of constructed time and philosophical temporality is exemplified by *Breaking Bad's* Walter White, a fifty-year-old high school chemistry teacher forced to acknowledge his own mortality. Within the narrative that ensues, Walter attempts to recoup wasted time, build a surplus of future time, efficiently utilize present time, and create alternate realities to foster simultaneous time lines. In a sense, each one of these endeavors allows Walt to defy that which we have constructed as "clock time" and manipulate his past, present, and future.

The presence of narcotics as narrative subjects on television or in cinema is not exclusive to *Breaking Bad*, and neither are their referents to 'right' and 'wrong,' or 'good' and 'bad.' In 2005, *Weeds* popularized this conflicting dichotomy by offering Nancy Botwin, the self-entitled, newly-widowed housewife who peddles drugs throughout her fictional suburb. As for *Breaking Bad*, it seems Vince Gilligan made a calculated decision to employ methamphetamine as the drug of choice. Methamphetamine (MA) creates one of the first thematic connections to our anxiety over time. To illustrate, one could look at the short-term effects of meth usage, which becomes a means by which we can stretch time. As Gonzales, Mooney, and Rawson (2010) note, "The desirable short-term effects of MA, or the initial rush, are characterized by increased energy and alertness, and elevated positive mood state, and decreased appetite. [. . .] Compared to other stimulants . . . the half-life of MA is quite long, ranging from 8 to 12 hours" (385-98). As a result, the short-term effects of meth serve to defy the established "clock time," making it irrelevant and stretching any time at hand into energy-filled endeavors. Within *Breaking Bad*, the appearance of shotgun-toting, shovel-happy junkies might not advocate the use of meth to stretch what little time is at hand, but—in real life—it's apparent that career addicts and criminals are not the only ones indulging in the substance. "Amphetamine-type substances are the second most widely abused drugs after cannabis," state Maxwell and Rutkowski (2008) in their study of the prevalence of methamphetamine abuse (229). Furthermore, studies find that "Women are more likely to start using stimulants to lose weight," battle depression, and methamphetamine use is growing in certain occupations (Maxwell and Rutkowski, 2008, 229) and students looking to achieve greater academic success with all-night cramming sessions (Gonzales, et al. 2010). If we discount the full-blown addicts, we can see an anxiety over time in the subsets of women, time-sensitive occupations, and students. Theoretically, women are attempting to lose weight in a shorter period of time to extend their aesthetic capital; the farther a truck driver travels in one sitting, the faster his or her load is delivered, and the sooner he can begin another run and earn more money; the student avoids sleep to absorb that much more information, ideally, to succeed on each test and accomplish as much as possible.

Something else of interest is Walt and Jesse's method of producing methamphetamine. Admittedly, I have no knowledge or experience of the required procedure, but, in the show, Walt uses his chemical knowledge to circumvent the time typically required to manufacture meth. Therefore, his method also defies the average "clock time" required for production. In addition, the chemicals themselves often serve to erase moments in time for both Walt and Jesse. This is most apparent when they use barrels of hydrofluoric acid (an ingredient in meth production) to dissolve certain deceased individuals: Krazy-8, Emilio, Victor, the super lab itself, Mike, and a young boy.[2] Furthermore, Gilligan's decision to use methamphetamine is possibly related to its spread throughout the country. As methamphetamine has gained in popularity, it has gone from a "small local problem and spread exponentially from west to east over a twenty-year span" (Gonzales, et al. 2010, 388). And, while "The indicators show that the problem is greatest in the western parts of the countries," it is "moving eastward." The importance here—for our perspective—is that the progression of meth is a way for Gilligan to break down the typical East-to-West progression that founded this country. In other words, the introduction of methamphetamine, its nefarious connotations, and the algorithm that it marries with modern capitalism creates an imagery of time doubling back on itself, effectively erasing the initial progression from East to West, instead creating a chaotic devolution that makes the time spent on the initial expansion a zero-sum game.

The starting point of this reverse progression is also worth noting. Set in Albuquerque, the series exists in a location that, with the exception of August, experiences very little precipitation and has 330 days of sunshine a year. Here, the weather's constancy creates a variety of symbolism. First, the series has been shot as if it were perpetually daytime. Nebulous clouds flit across the sky in time-lapse photography, but the sun hardly sets. If it does, the darkness is momentary, illuminated by the lights of buildings or the desert-bound RV/meth lab. This constancy fosters a perpetual present, undifferentiated from the day before or the day after.

Furthermore, the setting limns an economic corollary on the convoluted algorithm that is modern capitalism, in which "people sense that the time available to them is inadequate for their existence" reminding us that "time equals money" (Moshe 2012, 69). A prime example of this is illustrated in the time-oriented episode "4 Days Out" (5/3/2009). Jesse and Walt travel into the desert to cook meth over a weekend; together, they work against the clock, defying natural time in order to cook the product and earn large stacks of cash. In our own universe, we see this exhibited in office buildings that stay open beyond sundown, but the same post-sundown work ethic is further exemplified by the meth super lab that we're introduced to in season three. This windowless, Vegas-casino-like workspace eliminates both day and night. Fluorescent bulbs replace the sun, but create visibility twenty-four hours a day. In the lab, Walt and Jesse concoct their batches focusing on production and the amount they can produce before they leave the lab. Lab time revolves around the temporal anxiety of producing a specific amount of meth within a prescribed time schedule. For Jesse, Walter, and their boss, Gus, time and economics are linked and translate into the efficacy of production and return on investment. At the same time, for Walt, the anxiety over time spent on production also correlates, initially, to the time that he has left.

RECOUPING LOST TIME

In the pilot, Walt learns that he has cancer, a diagnosis that sends his thoughts in a variety of directions, but mostly toward his *time remaining*. Walt's recognition of his own mortality impels a number of different actions, but the first is to provide security for his family. As the viewer, we meet a character cognizant of the end of his life. In these moments, Walt embodies what Delueze refers to as "the death instinct," when time is "empty and out of joint" (111). This death instinct rearranges Walt's view on time, transitioning his present into the imminent future. Each moment of his present becomes his past as he inches closer and closer to death. In *Being in Time* (1927), Heiddeger notes "The event of death, which is the possibility of radical nonexistence, is futural, not in the sense of being 'not yet' in time but as something ever present yet seemingly coming from nowhere" (Heidegger, qtd. in Widder 2008, 166). If we look at Walt through this lens, we see inevitable death lingering within his present. At the same time, his knowledge of his death also impels him to reflect on the past, which, if Deleuze is correct, "no longer exists, it does not exist, but it insists, it consists, it *is*. It insists with the former present, it consists with the new or present present" (82). Simply put, Walt's past brings him to his present, but his present does not elide the past; rather, his past—or his just past—influences the decisions he will make, thereby influencing his future (Gallagher 1998).

In a sense, Walt becomes a prisoner, forced to acknowledge the time spent up to and including his current state and the time he has remaining. As a high school chemistry teacher and a part-time cashier at a car wash, Walt is far from affluent. Therefore, in an inverse of "time equals money," Walt procuring additional income equals "time." In one sense, the money he needs to earn will provide his family with a future. At the same time, the money that Walt craves also extends his time, despite his death. What I mean to suggest is that the money becomes his legacy, and, after his passing, the financial security he provides for his family signifies an extension of his life in the form of capital. This cynical commentary imagines the human body as a machine to produce inheritance (and relegates the body's worth to market value), but I believe this is an appropriate correlation in that the money that Walt wants to provide his family is akin to the "growth, decay, and transformation" of all living things that he lectures about to his students in the pilot episode. Walt has grown from child to adolescent to adult; at the age of fifty and upon his diagnosis, one could say that he has begun to decay; and, the money that he hopes will signify his existence is his transformation.

As Walt looks toward the future and the success that money will symbolize, he is also forced to look at the insisting, consisting past that brought about his present, which shifts Walt's focus from *time remaining* to *time lost*. In the pilot episode, it is clear that Walt's intellectual acumen surpasses his financial success. Interestingly, his intelligence is often perceived as a social detriment. His brother-in-law Hank remarks about the gigantic size of Walter's brain suggesting that his intellect has categorized him as a societal runt. Walt first laments his time lost in ". . . And the Bag's in the River" (2/10/08) as he and Jesse are sponging the dissolved remains of Emilio from the second floor of Jesse's home. At this time, Walt flashes back to a conversation he had about the elements in the human body. While mordantly comical, this scene introduces Gretchen, his previous love interest. The connection here is not solely to show that someone existed prior to Skyler, but to illustrate the heights from which Walt has fallen. While not fully exposited, it seems his departure from his field coincided with Gretchen falling in love with Elliot, Walt's partner. In a later episode, when Walt is surrounded by successful scientists who work for Gray Matter Technologies, the company owned by Gretchen and Elliot that Walt helped build,[3] he graciously notes that he drifted into teaching, but this is ominously prefaced in an earlier episode when he ponders the paths one takes in life.[4] Within this lament, Walt becomes a character who lives his remaining life in a vacuum of regret.

For Walt, Gretchen and Elliot represent the success and wealth that he could have achieved. From his perspective, they both removed him from their equation in order to build their own empire from his work.[5] Whether or not this is true is up for discussion, but Walt sees himself as an overqualified high school chemistry teacher and a man who has watched others pass him by in life.[6] Therefore, the money reaped through meth manufacturing provides Walt with the financial status that he feels was swindled from him. It also puts him once again at the forefront of a field. While taboo, the blue stuff that Walt produces becomes the purest methamphetamine that the market has seen. Walt's intellect is highlighted, but its emphasis is bred from nefariousness. This is another interesting commentary on capitalist society in that Walt's intelligence—on a legitimate level—has become undervalued in an economic hierarchy that requires "management and technical positions that can be open to everyone because they do not require genuine expertise" (Widder 2008, 153). Walt, a former contributor to research awarded the Nobel Prize, becomes equated to anyone with a pedestrian understanding of chemistry. The illustration here is that Walt's intelligence is unappreciated placing him financially behind others in society because expertise is unnecessary. Walt's knowledge and expertise, however, at least up through the middle of season four, enables his capital value to soar. Without him, there is no blue stuff. Without the blue stuff, his customers search for different dealers.

In a sense, Walt's success with the blue stuff, despite his devalued intellect, might place him within a movement of modern nihilism, which Nietzsche defines as "a condition in which delegitimated values of the past remain embedded in an incompatible present" (qtd. in Widder 2008, 143). For Walt, these delegitimated values include knowledge, education, innovation, and integrity. The first two are belittled socially and disrespected at the high school level. His innovations were poached by Gretchen and Elliot, and this ties directly in to Walt's views on integrity. Granted, at one point Gretchen notes that the money from Elliot and her belongs to Walt,[7] but she doesn't cut him a check or offer reparations. Gretchen's offer is as perfunctory as Walt's deflection of her sentiment. This conjures in Walt a feeling of the aforementioned "time squeeze." Following his diagnosis, he spent time examining his life and the time he has remaining. After speaking to Gretchen, Walt's desire to squeeze time "is evoked as a result of the individual's tendency to compare his or her standard of living a quality of life with those of others, out of ambition to arrive at the same quality of life" (Moshe 2012, 69). Walt's decision to recoup his lost time offers reconciliation to his contemplation about the paths one takes in life. Gretchen's conciliatory admission of Walt's contribution to their company jogs within Walt the memory of his moment at the top, as well as perhaps their romance. Having lost these in the shuffle of his current present, Walt announces to his family that he refuses to become a dying man just marking time till he dies.[8] It also foreshadows Walt's need to tangent from his current existence. In order to recoup lost time and achieve the success that he felt was ripped from him in the past, Walt needs to create an existence that maintains his role as dying patriarchal provider but shuns the role of simply marking time.

CONSTRUCTING SIMULTANEOUS REALITIES

These dual existences allow him to earn enough money to extend his legacy as well as provide him with the financial and intellectual gratification that he lost to his past. At the same time, this dual existence allows him to grow as a separate identity, not solely for financial or intellectual gain, but as a means to begin a new past, present, and future. One existence remains Walter White, husband of Skyler, father of Walter Jr. The other is Heisenberg. Logistically, Heisenberg is an identity that will keep the DEA at bay. The choice of the Heisenberg alias runs much deeper than a simple subversion. To contemporize Walt's decision to become Heisenberg, it might be best to think of his new identity as a version of an avatar, a visual representation with which "you can set about reworking . . . aspects of life that may not have gone so well in the real" (Turkle 2007). Sherry Turkle (2007) summarizes the tendencies of those who create avatars in virtual environments, observing "The plain represented themselves as glamorous; the introverted could try out being bold. People built the dream houses in the virtual world that they could not afford in the real." The tendencies of those in Multi-User Domains are akin to Walt's motives for the creation of Heisenberg in that his visage allows Walter to be the bold, badass dad that shadows his typically meek self, earn the type of money he was unable to as a chemistry teacher, and, most importantly, be what he *could have* been.

Werner Heisenberg, the Nobel Prize-winning German theoretical physicist, is best known for his uncertainty principle, a symbolically appropriate theory that juxtaposes that which is known and is probable to happen in an experiment and the variables that are unknown. According to Heisenberg (1999), the probability function within an experiment "represents a tendency for events and our knowledge of events" (46). The principle's relation to *Breaking Bad*'s Walt is rather clear. Despite his best attempts to control his situations and foresee an outcome, unforeseen variables present themselves and spin a number of the narratives within the series into chaotic climaxes. Moreover, each occurring variable illustrates a merging of the feared Heisenberg and Walt, the meek chemistry teacher. This convergence of identity parallels Heisenberg's note on dualism: "Generally, the dualism between two different descriptions of the same reality is no longer a difficulty since we know from the mathematical formulation of the theory that contradictions cannot arise" (50). In 1958, Heisenberg was referring to different perceptions and subsequent descriptions of an experiment observed by more than one scientist. However, his theory can also be applied to Walt, whose physical body and actions relate to the "same reality." When Walt goes home at night, his actions as Heisenberg are not erased; they're merely withheld from his family. The same can be said when he dons Heisenberg's hat. His family is not erased; their existence is merely withheld from people like Jesse,

Tuco, and Krazy-8. However, these realities are simultaneous and ever-present. The most significant aspect of Heisenberg's theory is when he notes that "contradictions cannot arise" (50). Essentially, Walt and his Heisenberg do not exist separately. The emergence of Heisenberg erases the contradictions that were fostered within the Walt who became a chemistry teacher rather than a man at Gray Matter Technologies. Admittedly, this is a cynical look at Walt, and I'm aware that it suggests that pre-cancer Walt was less a docile, meek father, and more of a violent, cutthroat narcissist, but by the end of season four, I'm not sure that this assumption is as much of a stretch as it would have been during the first half of season one.

To re-contemporize our look at Walter through a Heisenbergian lens, we can once again visit Turkle (2011), who notes "When identity is multiple in this way, people feel 'whole' not because they are *one* but because the relationship among aspects of self are fluid and undefensive. We feel 'ourselves' if we can move easily among our many aspects of self" (194). Even though she is still referring to a virtual environment, Walt's comfort in the emergence of Heisenberg and the ease with which he fluctuates can be seen in Turkle's assessment of fluidity and the aspects of self.

Walt's transition to Heisenberg allows him to create simultaneous living presents. As Deleuze (1994) asserts, a single living present includes "both the past and the future: the past in so far as the preceding instants are retained in the contraction; the future because its expectation is anticipated in the same contraction" (71). For Walt, the man dying of cancer, his path from chemist to chemistry teacher and through his diagnosis initially impels him to manufacture crystal meth to generate enough capital to leave a legacy to his family. At the same time, the creation of Heisenberg produces a second living present in which Walt-as-Heisenberg is allowed to erase his decision to leave behind his role as chemistry genius—and the correlated financial gain. The generation of a second present can be seen in Delueze's (1994) claim that "Two successive presents may be contemporaneous with a third present, more extended by virtue of the number of instants it contracts. The duration of an organism's present, or of its various presents, will vary according to the natural contractile range of its contemplative souls" (77). Deleuze refers to the emergence of multiple memories during any living present, but in the case of Walt, his memories—in the form of flashbacks—further drive him to intensify his relationship and actions to his second identity, which further connects to Deleuze's idea that "a phenomenon such as need can be understood in terms of 'lack,' from the point of view of action and the active syntheses which it determines" (77). Simply put, Heisenberg's arrival signifies that which Walt is deprived of: capital, power, and success. This leads us to a metempsychosis within the narrative, wherein "each is a passing present, one life may replay another at a different level, as if the philosopher and the pig, the criminal and the saint, played out the same past at different levels of a gigantic cone" (Deleuze 1994, 83). For Walt, a similar past exists for both himself and his Heisenberg, and it is this similar past that compels each to act and become one interloping and converging character.

This common past occupies a moment in time of *what could have been* (Heisenberg) and *what is* (Walt). Time signifies a fracture in the "I" that bifurcates pre-diagnosis Walt into post-diagnosis Walt and Heisenberg, something that allows Walt to atone for his formerly callow and pusillanimous demeanor, which is alluded to most notably in the conflict between Walt, Elliot, and Gretchen. The confidence that Walt exudes with Gretchen while talking about the elemental composition of the human body is palpable as is his passion when he leans in for a kiss prior to the end of the flashback.[9] However, Skyler and Walt's presence at Elliot's birthday party reeks of discomfort and anxiety, much like the way that Walter perfunctorily responds to Gretchen's claim about his half of the money. For a better look at pre-diagnosis Walter, we can build from David Hume's (2000) notion that personal identity is a fiction, with "nothing really belonging to these different perceptions, and uniting them together; but is merely a quality, which we attribute to them" (loc. 3825). If this is the case, then Walt's identity as "Walter" is merely a pervasive construction of the perceptions that surround him, placing his *self* in what George Mead referred to as the "attitude of the other" (Gallagher 1998, 50). This attitude of the other is even present within the series' title. The present continuous "breaking" suggests a process, one that is ongoing and—depending on how season five ends—infinite. Critical to the discussion of attitude is the adjective "bad." The notation of bad both establishes a stereotype for the business Walt is entering and the stigma that surrounds Walt –'good.' I have no objection to Walt being largely seen as a 'good' father, 'good' husband, or all around 'good' guy, pre-diagnosis. As the series progresses, however, this label becomes wonky and misleading, suggesting that the façade that Walt wears is once again linked to social expectations, or the attitude of others. Regarding this attitude, we can turn again to Mead who further believes "since we are already a product of other relations, our own experience of time is already conditioned by others" (Gallagher 1998, 113). If this is the case, then we can also interpret Walt's Heisenberg as a means to recoup his time spent as a social construction of those around him.

Ironically enough, Walt's alter ego fashions a scenario similar to his previous existence: the violent, powerful, narcissistic Heisenberg is a product of the attitude of others. In "Negro y Azul" (4/19/09) a narcocorrido[10] illustrates the constructed attitude of others toward "Heisenberg's fame," as the "gringo boss," with the blue stuff that "no one could stop it if they wanted to." This ballad seems to set Walt on the path that culminates in a confrontation with Skyler in "Cornered" (8/21/12) in which she asserts that he is not a criminal, but rather a man caught in an untenable position. Aghast and growling, Walt retorts, telling her that he is not the one in danger, rather he has become the danger. While this scene showcases Cranston and Gunn's acting abilities, it also serves to illustrate Walt as an egotist. But, his ego is a product of those around who exhibit fear at the name of Heisenberg.

In the end, the emergence of Heisenberg allows Walt to start over by creating a simultaneous second present, providing him with money he missed, power he gave up, and the credit that had been taken away from him. It also provides us with a glimpse into Walt's true character that had been buried by various social constructs and external attitudes. All of this culminates into a hero cum villain that Nietzsche (1974) warns us about when he posits "Whoever is dissatisfied with himself is continually ready for revenge, and we other will be his victims" (290). Looking at Walt through a combination of Meadean, Deleuzian, and Nietzschean lenses might help us better understand how Walt transitions into a ruthless villain bent on obtaining control by deceiving Skyler, manipulating Jesse, watching Jane die, poisoning Brock, and murdering Gus and Mike. And, perhaps Skyler asking Walt "Is that you?" should be seen as much less about a man who faces his own mortality and more about a man attempting to recreate himself in the time he has left.

Even though Heisenberg is the most blatant multiple existence within *Breaking Bad*, other characters experiment with their own multiplicity. Jesse is known as Captain Cook, Gus is Gustavo in a former life. Walter Jr. is Flynn to differentiate himself from his father. Jesse's friend Christian is Combo; Brandon is Badger. And, Skyler's sister Marie assumes the names Torri, Charlotte, and Mimi. Each of these pseudonyms has a purpose to differentiate the established identity from the one being portrayed, but Marie's assumption of other identities seems to be most similar to Walt's need to reinvent himself. In one sense, a pseudonym allows Marie to absolve herself of thievery, placing the crime on a separate identity. However, the names also provide Marie with a life that is not her own, something that is most apparent in "Open House," (7/31/11) when she passes herself off as a hand model with a former astronaut for a husband. She also pretends to be from London with a husband who's an illustrator. Most intriguing about these most recent delusions is that Hank becomes a subject of her fiction as well, suggesting that Marie's need for reconstruction is not exclusive to her person, but to everything that surrounds her. At the same time, her addiction to deception, shoplifting, and thievery build the foundation for a commentary on the prevalence of 12-step programs within *Breaking Bad*.

THE TIME CIRCUIT OF 12-STEP PROGRAMS

Though we never see Marie go to meetings, Hank alludes to them. However, Jesse, his ephemeral girlfriend Jane, Badger, and Skinny Pete all enter and exit 12-step programs repeatedly for their addictions. Admittedly, the connection between these programs and the anxiety over time that has been discussed throughout this project might not be clear. However, if we look at the programs metaphorically through a Freudian lens, it becomes clear the programs into which each character enters becomes a circuit of failure that ultimately correlates to varying amounts of time lost in futilely reinventing one's self. Freud (1920), in his psychoanalytical theory, looks at ladders, ascents, and steps, suggesting "that they have the rhythm of walking as a common characteristic; perhaps, too, the heightening of excitement and the shortening of breath, the higher one mounts" (loc 2126). Admittedly, Freud is discussing dreams, but in the same way that steps in a dream signify fulfillment, completing the steps within *Breaking Bad* equal the fulfillment of becoming clean. However, like gym-goers on a Stair Master, the characters within the series never reach the final step, consistently relapsing and starting over in a perpetual, time-sucking circuit. On the one hand, this might speak to an inability to change—something that would also support the notion that Walt has always been Heisenberg in disguise. On the other hand, these steps also relate to the convergence of past, present and future. The past and its memories bring the addicts to their present decision to change their lives, which, theoretically, provides them with the desired future. Considering the dangers of methamphetamines and heroin, climbing these steps builds a surplus of time for the future that—if they remain addicts— would most probably be depleted. The problem inherent in this circuit is that future time is wasted because the surplus becomes occupied by the characters' repetition of the same steps in order to reach the final one. The past and their past drug use continue to haunt their present (attempts in the program) and disrupts their intended future (living habit-free), thus creating a veritable time suck.

The occurrence of addiction and treatment within the narrative is a central theme, and the attention paid to addiction in seasons two and three suggests that Vince Gilligan has no intention to write them off as mere twists and turns. "Grilled" (3/15/09) marks the first reference to a 12-step program (Marie's). This season also introduces us to Jane, Jesse's girlfriend and landlord, a former heroin addict working her way through recovery. A number of conflicts ensue on account of Jesse's line of work and Jane's sobriety, but most intriguing is that Jane relapses during "Phoenix" (5/24/09)—the twelfth episode—signifying a fracture in her steps, a symbolic inability to complete the twelfth step, and entry into the aforementioned circuit of failure. Her eighteen months spent in sobriety and the trust she rebuilt with her father is painfully obviated and neatly euphemized as a 'backslide.' Season three begins in a similar fashion as we encounter Jesse in media res of his 12-step program, clean for forty-five days and proudly displaying the coin from this rearview mirror as he drives his car. This in and of itself is a visual symbol of the past, present, and future converging at one time: Jesse's forward motion (driving toward his destination) is simultaneously depicted with his present state of sobriety (forty-five days) as the travelled-on road (past) disappears in the mirror. However, by the end of the third season, Jesse, too, backslides in "Half Measures" (6/6/10) — the twelfth episode.

The occurrence of both relapses in a twelfth episode can hardly be coincidence. Rather, it's a way of demarcating time lost during each season. Through eleven episodes, Gilligan exhibits struggling characters to root for. As Walt makes his journey closer to being an anti-hero, Jane provides us with hope for Jesse, while Jesse in season three fuels an additional hope that he might put himself on the straight and narrow. However, both of these scenarios come to a crashing halt. Unfortunately for both Jane and Jesse, their efforts are all for naught. In both situations, the time spent in programs and sobriety is wasted; concurrently, their choices result in unintended action — Jane asphyxiates on her own vomit; Jesse fails to kill the two men. Thus, their attempts are similarly thwarted, and they remain caught in a circuit of failure.

Jane's death compels Jesse to enter rehab, but it also triggers an emotional decline that shifts his desire for fat stacks of cash into indifference. This creates a marked juxtaposition with Walter, who transitions from a man with dwindling time attempting to recover lost time into a man living on borrowed time. This "borrowed time" further allows Walt to *become* Heisenberg and marks a shift in the trajectory of his persona. Throughout the first two-thirds of the second season, Walt's cough becomes more prominent, and accompanied by blood, encouraging him to spend his spare time cooking enough meth to generate over half-a-million dollars as his share of the profits. This weekend of meth cooking occurs in the appropriately titled "4 Days Out." As Walt believes he is on the verge of death, these four days become the time allotted to recoup all lost time, meaning that Walt is essentially buying time for his family with his days in the New Mexico prairie. However, for this discussion, the importance of this episode is its closing scene in the oncologist's office, where Walt learns that his cancer has gone into remission. Regarding the prognosis, the doctor emphasizes that they're not out of the woods yet, but still have some options including more time. The doctor's response highlights the importance of the time that Walter has left, and in this moment, the time spoken of shifts from dwindling and fleeting to *borrowed*, and similarly signifies a rebirth. This interpretation can be garnered from Walt's prognosis, but also from separate moment that involves Skyler's visit to her OB/GYN within the same episode. The moment is brief, but her doctor notes that the baby is fine and will arrive according to plan, in its own time. In one sense, the gestating child is the antithesis of Walter's ostensible decline in the prairie; however, its inevitable arrival parallels Walter's rebirth upon hearing his prognosis.

The transition in Walt's character is not sudden but builds through the rest of the second season, beginning when, during a party to celebrate his remission, Walt feeds his son a few quick shots of tequila, leading to his getting sick and vomiting in the pool. Giving his son a few shots does not vilify Walt, but his anger toward the more ostensibly masculine Hank presents itself when he declares, "My son. My bottle. My house." The scene is brief but signals an uprising of subconscious feelings, as if the private world of Heisenberg begins to emerge in the public world of Walter. This newly blended persona coincides with Walt's prognosis and can be seen as a form of reinventing himself and creating a new time line that publicly deviates from his former one as school teacher and cancer patient. Throughout this same episode, Walt's second chance at a new identity is mirrored through Jesse and Jane's discussion of superheroes, particularly Rewindo, a hero that Jesse drew. Rewindo's superpower is simply the ability to turn back time. For Jesse, it's clear that his relationship with his mother and father was lost in the transgressions of his past, and his creation of the fictional Rewindo signifies his desire to place his own persona into a remission of sorts. Perhaps Jane and their ventures to museums to look at Georgia O'Keefe paintings will allow him to recoup lost time and begin anew. Regardless, both Walt and Jesse begin to lament their past decisions and strive for new time lines.

A clash between Walt's previous time line and his Heisenberg time line presents itself in "Phoenix" (5/24/09). Earlier, the significance of this episode has been discussed in its relation to twelve-step programs, but here we can look at Walt's binary existence as both father and Heisenberg. Walt, having negotiated an exchange worth $1.2 million for his duffel bag of methamphetamine, speeds through New Mexico to make the drop. At the same time, Skyler goes into labor, thus positioning Walt at a crossroads. He is able to simultaneously exist momentarily by using a cell phone to communicate with his family—lying that he is stuck in traffic—and maneuver through New Mexico in order to fulfill his part of the meth deal. However, his dedication to one ultimately elides his presence in the other. Here, Walt positions money and his role as Heisenberg above the birth of his child. We could certainly castigate him for misplaced values, but it is more important to think of this moment as the moment he veers away from his former life. Yes, the Whites still exist, but he is no longer treading the same path that they do. Instead, he has elected to pursue his role as Heisenberg, even though his mortality is no longer directly in front of him.

What might be the most damning part of his transition occurs prior to his delivery when he attempts to contact Jesse in order to obtain the bag of cash under Jesse's sink. When Walt arrives, Jesse and Jane are both passed out. As Walt recovers the money, Jane begins to vomit and, as Walter watches, asphyxiates. Walt's refusal to tilt Jane's head to the side is additionally symbolic of his transformation. Granted, she was black-mailing him for the money he owed Jesse, but this isn't Walt's motive. Rather, I would suggest that her influence on Jesse threatened to impede their business together and Walt's overall view of his own potential success. Jane's presence threatened to remove Jesse from the picture, thereby removing Walt's partner and potentially reverting Walt to his previous time line. It seems apparent that Walt could function without Jesse, though there always feels like an underlying desire for Jesse to be present. In part, this might be because Jesse functions as the doppelgänger-son of Heisenberg. Walt Jr. is a sixteen-year-old with cerebral palsy who prefers to be called Flynn to elide any similarity to his father. Jesse is, however, essentially, without family and an empty vessel into which Walt-as-Heisenberg can impart knowledge that he's unable to pass to his biological son—not on account of intelligence, but because of its illicit nature. I admit that this dynamic creates a contradiction, one that blends fatherhood (an element of Walt's previous time line) with Heisenberg (his current and future time line). This potential discrepancy, how-ever, can be remedied if we consider that the desire to be a father was present in Walter White, chemist, before he became Walter White, high school chemistry teacher. To echo Deleuze's thoughts, the desire to be a father exists in both passing presents that now persist on different levels in the future (83).

BUYING TIME

These climactic moments lead us to "ABQ" (5/31/09), in which Walt has surgery and his doctor notes that he has acquired more time for himself. Here, the time in question is still borrowed and will be funneled into Walt's work at the new super lab and for his boss, Gus Fring. While Walt is once again the chemist earning more than the money he was due from Gray Matter Technologies and positioning himself at the forefront of his newly found field, there is a sad irony within Walt's ascension to this new position. As the series progresses, the borrowed time and new time line that Walt receives via Heisenberg circuitously becomes *time remaining* when the super lab becomes a metaphorical form of cancer, wherein Walt's time is subsumed into Gus's industrialized time and operation. Basically, each moment that Walt spends making meth for Gus brings him closer to his own death. In part, this is illustrated in Gus's growing unpredictability, often shown in shifts from sedate, organized manager, to box cutter wielding murderer.[11] Prior to this, Walt hits a ceiling; he can't improve on the ninety-nine-percent, and the unbelievable amount of money he earns no longer provides him with security. Rather, the time that he spends generating this money actually depletes time from his future life, primarily because of Gale Boetticher and Jesse Pinkman, Walt's de facto protégés, who are, at different times, groomed to take his place. Walt-as-Heisenberg echoes his former self: the high school chemistry teacher widget replaced by someone able to follow a lesson plan, or, in this case, a formula. Here, Walt, too, is trapped in a circuit of failure from which he cannot escape. The episode that best exemplifies his recognition of his own endeavors is "Fly" (5/23/10). Walt's insomnia begins to rattle his brain, and he searches feverishly and futilely for a single fly that has infiltrated the super lab. His venture could certainly be seen as the precursor —if not the moments of—a nervous breakdown, but there's a sardonic significance in the fact that Walt, who no longer has to worry about money, spends (nee wastes) part of his depleting time trying to evict a housefly, a creature whose very existence exemplifies temporality.

And here, perhaps we can draw from Nietzsche's (2012) when he says "the mosquito, then we would learn that he floats through the air with the same self-importance, feeling within itself the flying center of the world." Whether Gilligan intentionally lifted the theme from Nietzsche, I'm unsure; however, there is a philosophical connection here about self-importance within both insects and man: it exists in both, despite temporality and futility. Within the episode, the fly seems to have no apparent purpose other than to bother Walt and to eventually die. Similarly, Walt often aggravates Gus, his family, Jesse, and his death comes sooner as the hours tick away. In the game of cat and mouse both are caught in a circuit of uselessness: the fly is trapped in the lab; Walt is not making any product. Both see their timelines growing shorter and shorter—and we watch both do so as well.

THE AUTEUR'S MANIPULATION OF TIME

It is apparent that our cultural obsession with time has bled into the characters and thematic elements of *Breaking Bad*. Moreover, it is apparent that Gilligan plays with time as a narrative device throughout the series. To begin, television (and film) might be the perfect medium in which to examine the push-pull of time, particularly, if we consider J. M. E. McTaggart's argument that there is no such thing as time. Rather, that there are only two descriptions of time: the A-Series and the B-Series (Gallagher, 1998, 112). The A-Series consists of what we consider past, present, and future in a historical time line: World War II happened in the past; I am typing a paper in the present; January 17, 2124 will occur in the future. The B-Series is our recognition of events that happen earlier, currently, and later: earlier, I brushed my teeth; now, I am typing a paper; later, I will eat dinner. *Breaking Bad* and other television shows follow these series to construct their narratives. The narrative of each episode is comprised of events that happen earlier (the beginning of the episode) and later (the end of the episode). At the same time, *Breaking Bad*, through flashbacks or flash-forwards that begin each episode, simultaneously manipulates our perception of time and injects moments that constituted the past, present, or future. As Spencer Shaw (2008) suggests, "Our sense of immanence and consciousness is intrinsically bound up with the continuity of objects, in the continuum of experience" (82). Simply put, our awareness and interaction with the present narrative derives from our previous experiences with past narratives. This might seem obvious, but Gilligan throws off this continuum by offering glimpses of moments that infect the narrative that has been established through the preceding episodes (A-Series) as well as what we will see during the current episode (B-Series). The inclusion of these brief snippets of past and future are not simply to keep us on the hook, but to create an uncanny recognition of our viewing past within the series. In a sense, Gilligan is playing with our memories of events much in the same way that Walt's memories play with his perception of the present.

Often, moments resemble other moments but don't repeat them. As Deleuze (1994) notes, "repetition is never a historical fact, but rather the historical condition under which something new is effectively produced" (90). Gilligan carefully treads within this hypothesis in his recurrent use of similar images without copying an introduction or closing to each episode. At times these images are subtle like the echoing of Jesse's "45 days sober coin" that hangs from his mirror with the "Fighting Terrorism Since 1492" tag that hangs from the police officer's rearview mirror in the same season.[12] Both of these images speak to the aforementioned unfulfilled steps (Jesse is continues to battle sobriety/the police force continues to battle terrorism), but they also signify the convergence of past, present, and future.

At other times, episodes begin with the half-charred face of a pink teddy bear and an eye. In "Seven Thirty-Seven" (3/8/09), "Over" (5/10/09), and "ABQ," all offer a version of this imagery, suggesting, in the presence of the eye, that someone is always watching, a foreboding notion that comes to fruition with the ubiquitous presence of cameras in Walt's super-lab. But the half-charred face amidst the absence of the pink teddy bear's eye creepily foreshadows the demise of Gus Fring in "Face Off" (10/9/2011). Like the pink teddy bear, Gus appears whole and nearly unharmed until the camera captures the right side of his face and sees its skeletal remains before he collapses in a heap. This image appears one more time in "Live Free or Die" (7/15/12) as Walt sits at a diner counter and arranges strips of bacon into the number 52. Although this conveys a lapse in time (a little over one year since the events of season four and two years from the beginning of the series), the iconography is similar to that of a skull, with an over-easy egg creating an eye on the left and a mass of food erasing the eye on the right, much like the last time we encountered Fring. Unlike the thirty-second recap that reminds us of important events from the previous episodes, these uncanny images remind us of moments within the series without blatantly making us relive them. Perhaps they were important, or perhaps they conjure previously seen characters. Regardless, they trap us—much like the characters—in a circuit of time in which the past is impossible to escape as it persists in the iconographies of the present and will continue to resurface in the future.

It seems that the most blatant use of these flashbacks and flash-forwards is to confuse our judgment of characters within a season and a present episode. This leads to exciting twists and turns throughout the narrative, but it also brings us back to Henri Bergson, who, in a bit of a riff on the early twentieth-century practice of associationism in psychoanalysis, suggests "placed in the actual, it exhausts itself in vain attempts to discover in a realized and present state the mark of its past origin, to distinguish memory from perception, and to erect into a difference in kind that which it condemned in advance to be but a difference in magnitude" (loc. 22358). In other words, the process of seeking out one's past exacerbates the moment for which the person searches. In turn, this leads us to wonder whether the "remembered sensation becomes more actual the more we dwell upon it" and whether "the memory of the pain, when it began, [was] really pain" (Bergson loc. 2358-2369). The significance here, in regard to *Breaking Bad*, centers mostly on Walt and the aforementioned anger and regret that impel him to become Heisenberg. The motives for this split identity have been discussed thoroughly, but the flashbacks employed throughout the series beg us to wonder about the accuracy of these snippets of memory: we are unsure why Walt left Gray Matter and can only speculate. We are unsure how Walt and Skyler became married: there's a saccharine retelling of their initial courtship, but then a gap exists before we see Skyler pregnant with Walt Jr. Most importantly, these flashbacks only pepper Walt as an anti-hero and slightly occlude our view of him as the man diagnosed with cancer through the first three and a half seasons. His narcissism becomes more apparent toward the end of season four, but Fring is still framed mostly as the villain despite the fact that Walt poisoned Brock and brought his potential reckoning upon himself. Artistically, Gilligan uses these brief moments of memory and foreshadowing to create characters and storylines, but he also utilizes them in an effort to manipulate our judgments of characters and cast us deeper into the seemingly perpetual circuit of time and repetition.

Something as a final note here might be for us to question why we continue to watch the series. In a way, Gilligan has already exposed the finale. In "Negro y Azul" the time condensing musical introduction offers us images of a dead Heisenberg, donning the symbolic black cap that Walt recovers on his fifty-first birthday in "Fifty-One" (8/5/12). I'm not here to advocate Walt's demise or his survival; rather, I find it interesting that the show itself is manipulating our sensibilities of time, giving us answers and then luring us to watch the preceding events. Much like the way *24* provides a clock to rile our curiosity that builds to the end of the series, Gilligan baits us with the inevitable and appears to be slowly elucidating the fall, combining, at once, our knowledge of the past, our viewing of the present, and our awareness of the future.

Within *Breaking Bad*, Walt's existence, encounter with his own mortality and struggles to atone for his past connect to our modern anxieties over time and our continuously-in-flux identities. Our obsession with achievement and "clock time," combined with the rising phenomena of hurry-sickness and time squeezing, perhaps provides a rationale for our always-on, always-connected culture that relishes in cell phones, social networks, and virtual representations of ourselves. While I don't believe that Gilligan is prophesizing a ubiquitous nihilism movement of joyous sadism and narcissism, his depiction of a character who ponders and laments the "paths we take" is eerily akin to our obsession over the past, present, and future, that define our own lives.

NOTES

1. Lyrics taken from Justsomelyrics.com from Mick Harvey's song, "Out of Time Man."
2. The episodes in which dead bodies are dissolved include ". . . And the Bag's in the River" (2/10/08), "Box Cutter" (7/17/11), "Face Off" (10/9/11), "Dead Freight" (8/12/12), and "Gliding Over All" (9/2/12).
3. This occurs in the episode "Gray Matter" (2/24/08).
4. Walt's comment occurs in the episode ". . . And the Bag's in the River" (2/8/08).
5. This comment occurs in the episode "Peekaboo" (4/12/09).
6. This observation is made in the episode "Bit by a Dead Bee" (3/22/09).
7. Gretchen's comment occurs in the episode "Gray Matter" (2/24/08).
8. Walt makes this declarative statement in the episode "Crazy Handful of Nothin'" (3/28/08).
9. This flashback occurs in the episode ". . . And the Bag's in the River" (2/8/08).
10. A narcocorrido is a Mexican ballad centered on the exploits of drug traffickers in Mexico.
11. Gus demonstrates to Walt and Jesse his penchant for cold-blooded murder in the episode "Box Cutter" (7/17/11).
12. This image occurs in the episode "Caballo sin Nombre" (3/28/10).

WORKS CITED

Bergson, Henri. (1929). *Matter and Memory*. London: Allen and Unwin. Kindle ebook, 2012.
———. *Time and Free Will*. (1910). London: Allen and Unwin. Kindle ebook, 2012.
Deleuze, Gilles. *Difference and Repetition*. London: Athlone Press, 1994.
———. *Cinema 2*. Minneapolis: University of Minnesota Press, 1989.
Freud, Sigmund. (1920). *Introductory Lectures to Psychoanalysis*. New York: Horace Liverlight. Kindle ebook, 2012.

Gallagher, Shaun. *The Inordinance on Time*. Evanston, IL: Northwestern University Press, 1998.

Gleick, James. *Faster*. New York: Random House, 2000.

Gonzales, Rachel, Larissa Mooney, and Richard A. Rawson. 2010. "The Methamphetamine Problem in the United States." *Annual Review of Public Health*. 31. 385-398. doi: 10.1146/annurev.publhealth.012809.103600.

Harvey, Mick. "Out of Time Man." http://www.justsomelyrics.com.

Heideggar, Martin. *Being and Time*, translated by John Macquarrie and Edward Robinson. New York: Harper, 1962 (1927).

Heisenberg, Werner. *Physics and Philosophy: The Revolution in Modern Science*. New York: Prometheus Books, 1999.

Hume, David. *A Treatise on Human Nature*. London: Oxford University Press. Kindle ebook, 2000.

Husserl, Edmund. *On the Phenomenology of the Consciousness of Internal Time*. London: Kluwer, 1991.

Leong, Susan, Teodor Mitew, Marta Celleti, and Erika Pearson. "The Question Concerning (Internet) Time." *New Media and Society*. 11. (2009): 1267-1285.

Maxwell, Jane Carlisle and Beth A. Rutkowski. "The Prevalence of Methamphetamine and Amphetamine Abuse in North America: A Review of the Indicators, 1992—2007." *Drug and Alcohol Review 27*. (2008): 229-235.

Moshe, Mira. "Media Time Squeezing: the Privatization of the Media Time Sphere." *Television and New Media*. 13:1. (2012): 68-88.

Nietzsche, Friedrich. *The Gay Science, with a Prelude in Rhymes and an Appendix of Songs*. New York: Vintage, 1974.

———. 2012. "Truth and Lies in an Extra-Moral Sense." http://academics.eckerd.edu/instructor/starkjl/jls--inactive/405/September13/Nietzsche.pdf.

Shaw, Spencer. *Film Consciousness: From Phenomenology to Deleuze*. London: McFarland and Company, 2008.

Swift, Jonathan. (1892). *Gulliver's Travels*. London: George Bell and Sons. Kindle ebook, 2012.

Turkle, Sherry. *Alone Together*. New York: Basic Books, 2011.

———. "Can You Hear Me Now?." *Forbes*. 7 May 2007. http://www.forbes.com/free_forbes/2007/0507/176.html.

Widder, Nathan. *Reflections on Time and Politics*. State College: Pennsylvania State University, 2008.

THREE

Heisenberg: Epistemological Implications of a Criminal Pseudonym

Alberto Brodesco

PROFESSIONS

Who is Walter White? What is his profession? The early impressions that *Breaking Bad* give of its main character's occupations are very contradictory. The first time we see him, in the cold open of "Pilot"[1] (01/20/2008), he is driving a RV in the desert in his underwear; then he is at home, in front of a plaque commemorating his contribution to research having been awarded the Nobel Prize; we learn later that he teaches chemistry at the J. P. Wynne High School; after school he reaches a car wash, where he works as an employee to supplement his income. The four jobs do not match each other at all.

As summarized in the above scheme, the illegal work performed inside the RV is in obvious contrast with all the other three legal activities. The work at the school is compatible with the one at the car wash, if we assume that the teacher is underpaid and he needs to moonlight. But in relation to his Nobel Prize research this job in education raises some questions. Why should a top level researcher settle teaching in a high school? What's even more perplexing is the arrow between the Nobel and the Car wash. Why should such a scientist work part-time at a car wash? *Breaking Bad* is a tale of schizophrenia. Teacher, car wash employee, Nobel prize co-winner, methamphetamine manufacturer, criminal. Walter White is all of these characters. It is impossible to identify this man with a single and recognizable profile. In a society that often bases its judgment and attribution of social value on profession, it is very difficult to decide

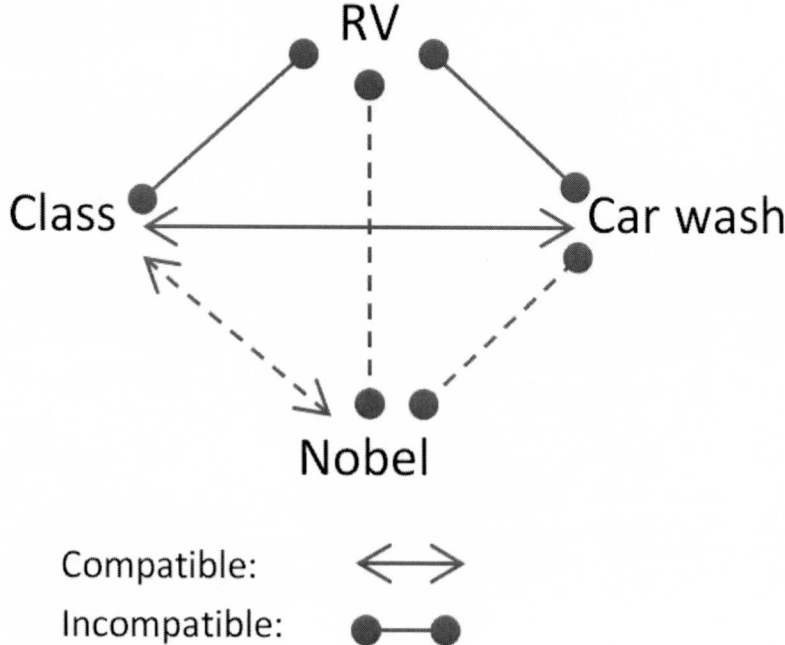

A scheme of the compatibilities of Walter White's occupations.

if White is a successful man or a loser. This indeterminacy or uncertainty that will develop further and further through the five seasons of the series is one of the great textures of *Breaking Bad*'s plot.

Following Walter we ultimately enter or get to know very different scientific milieus—legitimate ones like the classroom or Gray Matter company and illegitimate ones, like the RV and Gustavo Fring's drug laboratory. But in these "professions" there is not just a division between legal and criminal activities but also one between big and small (or smallest) science (see Price 1963), the first leading to awards and glory, the latter writing formulas on a blackboard in front of a class of bored students. For the high school job Walter White is evidently over qualified. His big science becomes small when transferred into a classroom and returns big again when (illegally) transported into the RV. There, out of place, applied to drug manufacturing, Walt's chemistry majestically gets back its strength and creativity.

Teaching seems indeed to provide just frustration to Mr. White. The only real restitution he gets from his high school employment is, quite ironically, that he recognizes a drug dealer escaping from a window as his former student Jesse Pinkman. In "Green Light" (4/11/10) Walter will definitely leave the school. White is now a full-time criminal and a full-time scientific genius. To give the viewer an idea of Walter's professional dissatisfaction, the pilot permits a close look at the Nobel Prize plaque. Walter wakes up early on the morning of his fiftieth birthday. In the dining room, he exercises on a primitive stair-master, in front of which is appended a framed paper that says "Science Research Center, Los Alamos, New Mexico hereby recognizes Walter H. White, Crystallography Project Leader For Proton Radiography, 1985, Contributor to Research Awarded the Nobel Prize." From this plaque we gather significant information. Walter White worked, when he was around twenty-seven years old, in a nuclear physics program at Los Alamos.

If we leave the fictional world and take a look at the real Nobel winner list, we can verify that the Chemistry prize in 1985 went to Herbert A. Hauptman and Jerome Karle with the following motivation, "for their outstanding achievements in the development of direct methods for the determination of crystal structures."[2] This is certainly a clue to Walter White's meth crystals. But given the "Proton Radiography" specialization of Walt's study we may also take a look at the Physics Nobel Prize of the same year, awarded to Klaus von Klitzing "for the discovery of the quantized Hall effect."[3] We are in the field of quantum mechanics. In light of Walter White's further career we take note of both of these pieces of information. The plot does not specify the pathway that drives White from Los Alamos Science Research Center to J. P. Wynne High School. Between the two there is certainly Gray Matter, a successful technology company deserving a *Scientific American* cover ("Gray Matter," 02/24/08) co-founded by Walter White with a friend of the time, Elliott Schwartz. For unknown reasons, Walt later left this position. He will accuse his former associates of having built an empire on his work ("Peekaboo" 4/12/09). The huge success of Gray Matter is an additional element leading Walt to drug manufacturing. As he explains to Jesse ("Buyout" 8/19/12), he had sold his share of the company to Elliott for $5,000, while Gray Matter now had a net worth of $2.16 billion. In front of this empire, Walter strives to build another, a criminal one.

In "Full Measure" (6/13/10), we see a flashback of Walter and a pregnant Skyler entering their new house, approximately in 1990, when Walt was working at the Sandia National Laboratory, a real life Albuquerque-based company dedicated to nuclear science and weapon research. Skyler manifests her worries about the house being too ambitious for their income, but Walter chides her for being too cautious. Being the teaser of the crucial third season finale, this apologue gains a double meaning. In a first sense Walter's vision of his future was wrong. His career was a failure, at the point that he had to 'break bad' in order to find success and wealth. In a second sense he has indeed 'gone up,' but in a very different way than expected.

The route leading Walter White to become a drug producer is therefore established by a series of coincidences. The cancer diagnosis, of course, but also a sum of professional disappointments and personal ambition. Walter considers himself a scientific genius. He will build his reputation as an outlaw on chemistry. A Nobel-awarded intelligence is employed to produce the purest methamphetamine for all the southern states. Already in the first episode of the series we see that his new occupation invigorates him, even sexually. In an early stage of his criminal career Walter White chooses the name of the great German physicist Werner Heisenberg as a criminal pseudonym—as we will see, a choice full of implications.

SCIENTIFIC RATIONALITY AND ITS MISHAPS

The signs of Walter White's scientific genius are not limited to a plaque on a wall, nor to manufacturing maximum quality meth. The developing of the plot shows that a great part of his criminal success depends on his intellectual brilliance. Scientific skills or tools are often displayed in different contexts as devices that get Walter (and Jesse) out of danger. Science assumes the form of 'MacGyverisms'—tricks, smart solutions, magic combinations of objects or chemical elements that provide a way-out from very troubling situations. In the pilot Walter produces a chemical explosion with red phosphorous and consequently poisons the two gangsters (Emilio and Krazy-8) trapped inside the RV with a toxic gas; in "Cat's in the Bag . . ." (1/27/08) Walter tells Jesse how to dissolve a corpse using hydrofluoric acid in combination with a plastic container; in "Crazy Handful of Nothin" (3/2/08) Walter intimidates the drug boss Tuco by using explosive fulminated mercury. The day after this successful criminal act Walter teaches his class about chemical reactions that produce rapid explosions, mentioning the example of fulminated mercury. We witness again to confusion or overlapping between different approaches to science, its legitimate knowledge and its illegitimate use. The lesson also addresses the audience of the series. The classroom is used as a kind of 'footnote' to explain the chemistry upon which Walter's tricks are based. In "4 Days Out" (5/3/09) Walter and Jesse are stuck in the desert. The RV battery is dead, there is nothing within walking distance and their cell phones are not working. Nervous and frightened, Jesse screams at Walt to think of a scientific response to the situation. He does. A surrogate battery is built using coin zinc. In "Buyout" (8/19/12), Walter, tied by Mike to a radiator, chews a line cord, and uses the wires to burn the zip-ties that hold him captive. But Walter's scientific knowledge includes also the field of biology. He knows how to extract the ricin from castor beans ("Seven Thirty-Seven" 3/8/09; "Problem Dog" 8/28/11) and how to synthesize poison from a plant, the Lily of the Valley ("End Times" 10/2/11; "Face Off" 10/9/11).

It is on this strict mastery of scientific rationality that Walter White builds his criminal success (and survival). The guideline of Walter's actions is instrumental rationality, which postulates an agent who conceives an end and combines a series of means to fulfill it.[4] Foreshadowing death after his lung cancer diagnosis, all he wants to do is leave his family financially safe. The target of Walter White's instrumental rationality is in fact, all too simply, to make money—his wife is pregnant, his teenage son was born with cerebral palsy and his bank account is almost dry. His decision to make money producing drugs can be questionable, but this is nonetheless a very lucrative business. It is fast and easy money for a master chemist like Walter. In that initial moment the choice of manufacturing methamphetamine is objectionable but mostly lucid. Walt applies his scientific rationality also in the drug distribution strategy, where he acts as a perfect *homo economicus* deciding that they need to charge more for their product and control the market.

Episode after episode this 'stronger' rationality seems to weaken. Walt's behavior will soon shift from instrumental rationality to Weber's value-oriented rationality—the value being family. In the farewell video message to his wife and son in the very first scene of the pilot episode (1/20/08), Walter tells them that all of his actions were for the best of the family. The rationality of his actions is shaken by the adversity of the field he is moving in: the Albuquerque criminal world, the Mexican cartel, the DEA investigation, etc. Having to deal with such complexity (also on the home front, he has to worry about Skyler, Hank, and Jesse), the saner choice would be to retire from this business as soon as possible. But the (alleged) interest of the family is more important than the evaluation of risks. In this type of value-oriented rationality actions are rational only from the subjective point of view of the actors.

At least until season five, Walter's *amoral familism* is principally responsible for his breaking bad. What defines amoral familism is the will to "maximize the material, short-run advantage of the nuclear family" (Banfield 1958, 85) without any consideration whatsoever about what is good for the community or society. Walter White achieves his aim to leave money to his wife and provide for his kids' college tuitions at the price of causing suffering and death outside of his family, finding in the ideology of family justification and self-absolution. When Skyler is traumatized by Ted Benekes' awakening in the hospital, Walter tries to tell her everything is fine because our actions were all for good reasons—to protect the family. That is a perfect formulation of amoral familism. With his good intentions Walter goes far, possibly too far. As Skyler herself soon realizes, she must protect the family from the man (Walter) who threatens it through his protective actions

In "Mas" (4/18/10), Gus Fring says to Walter that he shares his ideas about family and masculinity by stating the importance of the man serving as the provider and caretaker of his family. It is amoral familism that renders Walter equivalent to a mafia member or a narco-trafficker. In "One Minute" (5/2/10) a flashback brings us to Mexico. In front of a dispute, Tio tells his two small nephews that family is everything. The agreement with Walt's statements is total. White can speak with criminals like a peer.

In season five, this 'minor' value-oriented, familistic rationality crumbles. Walt's logic is overcome by ambition and by a Nietzschean will to power (Wright 2012). Walter gets to embrace the third type of Weberian action, the emotional or affective action, produced by a mood or a disposition. Being a scientist, Walter White is not immune from *hubris*, a loss of rationality in the heart of rationality itself (Frayling 2005, Brodesco 2008), occurring when scientific calculation is overwhelmed by a personal tension. Hubris puts in danger human lives (including the scientist's) and scientific progress. Walter White is far from being a stereotypical mad doctor. Differently from most science-fiction and horror mad docs, Walter is not led by an insane desire to defy nature's boundaries. But hubris affects his rationality nonetheless, leading him to peril. Both Walt's instrumental and value-oriented rationality begin to crumble in the first episodes of season four. In "Shotgun" (8/14/11) Hank, at dinner at the Whites' home, talks about the case of Gale Boetticher, Walt's former assistant recently found dead. Hank says he thinks Gale was not merely a cook, but a superior meth chef and genius. Knowing well that the genius plain and simple is instead himself, Walt cannot keep from telling his brother-in-law that those chemically perfect blue meth could not have been produced by Gale. The lab notes that the police had found at Gale's house are dismissed by Walt as mere copies of another person's work. Against every rationality, Walter lets the DEA know that Gale was not the mastermind behind the meth operation. He is so proud of his product that he cannot hold back.

This scientific narcissism is certainly a minor symptom of a mad doctor syndrome. As prescribed by mad science tradition, hubris goes beyond control and begins to act against the interest of the individual (Skal 1998). Walter seems here to share the same hubris as an epic hero renowned for his intelligence. Leaving Polyphemus' cave, Ulysses could not resist from telling the Cyclops that his real name was not Nobody, hence exposing himself and his comrades to danger.

> The artful Odysseus cannot do otherwise: as he flees, while still under the sphere controlled by the rock-hurling giant, he not only mocks Polyphemus but reveals to him his true name and origin, as if the primeval world still had such power over Odysseus, who always escaped only by the skin of his teeth, that he would fear to become Nobody again if he did not reestablish his own identity by means of the

magical word which rational identity had just superseded. (Horkheimer and Adorno 2002, 53)

This fear to "become Nobody again" perfectly applies to Walter White's case. In "Buyout" (8/19/12) Walt speaks frankly with Jesse. He tells him that his wife has just said that she is waiting for his cancer to come back; that Gray Matter, the company he has left for dimes, has presently a billion dollar turnover. It is no longer a question of family or money, but building the business into an empire. Family seems to have acted ever since as a cover for his now declared hubris.[5]

Scientific hubris has become criminal hubris. Walter White does not just want to produce his blue meth but to build an industry as successful and remunerative as Gray Matter. In "Gliding Over All" (9/2/12) Skyler leads Walter to the garage where his illegal incomes are stocked. She tells him that they will never be able to spend all that cash. If Walt's rational ambition is to leave money to his family, that is far too much. Faced with mountains of dollars the complete irrationality of his actions is apparently evident even to Walter. Other than being loads of money it is a symbol of excess, a manifest revelation of Walter White's ultimate hubris.

HEISENBERG

The turning point comes in the episode, "Crazy Handful of Nothin" (3/2/08). Walter White has just shaved his head to prevent the hair loss that is the consequence of chemotherapy. He now has a goatee. He sits a few seconds in his car in meditation. Then he grabs a pack of crystals and moves in the direction of a building painted with graffiti, with small groups of gangster-looking men chatting in front. That is the headquarters of Tuco, the local drug boss. The camera, positioned inside the building, frames Walt in medium shot. We see his silhouette through two kinds of colored windows, passing from yellow to red. He advances again into a yellow background, as though he was going back and forth from risk to danger. Walter asks a gang member to see Tuco. The handheld camera trembles. Walt stares at a surveillance camera. We see him through its cold lenses. A gang member body searches Walt and takes the crystals. The product brought in by Walter is now analyzed by Tuco. The camera finally follows Walter as he enters Tuco's room. A reverse-shot shows him advancing with resolution. Tuco asks him who he is and Walt replies, "Heisenberg."

Werner Heisenberg (1901-1976) is the German theoretical physicist awarded with the Nobel Prize in 1932 "for the creation of quantum mechanics."[6] His name is tied to the uncertainty principle. The choice of the Heisenberg criminal name is full of consequences. This alias acts like a spoiler that provides an interpretative frame for Walter White's actions. Tuco asks Walter what he wants. The audacious answer is 50,000 dollars.

He has entered with belligerent intentions into the headquarters of a dangerous criminal. To be even more convincing he makes use of an explosive, blowing up Tuco's office. The crystals were not meth but fulminated mercury. The transformation of Walter White into Heisenberg undergoes several changes in look and attitude. Walter White's choice of Heisenberg's name can surely be attributed to his will to wear the mask of a revolutionary scientific genius. But the name he picks is Heisenberg, not Newton, Mendeleev, Tesla, or Einstein. There are at least five main applications of Heisenberg's figure and his notorious uncertainty principle that can give an explanation for such an adoption. The first can be applied to the character's conscious or unconscious intent, while the other four are principally attributes of the film narrative and its connotative strategies.

As a first element it is interesting to note how the announcement of the criminal name is made in a controlled context, under the gaze of a video surveillance camera, an angle "synecdochic of our time" (Tziallas 2010, 17; Lyon 2006). White and associates also later ("Live Free or Die" 7/15/12) will have trouble with the surveillance regime. They will have to destroy the video data stored in Fring's computer, now in the possession of the DEA. The surveillance camera is a symptom of control, of the captivity of Walter's existence. Life events forbid Walter to express his talent. The choice of the Heisenberg name is an exit strategy. Video surveillance can be compared to scientific scrutiny in its aim to record reality and render it objective. Heisenberg's principle unsettles it all. Reality escapes, hiding data while showing another. As with a microscope, the surveillance camera cannot record everything. Heisenberg's uncertainty offers an escape from the ideal of transparency and predictability of the surveillance regime. The name of Heisenberg is a guarantee of the complexity of reality. The disciplinary institutions that pretend to be in control cannot have total access to the truth of human lives. The observed subject has traits that make him/her ontologically impossible to be scrutinized in all of his/her intentions and will. Even after being checked and body-searched, Walter is able to introduce explosives in Tuco's headquarters. There is a misinterpretation in the observation of the crystals (not meth but fulminated mercury) that Walt is carrying with him. Walter White, now Heisenberg, manifests his unpredictability.

A second point is related to the 'political' doubts raised by Werner Heisenberg's behavior during the Second World War. When, in "Negro y Azul" (4/19/09), Walter White has a meeting with Jesse's pals and dealers at the National Atomic Museum and introduces himself as Heisenberg, some strong and perturbing resonances come to mind. Real Heisenberg's participation in the development of the national-socialist atomic project is one of the most debated themes in the history of science.[7] As the plaque in the living room showed in "Pilot," Walter White worked at Los Alamos. We also know that he was employed at the Sandia National Laboratory, dedicated to weapon research and nuclear science. Walter White is for two seasons the scientist in residence of Fring's drug industry, manufacturing a drug that causes psychological and physical harm to masses of people. Political naivety or an apolitical attitude become political guilt.

Thirdly, Werner Heisenberg put an end to the concept that science is the "attempt to extract order from confusion" (Lindley 2008, 1). With Heisenberg, science got to admit ambivalence. Debating with his mentor Niels Bohr, the young German physicist resolved to call his principle "uncertainty." There are variables that an experimenter cannot measure at the same time. If he gets to describe the behavior of one, the second fades. The more precise you get to measuring one aspect, the farther you will find yourself from the other. "Uncertainty" does not mean that a measurement cannot be precise or that science has to submit to chaos. It reveals the necessity to choose between obtaining knowledge about one feature over another—this is what Bohr calls the "principle of complementarity" (see Gilmore 1995, 47). A scientist has to face the impossibility of being in full mastery of his variables and their effects. He can control some determinations of his experiment, but others will remain uncertain. Walter White could not even remotely predict that the actions (to let a young girl die) carried out in episode "Phoenix" (5/24/09) would lead him to be involved in the collision of two airplanes and the death of 167 people in "ABQ" (5/31/09).

The fourth point is tied to the consequences of the uncertainty principle.

> The acquisition of knowledge about a system by an observer, even inferential knowledge, can somehow change the behavior of that system or at any rate what the observer subsequently sees in a way unprecedented in classical physics, where the observer plays no special role. (Colin 2004, 39)

Walter White tries to act like an 'external' experimenter in the world of drug dealing but his entrance into the field changes the entire domain, making it impossible for him to stand outside. In the first place the distribution of his product will cause a change in the whole balance of the commerce. The blue meth will upset the market of the southern states. In the second place, since the pilot, Walter will not be able to just cook but will get involved in the criminal activities at all levels. An amazing exemplification of the 'external observer' illusion can be found in "Caballo Sin Nombre" (3/28/10), where the two Mexican cousins of the cartel wait in Whites' bedroom for Walter to come out of the shower. One holds an ax in his hand. Walter believes he is an observer, outside of the drug wars being waged between the cartels, but the two cousins (and their ax) act like a revelation. Knowingly or not (he will not see the cousins sitting on his bed), Walt is part of the field. He has produced a consistent change in the international drug business.

The uncertainty principle, the fifth and final point, implies that two mutually exclusive behaviors may happen simultaneously, as displayed in the (in)famous quantum mechanical "Schrödinger's cat" paradox, where a cat inside a box is alive and dead at the same time (Bruce 2004). In a similar way, we are unable to decide upon Walt's conduct, simultaneously 'good' and 'bad.' The most important perspective on the choice of the Heisenberg pseudonym relates probably to this ethical judgment on Walter White's actions. Can we absolve Walter White from producing drugs and becoming a murderer because he set out with the best intentions and all the bad done was accidental 'collateral damage?' Or should we consider him morally guilty? This uncertainty or indeterminacy about Walt's morality is possibly the most debated topic of the whole series.

Before analyzing this particular feature, we must say that the viewers' perspective on White's ethics is subjected to a major development season after season.[8] We can recognize, from season one to season five, a continuous increase, in blogs and message boards, in the number of commentators that judge Walter morally guilty. "Cornered" (8/21/11) shows in this sense a precise coming out, with Walter declaring, "I'm not in danger. I am the danger." From then on, it is a descent into the abyss. In season five the screenwriters' will to insist on Walter White's wickedness is manifest. In "Buyout" (8/19/12) Walter happily whistles after having told Jesse that he is very afraid and sad for the death of Drew, the young boy shot in the desert because he witnessed the train robbery. But, as I have already stated, season five does not cancel seasons one through four.

In a series where the idea of "badness" is included in the title, the audience divides between those who absolve Walter and those who condemn him. As with Schrödinger's cat, the observer has to face a superposition of states. The official AMC *Breaking Bad* blog has published, after episode one of season five, a very interesting poll on this subject.[9] Two of the questions posed by the survey deal with Walt's morality.

7. Morality Meter: "Good" Skyler playing the heavy with Ted is . . .

    a. Virtuous—4.25 percent
    b. Questionable—16.37 percent
    c. Ethically Corrupt—12.15 percent
    d. Villainous—17.6 percent
    e. Heisenberg—49.64 percent

[. . .]

10. Morality Meter: "We're done when I say we're done." Walt pushing Saul around is . . .

    a. Virtuous—1.89 percent

b. Questionable—2.56 percent
c. Ethically Corrupt—2.29 percent
d. Villainous—14.91 percent
e. Heisenberg—78.35 percent

This use of "Heisenberg" as a synonym of "I can't decide" in a moral evaluation is really intriguing. The "Heisenberg" answer is in the place usually occupied by "no opinion / don't know." The German scientist's name stands for uncertainty. "Heisenberg" means two opposite situations (moral and immoral) happening simultaneously.

The trouble with judging Walt's behavior depends upon two impossibilities. Cinematographic identification always leads the viewer to support the main character to some extent.[10] "We are all Walter White. . . . [He] came along and gave us all hope. . . . Walter White remains our hero, and we root for his success, and the defeat of his foils" (Koepsell and Arp 2012, vii). As this citation demonstrates, secondary identification gets us indeed "too close" to the (evil) subject. We are conscious of it, and possibly afraid. The reaction to this concern may manifest in the assumption of an ironic spectatorial agency (i.e., to fully endorse White's 'breaking bad') or in taking distance from identification, attempting a rational analysis of Walter White's actions. But the second impossibility deals exactly with the vanity of searching for an objective standpoint, for a perspective that permits one to hold together the several variables of this complex field. Walter is fifty-years-old, his wife is pregnant, he has a teenage son with a disability, he is frustrated with a job for which he is certainly overqualified, he gave up working with a flourishing industry for unknown reasons, and, most of all, he has cancer with few, if any possibilities to recover. Every mean of understanding gets lost in the uncertainty generated by the multiple crossing of these factors.

In "Full Measure" (6/13/10), should Walter murder the innocent Gale Boetticher, if the alternative is probably being killed himself? And before, in ". . . And the Bag's in the River" (2/10/08), should Walter murder Krazy-8 or not, knowing that Krazy-8 would probably exterminate his entire family if he lets him go? Walter forgets to write that fundamental adverb, *probably*, when, pondering this killing, he makes on his notebook a list of pros and cons. But the future Heisenberg should be aware of the central role of probability. Werner Heisenberg writes in fact that a correct experimental procedure is based on probability function, that represents "a mixture of two things, partly a fact and partly our knowledge of a fact" (Heisenberg 2000, 15).

It is presumptuous to judge these cases from an external point of view and impossible to assume his standpoint. How can we enter the mind of a mortally sick person who knows he is dying? Only a specific, individual, relative angle on the surrounding environment is possible.[11] As Giorgio Agamben (2004) writes speaking about the animal realm,

Uexküll's investigations into the animal environment are contemporary with both quantum physics and the artistic avantgardes. And like them, they express the unreserved abandonment of every anthropocentric perspective in the life sciences and the radical dehumanization of the image of nature. . . . Too often . . . we imagine that the relations a certain animal subject has to the things in its environment take place in the same space and in the same time as those which bind us to the objects in our human world. This illusion rests on the belief in a single world in which all living beings are situated. Uexküll shows that such a unitary world does not exist, just as a space and a time that are equal for all living things do not exist. The fly, the dragonfly, and the bee that we observe flying next to us on a sunny day do not move in the same world as the one in which we observe them, nor do they share with us—or with each other—the same time and the same space. (39-40)

HEISENBERG: USES AND MISUSES IN CONTEMPORARY TV SERIES

The name of Heisenberg, the uncertainty principle, Schrödinger's cat, and the quantum mechanics' "mystery" are recurrent topics in contemporary TV series.[12] Let us take a look at a few examples. In the episode "The Luck of the Fryrish" (3/11/01) of *Futurama*,[13] Professor Farnsworth goes to the races. Two horses cross the end-line perfectly tied-up. An electronic microscope is used to indicate the winner. The speaker declares that the winner is horse number three "at quantum finish." Farnsworth, who bet on another, complains, "No fair! You changed the outcome by measuring it!" In "The Monopolar Expedition" (5/11/09) of *The Big Bang Theory*,[14] the main character (a theoretical physicist) waiting for an important meeting says he will be, in between, a "Heisenberg particle." One episode of *Numb3rs*[15] is titled "Uncertainty Principle" (1/28/05). In the mother of all modern series, David Lynch's *Twin Peaks*,[16] one character explicitly quotes Heisenberg, "What we observe is not nature itself, but nature exposed to our method of questioning" ("Checkmate" 1/19/91). The Schrödinger's cat paradox is mentioned in *Futurama* ("Law and Oracle" 7/7/2011), *Six Feet Under*[17] ("In the Game," 3/3/02), *FlashForward*[18] ("Scary Monsters and Super Creeps" 10/29/09). Even in the pilot of *Eureka*[19] ("Pilot" 7/18/06) there are references to quantum mechanics. In *Lost's*[20] "Because You Left" (1/21/09) one of the main characters, Sawyer, confronts Daniel Faraday, a former Oxford researcher. The latter says, "We really do not have time for me to try to explain. You have no idea how difficult that would be for me to try to explain this . . . this phenomenon to a quantum physicist." In one of the first scenes of *Rubicon*[21] ("Gone in the Teeth," 6/13/10) we see the main character leaning on a bookshelf a volume on string theory.

Also, *Breaking Bad* makes a direct reference to physics by quoting the string theory. In "Live Free or Die" (7/15/12), Walter, Jesse, and Mike are trying to solve the problem of the video data archived in Fring's laptop now in possession of the DEA. They think about contacting a familiar junkyard operator to use his giant-size magnet. In the negotiation with the man, Walter asks him if it is feasible or not. The answer is, "Hey, we're living in a time of string theories and God particles. Feasible, do-able? Yeah, sure, why not? Expensive." As we can see, the use or misuse of Heisenberg's name and quantum mechanics principles has become very common in TV series and, more generally, in other fields that have nothing to do with physics—popular fiction, anthropology, sociology, literary criticism. Theoretical physicist and science writer David Lindley (2008) questions the legitimacy or necessity of mentioning Heisenberg in such heterogeneous contexts and for such various purposes, with just a metaphorical connection with Heisenberg's statements on measurement. He writes about a "curious annexation of an esoteric idea" that is used to say "that what you see varies according to what you are looking for, that the story depends on who is listening and watching as well as who is acting and talking" (7, 213). Lindley elaborates on the perspective.

> But this is easy to understand. Put a bunch of cameras in the middle of a tense and private situation, and people will start acting oddly. No one who has taken photographs at a wedding or tried making a home movie of a family reunion will be surprised by this. Why drag Heisenberg into it? . . . If Heisenberg's principle doesn't enter all that often into the thinking of the average physicist, how can it be important for journalism, or critical literary theory, or the writing of television screenplays? (213-214)

The answer we may give is that the recurrent presence of Heisenberg is a symptom of a cognitive apprehension affecting the contemporary media-sphere. Present-day American TV series incorporate in their narrative the complexity or incomprehensibility of the world, admitting an essential cognitive frailty. Richard Feynman's statement "I think I can safely say that nobody understands quantum mechanics" (quoted in Kumar 2009, 351) may easily and legitimately be reformulated as "I think I can safely say that nobody understands *Lost*." The structure and storylines of many TV series assume the shape of a puzzle, of a mind game.[22] *Lost*, *Fringe*,[23] *Alcatraz*,[24] *The 4400*,[25] *Dollhouse*,[26] and *Flash Forward* are all series that challenge "the reliability, necessity and readability" (Di Chio 2011, 178) of the worlds produced by fiction. Space-time complications, time travels and parallel universes—with all the logical paradoxes and philosophical questions implied—are some of contemporary series' favorite devices. Audiovisual products that ask for expanded plots can rely on the expansion of reality produced by sciences—especially by disciplines that move beyond common sense as relativity theory or quantum mechanics—to stimulate and defy the "*libido cognoscendi*" (Jost 2011, 30) of the viewer. Science is a tool that can be employed to multiply the storylines, authorizing the "coexistence, in a single universe of experience, of situations instead incompatible" (Coco 2006, 24), successfully mixing rationality and mystery, acting as a mediator between plausible and fantastic. Cognitive apprehension goes together with ethical doubt. Also *Breaking Bad*, although in a very different way than *Lost*, walks on the edge of uncertainty.

UNCERTAINTY

The cinema of Joel and Ethan Coen is a prominent source for Vince Gilligan and his team of writers and directors.[27] The title of "No-Rough-Stuff-Type Deal" (3/9/08) explicitly quotes a dialogue from *Fargo* (1996). In both *Fargo* and *Breaking Bad* an illegal but supposedly "simple" activity (a staged kidnapping and drug manufacturing) becomes very complicated because of the problems with controlling the complexity of reality—call it causality, theory of chaos, butterfly effect, or principle of uncertainty.

A *Serious Man* (2009), possibly one of the Coen brothers' most intense films, opens with a prologue. We are in a *shtetl* in Eastern Europe. One night a Jewish couple, husband and wife, is visited by a man, apparently an elderly man who had died three years before. The wife says he is a *dybbuk*, an evil spirit who possesses the dead person's body. The old man laughs at this idea, claiming to be through all evidence alive. The woman does not believe him. She stabs him in the chest. He does not seem to bleed initially but soon his shirt is covered with red. Was he really a ghostly presence? Did he deserve to be stabbed or did he just need help? Was he alive or dead? The "dybbuk" stumbles out in the dark and snow, leaving the couple and the viewers in the most total uncertainty about who he was for real. *A Serious Man* tells the story of a physics university professor, Larry Gopnik, who teaches his class the Heisenberg principle, whose mathematical explanation covers an enormous blackboard. "[The principle] proves that we can't ever know what's going on. . . . But even if you can't figure anything out, you're still responsible for this on the midterm!" At the beginning of the film, Clive, a student of Korean origin, visits Professor Gopnik to claim that the failing grade he had received was "unjust . . . I understand the physics. I understand the dead cat." Larry replies, "Even I don't understand the dead cat. The math is how it really works." Clive implores the professor to give him a passing grade or the possibility of taking the midterm again, but Larry refuses. When the student leaves, Larry finds an envelope with a bundle of money on his desk, a blatant attempt to bribe him. He confronts Clive again, telling him that his attempt of corruption will have severe consequences. Clive replies that his interpretation of the situation is "mere surmise, very uncertain." Later, at home, Gopnik receives the visit of the Korean student's father, who threatens to sue him *either* for falsely accusing his son to have left the money on his desk *or* for having taken that money. Gopnik replies, "It doesn't make sense. Either he left the money or he didn't." Mr. Park's memorable answer is, "Please. Accept the mystery."

Even if it is difficult (and possibly unnecessary) to tell exactly if *A Serious Man* has a direct influence on the development of *Breaking Bad*'s plot,[28] this scene certainly offers a lens to interpret the series. More than judging upon good and evil, taking pro- or anti-Walt positions, identifying with him or not, *Breaking Bad* suggests to "accept the mystery." The use of Heisenberg's name makes particular sense here, being that uncertainty is the most prominent trait of the series. Most of its characters are schizophrenic, in a sort of global generalization of Schrödinger's cat's paradox to all society. Walter is a teacher and a meth producer, Fring a fast-food owner and a drug lord, Marie a cop's wife and a kleptomaniac, Saul a lawyer and a criminals' accomplice, Skyler a mother and a manager of a money-laundering business. As Telotte (1995, 160) writes about *Twin Peaks*, "the order of our world begins to show just how threadbare and fragile it really is, while the signs that sustain that order, including the various codes of the television narrative, reveal a sense of meaninglessness or blankness that also haunts our world."

Most TV series base their success on uncertainty, on the addiction created by not knowing "what will happen next," on the suspension (institutionalized by the rhetoric device of cliffhanger) that makes you long for the following episode. *Breaking Bad* takes this concept a step further, structuring the whole plot around Heisenberg's name and embodying his principle in some way. Schrödinger's cat mental experiment insists on the superposition of two states, life and death. After his cancer diagnosis, Walter White enters exactly into this suspended contingency— alive and dead at the same time. As the Mexican band sings in a music video in "Negro y Azul" (2.7), "Ese compa ya esta muerto/No más no le han avisado" (that dude is already dead, he hasn't been told yet). In this condition, Walter White acts like a rational-minded scientist who moves in irrational ways, driven by amoral familism and hubris, under the rule of the most fundamental "uncertainty," the one about our own mortality.

NOTES

1. If we suppose that the diegetic time concurs with the year of broadcasting (2008).

2. Please see http://www.nobelprize.org/nobel_prizes/chemistry/laureates/1985/.

3. Please see http://www.nobelprize.org/nobel_prizes/physics/laureates/1985/ .

4. In Max Weber's theory of action instrumental rationality (*Zweckrationalität*) is opposed to value-oriented rationality (*Wertrationalität*), emotional or affective action (*Affektuel*) and traditional action (*Traditionell*) (Weber 1978). See Brubaker 1984.

5. The fifth season's strong shift in White's characterization does not cancel the interpretation that can be made of the first four seasons. An analysis of a TV series that

spreads along six years can legitimately take as its corpus the whole series, one single season or even one or more single episodes.

6. Please see http://www.nobelprize.org/nobel_prizes/physics/laureates/1932/index.html.

7. See Cassidy 2009. For a synthesis of the different interpretations of Heisenberg's contribution to Nazi research see Landsman 2002. This topic is also the subject of Michael Frayn's successful play *Copenhagen* (1998).

8. I have regularly visited http://blogs.amctv.com/breaking-bad, http://www.imdb.com/title/tt093747 and http://www.tv.com/shows/breaking-bad.

9. Please see http://blogs.amctv.com/breakign-bad/2012/07/episode-1-story-sync-poll-results.php. Final poll results.

10. See Christian Metz's (1982) classic theory, that distinguishes between primary identification (with the camera) and secondary identification (with a character). The sympathy for Walter is also induced by Bryan Cranston's previous comic roles in the sitcoms *Seinfeld* (created by Larry David and Jerry Seinfeld, NBC, 1989-1998) and *Malcolm in the Middle* (created by Linwood Boomer, Fox, 2000-2006).

11. "If we must blame anyone for the curse of relativism that supposedly afflicts modern thought (no one's story is 'privileged', as the sociologists like to say, above anyone else's; all viewpoints are equally valid), then probably we should blame Heisenberg more than Einstein. Relativity—the scientific theory of space-time, that is—indeed says that different observers will see events in different ways, but it also offers a framework by which these different viewpoints can be reconciled to a consistent and objective account. Relativity doesn't deny that there are absolute facts; that's what the uncertainty principle does" (Lindley 2008, 213).

12. I tried to map the presence of science in contemporary serials in Brodesco 2013.

13. Created by Matt Groening, Fox, 1999-.

14. Created by Chuck Lorre and Bill Prady, CBS, 2007-.

15. Created by Nicolas Falacci and Cheryl Heuton, CBS, 2005-2010.

16. Created by Mark Frost and David Lynch, ABC, 1990-1991.

17. Created by Alan Ball, HBO, 2001-2005.

18. Created by Brannon Braga, David S. Goyer and Robert J. Sawyer, ABC, 2009-2010.

19. Created by Andrew Cosby and Jaime Paglia Eureka, SyFy, 2006-2012.

20. Created by Jeffrey Lieber, J. J. Abrams and Damon Lindelof, ABC, 2006-2010.

21. Created by Jason Horwitch, AMC, 2010.

22. A genre recently elaborated within the field of Film Studies is the "mind game film," a movie—from *The Sixth Sense* (M. Night Shyamalan, 1999) to *Inception* (Christopher Nolan, 2010)—that inquires and defies audience's understanding, progressively unsettling and withdrawing the information and knowledge that text had delivered (see Elsaesser 2009).

23. Created by J. J. Abrams, Roberto Orci and Alex Kurtzman, Fox, 2008-2013.

24. Created by Elizabeth Sarnoff, Steven Lilien, Bryan Wynbrandt, Fox, 2012.

25. Created by René Echevarria and Scott Peter, USA Network, 2004-2007.

26. Created by Joss Whedon, Fox, 2009-2010.

27. Read this extract from a 2011 interview where Vincent Gilligan declares: "Film noir is a big influence: the classic noirs—I could watch *The Maltese Falcon* once a month, probably—as well as the Coen brothers contemporary ones as well" (http://blogs.amctv.com/breaking-bad/2011/10/vince-gilligan-interview.php).

28. The date of release of *A Serious Man*, September 2009, is six months earlier than the broadcast of season three.

WORKS CITED

Agamben, Giorgio. *The Open. Man and Animal*. Stanford: Stanford University Press, 2004.

Banfield, Edward C. *The Moral Basis of a Backward Society*. Glencoe: The Free Press, 1958.

Brodesco, Alberto. *Una voce nel disastro. L'immagine dello scienziato nel cinema dell'emergenza*. Roma: Meltemi, 2008.

———. "Tecnoscienza e serialità televisiva. Una mappatura." *Annuario scienza e società 2013*. Eds. Federico Neresini and Andrea Lorenzet. Bologna: il Mulino, 2013.

Brubaker, Rogers. *The Limits of Rationality. An Essay on the Social and Moral Thought of Max Weber*. London-New York: Routledge, 1984.

Bruce, Colin. *Schrödinger's Rabbits. The Many Worlds of Quantum*. Washington: Joseph Henry Press, 2004.

Cassidy, David C. *Beyond Unncertainty. Heisenberg, Quantum Physics, and the Bomb*. New York: Bellevue Literary Press, 2009.

Coco, Attilio. "Le serie tv e l'esperienza del transito." *Segnocinema* 142.

Di Chio, Federico. 2011. *L'illusione difficile. Cinema e serie tv nell'età della disillusione*. Milano: Bompiani, 2006. 24-27.

Elsaesser, Thomas. "The Mind Game Film." In *Puzzle Films: Complex Storytelling in Contemporary Cinema*, edited by Warren Buckland. 13-41. Malden-Oxford: Wiley-Blackwell, 2009.

Frayn, Michael. *Copenhagen*. London: Methuen Drama, 1998.

Frayling, Christopher. *Mad, Bad and Dangerous? The Scientist and the Cinema*. London: Reaktion Books, 2005.

Gilmore, Robert. *Alice in Quantum Land. An Allegory of Quantum Physics*. New York: Springer-Verlag, 1995.

Heisenberg, Werner. *Physics and Philosophy. The Revolution in Modern Science*. London: Penguin Books, 2000.

Horkheimer, Max, and Theodor W. Adorno. *Dialectic of Enlightenment, Philosophical Fragments*. Stanford: Stanford University Press, 2002.

Jost, François. *De quoi les séries américaines sont-elles le symptôme?*. Paris: CNRS Editions, 2011.

Keopesell, David R., and Robert Arp. "A Fine Meth We've Gotten Into." In *Breaking Bad and Philosophy. Badder Living through Chemistry*, edited by David R. Keopesell and Robert Arp. vii-ix. Chicago-LaSalle: Open Court, 2012.

Kumar, Manjit. *Quantum. Einstein, Bohr and the Great Debate about the Nature of Reality*. London: Icon Books, 2009.

Landsman, N. P. "Getting Even with Heisenberg." *Studies in History and Philosophy of Modern Physics*. 33. (2002): 297-325.

Lindley, David. *Uncertainty. Einstein, Heisenberg, Bohr, and the Struggle for the Soul of Science*. New York: Anchor Books, 2008.

Lyon, David, ed. *Theorizing Surveillance: The Panopticon and Beyond*. Cullompton, UK: Willan, 2006.

Metz, Christian. *The Imaginary Signifier: Psychoanalysis and the Cinema*. Bloomington: Indiana University Press, 1982.

Price, Derek J. de Solla. *Little Science, Big Science*. New York: Columbia University Press, 1963.

Skal, David J. *Screams of Reason. Mad Science and Modern Culture*. New York: Norton & Company, 1998.

Telotte, J. P. "The Dis-Order of Things in Twin Peaks." In *Full of Secrets: Critical Approaches to Twin Peaks*, edited by David Lavery. 160-172. Detroit: Wayne State University Press, 1995.

Tziallas, Evangelos. "Torture Porn and Surveillance Culture." *Jump Cut: A Review of Contemporary Media* 52. 2010. http://www.ejumpcut.org/archive/jc52.2010/evange-losTorturePorn/index.html.

Weber, Max. 1978. *Economy and Society*. Berkeley: University of California Press.

Wright, Megan. "Walter White's Will to Power." In *Breaking Bad and Philosophy: Badder Living through Chemistry*, edited by David R. Keopesell and Robert Arp. 81-89. Chicago-LaSalle: Open Court, 2012.

II

The Politics of *Breaking Bad*

Breaking Bad (AMC). Season 1 Episode 1: "Pilot." Airdate: January 20, 2008.
Shown: Bryan Cranston, Anna Gunn, RJ Mitte.
AMC/Photofest © AMC. Reprinted by permission of Photofest.

FOUR

Taking Control: Male Angst and the Re-Emergence of Hegemonic Masculinity in *Breaking Bad*

Brian Faucette

Man has all too long had an 'evil eye' for his natural inclinations, so
that they have finally become inseparable from his 'bad conscience.'
—Friedrich Nietzsche, *Genealogy of Morals* (1887)

The image of empty khaki trousers falling against the brilliant blue desert
sky, followed by the shot of an out of control Winnebago careening
alongside a dirt road in the desert driven by an average looking man
wearing tight white underwear and a gas mask, are the first few images
presented to viewers of the pilot episode of the critically acclaimed cable
series *Breaking Bad*, which premiered on January 20, 2008. These first few
moments are crucial to not only establishing the series' visual style but
also the complex and problematic themes that the show sought to explore.[1]

As series creator, Vince Gilligan, has consistently repeated in interviews and discussions of the series that the idea behind the series was to
take "Mr. Chips and transform him into Scarface."[2] What Gilligan identifies in using this tagline is two distinct types of masculinity: Mr. Chips
is a shy, good-natured schoolteacher who struggles to connect with his
students and women in the book written by English novelist James Hil-
ton in 1934. Scarface is a daring, violent figure who imposes his masculinity on the world using violence and intimidation in Howard Hawks'
classic gangster film of the same name. From the pilot to the latest episodes, the show has tapped into the cultural fear that America faced a

crisis of conscience and a perceived crisis of masculinity. In *Breaking Bad,* Gilligan combines these two types of masculinity in order to show how the fears of male angst that America has been dealing with since the late 1960s has resulted in the feeling within men that they are no longer in control—not of their homes or even themselves. Thus, Gilligan seems to imply for men like Walter and Mr. Chips to restore their authority they must embrace older models of masculinity based on violence, intimidation, and control in order to re-masculinize themselves and their lives during periods where 'traditional' modes of masculinity seemed to be under assault.

Sociologist Michael Kimmel (1996) states that "all across the country . . . men have been in full scale retreat, heading off to rediscover their wild, hairy, deep manhood" and then notes how for straight, white, American men "a siege mentality" developed as men struggled to redefine themselves and faced increasing competition for their jobs from global competition and challenges to their way of life from women and minorities (316, 330). Kimmel documents the history of the "self-made man" and its central role in the formation of American masculinity. He points out that in America manhood is "less about the drive for domination and more about the fear of others dominating us" because "throughout American history American men have been afraid that others will see us as less than manly, as weak, timid, frightened" (6). To combat this sense of insecurity Kimmel claims often American men define their masculinity not in relation to women but in relation to other men. To analyze the representation of Walter White's masculinity I use Kimmel's model of the "self-made man." Walter embodies the complex and contradictory models of masculinity that American men have faced as a result of changes in society, the economy, and the political system. The series presents an image of a man who attempts to reconnect with the model of the self-made man in order to take control of his own destiny.

After the cold opening of the pilot the viewer is introduced to the series protagonist, the dowdy Walter White (Bryan Cranston). He stands in the desert and in a medium close-up is shown staring into a camcorder as the sounds of sirens are heard in the background. With a look of desperation and fear he records a message to his family using the camera. He then covers the lens of the camera as the viewer hears the sounds of the sirens getting closer and the muffled sound of Walter's sighs. Following his recording, he regains his composure and then he is shown in a long shot standing in the middle of the road wearing only a green button down shirt, his tight white underwear, and shoes, as he points a pistol toward the oncoming sirens. His face is marked not with fear but with the look of desperation and pride. The scene shows how in an instant a simple family man like Walter White can be transformed and in effect performs a model of masculinity that is both confident and willing to embrace violent actions in order to maintain control.

Walter's transformation is an illustrative of Judith Butler's (1999) concept that gender is "performative." Butler argued that, "gender proves to be performative" (33). For Butler both masculinity and femininity are products of social expectations rather than a biological fact. Gender is best understood for Butler as a performance that is linked to questions of power, voice, and the continued production of what are perceived as "normative models" of gender behavior. Throughout the series the audience watches as Walter struggles to represent the traditional models of masculinity and in the process 'breaks bad' which also requires him to take control of his life, his family, and his talent, all of which he uses to assure himself that he is a man who is capable of being a provider and who can indeed take control when necessary.

R. W. Connell (2005) defines masculinity as "simultaneously a place in gender relations, the practices through which men and women engage that place in gender, and the effects of these practices in bodily experience, personality, and culture" (71). He then theorizes that in effect masculinity is best recognized as a form of hegemony. Drawing upon Antonio Gramsci's analysis of class relation, Connell employs the term "hegemony" to argue that "hegemonic masculinity" is best understood as the "configuration of gender practice which embodies the currently accepted answer to the problem of the legitimacy of patriarchy, which guarantees the dominant position of men and the subordination of women" (77). I use both Connell's definition of masculinity and his model of hegemonic masculinity to analyze the series and its complicated representation of American masculinity in the figure of Walter White who presents a model of masculinity defined by a need for freedom and control to reclaim masculine authority. It is this freedom from normal obligations and strictures that allows Walter to reclaim his masculinity.

Walter is at first shown to be ineffectual and weak, but as the series continues he shifts to a man who embraces the more traditional models of American masculinity that celebrated aggressive and ruthless behavior, especially in the business realm. And as Walter becomes more adept at managing the drug business in the series he asserts a type of hegemonic masculinity previously unavailable to him both in his business dealings and in his relationships with his wife and son. This reclamation of traditional masculinity, albeit by untraditional methods, reflects the inner desires of some men to reify what they perceive as having been lost.

THAT'S WHY THEY HIRE MEN: HANK QUESTIONS SMART MASCULINITY

The pilot episode establishes the major themes and problems that Walter faces as he struggles with feeling that neither his family nor his students respect him and that as a man he is inadequate as a provider for his family. His lack of income is depicted to be the result of his desire to play by the rules and be a law-abiding citizen, good husband, and father, roles, which in some ways allow him to be emasculated because people see Walt as a mild-mannered man and a loser. In truth, Walter is a genius; his boisterous, aggressive, masculine brother-in-law Hank who is a DEA agent, jokes about the large size of Walter's brain when he toasts him at his fiftieth birthday party. The idea of a man being associated with the "heart" and emotions is celebrated and ridiculed by Hank in the scene when Hank shows off his service weapon to the other men attending the party, including Walt's disabled son, Walter Jr. It is made clear that Walt Jr. idolizes his uncle and the excitement of his job. Still, Hank attempts to make Walt feel included by letting Walt handle his weapon. Walt, beer in hand, does not relish the opportunity the same way as his son and commenting on the weight of the gun to which Hank scoffs that's why they hire him thus indicating that only real men, like Hank, carry guns.

The gun in films and television often signifies masculinity and male potency. The gun can be read as a form of cliché for the male penis or it can be read as both a fetish and an object. Roderick McGillis (2009) states that the gun as "a symbol serves as a claming reassurance of the absent penis" and that as an object the gun "exists as something we imagine will satisfy us" (73). The gun validates Hank's masculinity and challenges Walt's because a man like Walt is not comfortable wielding a gun and feels the weight of the gun, and the responsibility of the weapon. For men like Hank the gun is an extension of their masculinity and their authority. Walt shows the first signs of dissatisfaction with his status as a man when his brother-in-law, son, and the other men laugh at him. In that moment he comes to realize that his family sees him as effeminate because he does not measure up to a man like Hank.

Hank's bluster and masculine bravado that overshadows Walt's birthday celebration is an example of the problems with hegemonic masculinity as it is most often based around the representation of men as boorish and violent. Hank not only shows off his weapon but also commandeers the party's focus to the television because he wants everyone to see his appearance on the local news as he was interviewed during a meth bust. Walt watches the footage as Hank sits in his chair and marvels at the piles of money that was seized. Hank tells everyone that it was a good day because they took in drugs, weapons, and nearly seven-hundred-thousand dollars in drug money off the streets. Hank jokes that drug-dealing is quick money, unless you get caught, not realizing that his brother-in-law is contemplating the possibility of making illegal drugs in order to protect and provide for his family.

The importance of being seen as a provider and protector is one of the key themes the series addresses as it presents an image of an America where it is no longer possible for most men to be the 'bread winner' without having more than one job. Despite the fact that Walt is a man with advanced degrees in science and a teacher, he is forced to work after school at a car wash to help keep the family afloat. Walt's wife Skyler (Anna Gunn) who is eight months pregnant reminds him to not let the owner screw him on his work hours again. Her statement shows her concern for the family but also indicates that in effect Skyler is the person who is in charge in the home, which is a situation that as the series moves forward it seeks to destabilize in an attempt to make Walt feel masculine and in control.

Kimmel's (1996) study of the history of manhood in America shows how American men have since the nation's founding been insecure and sought to use their political, social, and economic status within the home and in the world to ensure that they were in control of all aspects of their lives. In Walter's case his love of chemistry and expertise as a scientist mark him as different from men like Hank. However, when Walt tells his high school students that chemistry is ultimately the study of change, what he is really talking about is himself. He begins to realize that he is so dissatisfied with his situation in life because he is not in charge of his classroom, his income, his life, or his sexuality.

IS HE ASLEEP?: RECLAIMING CONTROL OF WALT'S SEXUALITY

As Walter and Skyler get ready for bed on the night of his birthday celebration Skyler offers him another present. As they sit together in bed she begins to stroke Walt's penis while she monitors the status of an item she placed for sale on Ebay on her laptop. Walt is startled at first by her willingness to pleasure him and asks what she is doing. Walt then tries to take charge of the situation and begins kissing his wife and trying to seduce her, but she rebuffs him telling him that her sexual actions are just for him so he should just relax and enjoy it. Skyler, however, becomes less interested in Walt achieving sexual satisfaction when she notices that her item on Ebay is reaching its target price and deadline. As she continues to rub Walt's penis, Skyler notices that he is not becoming aroused. She asks the question, "Is he asleep?" In this scene Walt becomes a passive figure who cannot even control his own orgasm, nor seduce his wife, who shows more interest in her Ebay bidding than she does her husband.

The importance of Walt's sexuality and its link to his own understanding of his masculinity is addressed in the last scene of the pilot when Walt climbs into bed, begins to passionately kiss his wife and then mounts her from behind, indicating that he is now the person in control in the bedroom. Where in the previous scene Skyler was in charge of the Walt's sexual satisfaction, Walt shows that he is beginning to transform into a more dominant male figure. This change shocks and thrills Skyler as she inquiries if her partner is Walt.

The connection between Walt's more aggressive sexual appetite, the possibility of his death, and his new criminal outlook is highlighted on several occasions after he steals equipment from the school where he works and coerces his former student, Jesse Pinkman (Aaron Paul), into making crystal meth with him. Walt uses his cancer diagnosis as an opportunity to take charge of his life and his fortune after seeing all the money that Hank seized in the raid. Walt bullies Jesse by criticizing his meth cooking skills and the poor quality of his product. Walt, however, soon discovers Jesse, like Hank, judges Walt's masculinity when he tells Walt, "you can dress up like a faggot, but not me" when Walt shows Jesse the safety goggles and aprons that he has stolen. Later, when Jesse questions Walt's motives after they agree to their partnership and the purchase of an RV to use as a mobile meth lab, Walt tells him that he has woken up. He has withdrawn his life savings from a bank to pay for the RV. Walt's statement and actions show that he realizes that men like him who obey the law and try to be model citizens and still struggle often are only able to get ahead in the world by relying on illegal means. When Walt tells Jesse he is awake, what he gives voice to is the realization that for men like him to take control they must embrace a model of hegemonic masculinity and in doing so it allows them to regain their agency.

Yet, what Walt fails to understand is that making the drugs is the simple part. All the other things that go along with it, such as making calculated and immoral decisions, he does not consider until he faces his own anxiety and mortality head on. Jesse introduces him to the dark side of the business and to insane people like Krazy-8 and Emilio who Walt is forced to deal with when they try to kill him and Jesse. It is after his brush with death that Walt begins to change and finds the confidence to be sexually aggressive with his wife. In the episode "A No-Rough-Stuff-Type Deal" (3/9/08) Walt sexually stimulates his wife underneath a table during a meeting with parents, local law enforcement, and school administration officials at the school where he works. As the group is being briefed on the dangers of the drug problem, Walt ignores the meeting and instead focuses on his own desires, desires that he satisfies after the meeting when he and Skyler have sex in his car in the school parking lot. Walt tells Skyler that their sexual encounter was so pleasurable because "it was illegal." Walt learns over the course of the first season that "illegal" acts can be pleasurable and in turn make him feel more masculine and thus enable him to be awakened from the stupor that crippled his male psyche.

HE'S A GOOD MAN ISN'T HE?: FATHER, HUSBAND, PROVIDER?

The last episode of season two "ABQ" (5/31/09) focuses on Walt's connection to his family, Jesse, and the business. In the episode Walt attempts to be supportive of his son who has set up a web site to help raise money for the family and for Walt's cancer treatments. However, it is Walt's masculine pride that continually damages his relationship with his wife and family. When Saul Goodman suggests using Walt Jr.'s website to launder the drug money, Walt complains that the website is simply another form of begging for money. Walt's status as husband and provider become critical to the formation of Walt's newer more aggressive masculinity in the series as he continues to juggle between his secret life of drug dealer and doting father and husband.

Stella Bruzzi (2005) shows the importance of the status of father in defining American masculinity in her book on fatherhood and Hollywood. Bruzzi points out that in America there is perhaps no figure or signifier more important to the formation and function of American masculinity than that of the father. In her analysis of contemporary models of fatherhood, she argues that the traditional domineering model has been transformed into a man who is flawed but who bases his own notion of fatherhood on traditional models that he no longer believes in nor emulates (Bruzzi 2005). Though Bruzzi focuses on the idea of the model of contemporary American masculinity as flawed in films, her conclusions can be seen in contemporary American television series like *The Sopranos* (1999-2007), *Friday Night Lights* (2006-2011), and *Breaking Bad* (2009-2013) as well. The focus on the father and a type of flawed masculinity in crisis comprises much of the contemporary television landscape.

Amanda Marcotte (2011) maintains that flawed masculinities play a critical role in the representations of masculinity on contemporary American television. She asserts that in today's television landscape most of the series like *Breaking Bad* feature men who struggle with their masculinity in a world where male authority is in decline and that often many of these men are shown to be deeply flawed individuals because they cling to older, traditional models of masculinity that have been challenged and problematized by shifts in society, and economics. Kimmel (2009) draws a connection between economic shifts and male status as provider and father when he states that, "most American men have simply continued to go about their lives, falling somewhere between eager embrace of women's equality and resigned acceptance" (15). He further notes that in this economy, "a man who is not a provider…doesn't feel like much a man at all" (17). It is this questioning of his status and sense of malaise as a man that Walt tries to overcome as he tries to adopt the role of provider and as a result take control of his life.

Walt recognizes that as a drug dealer he is better able to provide for his family than he ever was as a high school chemistry teacher. For example, in the season two episode "Over" (5/10/09), Walt decides to replace the leaky, inefficient old hot water heater with a new system that he pays for with money he earned from providing his product to Gus Fring. Walt does this in an attempt to show his concern for his family. In the process discovers that the hot water heater was leaking damaging the wood underneath it. Walt then sets about to repair it and becomes consumed by ridding the house of rot as he tries to protect his family's home and chief investment from further damage. For Walt, money is the route to masculine efficacy and allows him to rationalize all the violence he enacts as he continuously reminds himself that he has become involved in the drug trade in order to provide and protect his family.

The issue of money and Walt's ability to provide are explored when Skyler, while pregnant, returns to work in the episode "Negro y Azul" (4/19/09). What Walt fails to see is that his actions to maintain control of his cancer and the family are the very actions which drive a wedge in his marriage, to the point that Walt chooses to miss the birth of his daughter in order to deliver his product and become a part of Gus Fring's enterprise. In order to maintain control of his dual lives, Walt is forced to continually lie to Skyler who at the end of season two demands that Walt leave. When he refuses to do so, she stares him down and then drives off with the baby, leaving Walt alone with his money and the house. In short, Walt is able to reclaim his masculine authority but at the expense of his marriage, his children, his character and perhaps his own humanity.

Instead of trying to salvage his marriage and give up the life of deception, danger, and drugs, Walt decides to further entangle himself with Fring, who becomes Walt's chief adversary and primary employer when he offers Walt the opportunity to make millions of dollars cooking in an industrial lab that Fring has set up. In order to entice Walt, Fring shows Walt the industrial facility that he has built to manufacture Walt's product and then he tells him in the season three episode, "Mas" (4/18/10) that a man must be a provider to his family to be a true man. Fring plays on Walt's desire to be seen as a man who can provide for his family. Fring also understands that even though Walt and his wife's marriage is in jeopardy that there is nothing more important to him than making sure that his kids' future is better than their present. Yet, when Skyler discovers a large duffel bag of money she begins to piece together the fact that Walt is involved in something that is dangerous and criminal. Skyler consults a lawyer who tells her that Walt's actions could cost her the family. Skyler tears up as she thinks about the old Walt she knew and that she did not marry a criminal. Skyler tries to extricate herself from Walt, and his business. Yet, when Hank is attacked by killers working for the Mexican cartel and needs medical care, she convinces Walt to pay Hank's medical bills with monies he earns working for Fring. As a result of his gesture to help the family Skyler agrees to protect Walt as she looks past his criminal behavior. While Skyler does embrace Walt and his business, including helping him launder his money through the car wash they purchase, what she fails to understand is that the Walt she married is no longer the same man. He is now a brutal criminal who expresses his love through smothering intimidation rather than compassion and freedom.

THIS LINE OF WORK DOESN'T SUIT YOU: ADOPTING THE ROLE OF KILLER

In the episode ". . . And the Bag's in the River" (2/10/2008) the drug dealer Krazy-8, who survived Walt's chemistry experiment in the RV only to be held prisoner by Walt and Jesse in Jesse's basement, tells him that the drug business is not his line of work. He can see Walt's struggles to figure out what to do with him. When Skyler confronts Jesse about his relationship with Walt, Jesse openly challenges Walt's resolve to the business venture and his masculinity. He accuses Walt of not controlling his own family business. Again, the series shows that Walt has continually struggled to maintain control of his family and his life. When Walt begins to lie to Skyler about his strange behavior, he tells her that he has not been himself lately and begs her to give him a break. What Skyler does not know is that Walt is dying and now making drugs to provide for his family's future and as a result he now faces a variable he had not calculated; that is the possibility that he has killed one man and perhaps may need to kill another one. Walt's initial timidity illustrates how men like him have been walking through life in a daze and, when faced with real hard choices, they must be coerced into accepting violence as an option. In fact, Jesse chides Walt for not handling Krazy-8 after he agreed to dispose of the first body.

Sally Robinson (2000) argues that as a result of the progressive policies and movements of the 1960s and the adoption of neoliberal economic policies that many American men, especially white men, viewed themselves as victims who needed to rebel against the normative forces of society that they believed were responsible for imprisoning them and their masculine potential. According to Robinson, one of the key factors in the defining and formation of American masculinity post 1960 has been the need by many white middle-class and working class American men to reclaim control of their lives, social spheres, and in order to do so many of these men have often used violence, brutality, and intimidation to ensure that they remain in control. Kimmel (1996) notes that during the Reagan and Bush administrations that the form of American manhood that was regained was the "compulsive masculinity of the schoolyard bully" and was exemplar of "a defensive and restive manhood of men who needed to demonstrate their masculinity at every opportunity" (292). In the case of Walt, the viewer watches as he transforms from the dowdy chemistry teacher to a cold rational killer and drug pusher, who constantly demonstrates that he is masculine, but this transformation is not without its costs.

Before disposing of Krazy-8, who Walt wants to see the best in, he sits down with pad and paper and makes out a list of pros and cons for ways to handle the situation. He is still at this point trying to search for another option besides murder, but Jesse has informed Krazy-8 who Walt is and what he does for a living. What Walt searches for is a clear conscience without having to give up on the exciting and thrilling new feelings of confusion and satisfaction that he discovers after breaking bad. However, because Walt is intelligent, logical, and scientific, he is clearly adept at killing someone. He gets his excuse when he realizes that Krazy-8 has kept a piece of the plate that Walt broke to use as a weapon against him. Walt descends into the dark basement and pretends to unlock the chains holding the prisoner to a post. He grabs hold of the metal bar wrapped around his neck and begins to strangle him, even as Krazy-8 tries to stab him. Walt summons all his fury and takes the man's life without blinking an eye. Then, in an attempt to redeem his actions, he apologizes as he tries to rationalize his actions to himself and in the process maintain his humanity.

Walt, in the episode "Cancer Man" (2/17/08), begins to embrace the power of his rage when he destroys a cocky businessman's BMW at a gas station. Using his knowledge of chemistry, he caused the car to explode. This violent act was in retaliation for the man's rude behavior at Walt's bank and for taking the parking place that Walt sat patiently and waited for like other normal people. Walt's actions, no longer justifiable as self-defense or protection of his family, are linked to his own growing sense of indifference and anger. He begins to realize that everyone views him as a victim including Hank who tells him when Walt finally breaks down and reveals his cancer diagnosis to his loved ones. Walt's decision to reveal his diagnosis provides Walt with the opportunity to try and assert control in his own home when he tells his family that he needs to be in command of his destiny.

The idea of choice and freedom allow Walt to perform the role of dutiful husband and father even when he agrees to get help while at the same time it affords him the chance to further his aspirations of ensuring financial security for his family through the drug trade. Walt chooses to involve Jesse and himself with the psychotic Tuco when he realizes that on their own they cannot earn the sums of money that Walt anticipated. Still, Walt shows that he is not yet capable of managing the business and expectations, and thereby he questions Jesse's masculinity when he tells him, "to grow some balls." Walt's statement illustrates how he is beginning to change as a result of hegemonic masculine expectations exhibited by men like Hank.

As they try to build their business Jesse meets with Tuco to discuss their product but instead of buying the drugs Tuco beats Jesse up with a sack of money to send a message that he is a man who is not afraid to use violence and intimidation to maintain control. Tuco's brutal actions put

Jesse in the hospital and leads Walt to adopt a new image. He shaves his head, dons dark clothes, pants, and a porkpie hat after telling Jesse's friend Skinny Pete that he is the man. These actions indicate that Walt now understands he must assume control and responsibility for what happened to Jesse. Walt adopts the identity of Heisenberg when he meets with Tuco and then demonstrates that he too is a man capable of great violence when he smuggles an explosive designed to look like their crystal meth into Tuco's office and it explodes. Tuco laughs as he hands Walt the money and tells him that he has "balls." The men then agree to go into business together and Walt struts out of the office in his porkpie hat and dark glasses as Heisenberg rather than the mild-mannered Walter White. When Walt gets into his nondescript green car and holds wads of cash in his hands, he grunts loudly. He is both scared and excited by the fact that he has gotten the cash and in the process asserted control over the situation and ensured that men like Tuco will come to respect and fear him. It is these two qualities of masculinity, respect and fear that Walt was initially unable to instill in others. As his knowledge of the business and his own ambitions grow, it is these two qualities that he comes to rely on as he becomes accustomed to a line of work that Krazy-8 tried to convince him he could not be effective in.

Once Walt embraces violence and intimidation to maintain control of his life he resorts to it time and time again as he continues to consolidate his business, eliminate the competition and protect his family and interests at all costs. In the episode "Half Measures" (6/6/10), Walt kills two drug dealers by ramming one of the men with his car and shooting the other man in the head at point blank range in order to protect Jesse when he learns that his new business partner, Gus Fring has ordered that Jesse be eliminated. Walt demonstrates to Jesse that he is willing to do whatever it takes to protect him and the business and in a sense becomes a surrogate father to Jesse. Because of this level of devotion and his ability to manipulate Jesse, Walt is able to convince him to kill a rival chemist, Gale Boetticher, in the episode "Full Measure" (6/13/10). Walt discovers that both he and Jesse are expendable to Fring who provides them with a super lab to cook their product in and intends to eliminate them once he learns the secret of their formula. Walt orders Jesse to kill Gale, an action that traumatizes Jesse but one that Walt has become desensitized to. Jesse shoots Gale in the face at point-blank range to save Walt's life and his own, not realizing the consequences of his actions or that Gale was not the real threat to his own ambitions. In fact, Walt's true nemesis is Gus Fring, who like Walt embraces violence and intimidation to control his business and his family.

Walt, in the episode "Face Off" (10/9/11), demonstrates the dangers of his ambitions and resolve when he plants a bomb on the wheelchair of Hector Salamanca, an elderly Hispanic man who Walt first encountered when he and Jesse were on kidnapped by his nephew Tuco. From the moment they met, Hector was suspicious of Walt's actions and he recognizes that underneath the exterior look of a frightened man in glasses is a man who is capable of great violence and evil. It is no shock when Walt turns Hector into a bomb and uses him to kill Gus Fring as he seeks to take control of the business. Nor is it a shock to learn that Walt is no longer a safe, family man who respects children when it is revealed that Walt is the one who poisons Jesse's girlfriend's son in order to force Jesse to go along with Walt's plan to kill Gus.

After removing the threat to himself and his family by killing Fring at the end of season four, Walt is able to crow to Skyler in the episode "Fifty-One" (8/5/12) that he won. While Walt tells his wife that he has taken control of the drug business he also sends her the message that he has also won control of the home and his family. As Walt celebrates his victory, Skyler tells him that she is afraid of him and that she does not want him around her children because as Walt told her in season four episode six that he is now the danger. It is for this reason that Skyler tells Walt in season five that she no longer cares if he lives or dies. Moreover, Skyler removes Walt's motivation for 'breaking bad' when she takes away his children, a decision that challenges his authority. Yet, what Skyler fails to see until season five is that Walt is no longer the meek man who she could manage, instead he is now a forceful man who has committed innumerable acts of violence and mayhem to maintain control of his business and he understands how to use those same skills in his marriage and home.

In season five Walt's transformation from "Mr. Chips to Scarface" is completed when Walt sanctions the killing of a young kid who witnesses them rob a train in the episode "Dead Freight," (8/12/12) and when he kills Mike Ehrmantraut (Jonathan Banks), who had worked for Gus and then goes into business with Walt only to realize that Walt is a man who is solely driven by ambition and greed. After Mike challenges Walt's authority, he becomes a liability that Walt decides to handle in the episode "Say My Name" (8/26/12). When Mike refuses to provide the names of the men associated with Fring's operation, an angry, frustrated Walt shoots him with Mike's own gun. At the end of season five, Walter White, the former dowdy, law-abiding citizen, is displaced by his alter-ego Heisenberg, a man who reclaims his masculine authority both in society and at home through brutality, intimidation, and stubborn will power. His manhood is reclaimed by taking control of his home life, his relationships, and his business and this allows Walt to restore his masculinity and status as father, husband, and provider.

CONCLUSION: "I AM THE DANGER"

At the end of season five, the audience is left to wonder if men like Walt, who declare that they want to build empires, are capable of redemption. Walt's constant need to assert that he is a man and can provide for his family illustrates the dangers of the "self-made man" and "hegemonic masculinity" in the formation of American masculinity at a time of great upheaval at the social and economic level. These ideas, constructed around the argument that the only means for a man to achieve respect is through brusque behavior and, if needed, violence, were once accepted as normal, but have since the 1960s been questioned and challenged as women, minorities, and LGBT individuals struggle for equal rights. As I have argued it is men like Walt who use 'a perceived crisis' of masculinity as the rationale for returning to outmoded modes of male authority in an attempt to take control. Like the empty pants in the first shot of the pilot, Walt's transformation demonstrates that often in an effort to reclaim control men resort to empty rhetoric and performances of hegemonic masculinity because these modes have been crucial in the formation of the nation. At a time when America struggles to decide its future and the future roles of men in the twenty-first century, a series like *Breaking Bad* can provide viewers with a portrayal of what it means to embrace the idea of the self-made man and how, along with violence, the idea has been used and continues to be used by men to retake control of their lives and the nation.

NOTES

1. See David Lavery's online essay, "Bad Quality: *Breaking Bad* as Basic Cable Quality TV" *Critical Studies in Television.* http://www.criticalstudiesintelevision.com/index.php?siid=13805.
2. See Martin Miller's interview "The End Nears for Walter White of Breaking Bad" *Los Angeles Times* Sept. 1, 2012. http://www.latimes.com/entertainment/tv/showtracker/la-et-st-breaking-bad-vince-gilligan-20120901,0,0854913.story for a discussion of the show's initial development and the importance of the idea of Walt's character transformation from a mild mannered family into a cold blooded, ruthless killer.

WORKS CITED

Bruzzi, Stella. *Bringing Up Daddy: Fatherhood and Masculinity in Post-War Hollywood.* London: British Film Institute, 2005.
Butler, Judith. *Gender Trouble.* New York: Routledge, 1999.
Connell, R.W. *Masculinities.* 2nd ed. Berkley, CA: University of California Press, 2005.
Kimmel, Michael. *Manhood in America: A Cultural History.* Boston: Free Press, 1996.
———. *Misframing Men: The Politics of Contemporary Masculinities.* New Brunswick, NJ: Rutgers University Press, 2010.
Lavery, David. "Bad Quality: *Breaking Bad* as Basic Cable Quality TV." *Critical Studies in Television.* September 2010. http://cstonline.tv/.

Marcotte, Amanda. "How to Make a Critically Acclaimed TV Show about Masculinity." *Jezebel*. 2011. http://jezebel.com/5837945.

McGillis, Roderick. *He Was Some Kind of a Man: Masculinities in the B Western*. Waterloo, Canada: Wilfrid Laurier University Press, 2009.

Miller, Martin. "The End Nears for Walter White of Breaking Bad." *Los Angeles Times*. 1 September 2012. Latimes.com/entertainment/tv/showtracker/la-et-st-breaking-bad-vince-gilligan-20120901,0,0854913.

Nietzsche, Friedrich. "On the Genealogy of Morals." *Basic Writings of Nietzsche*. trans. Walter Kaufmann. New York: The Modern Library, 2000.

Robinson, Sally. *Marked Men: White Masculinity in Crisis*. New York: Columbia University Press, 2000.

FIVE

Not Your Average Mexican: *Breaking Bad* and the Destruction of Latino Stereotypes

Andrew Howe

Since its debut on AMC in early 2008, Vince Gilligan's *Breaking Bad* has been populated with increasingly complex depictions of Latin identity.[1] As a border narrative, many of the series characters are Latino. However, there is a wide variability in the portrayal of such characters, from the crazed, drug addicted Tuco to the suave businessman Gustavo Fring, and from the axe-wielding Salamanca cousins to their wheelchair-bound uncle, Hector. In establishing such a wide range of Latino characters, the series brings to the surface complicating social factors. For instance, although he is the drug kingpin for the American Southwest and has direct connections to the Mexican cartels, Fring is originally from Chile. Although little is offered about his background, he clearly has African ancestry, bringing an interesting racial component to the series' context. Likewise, the background offered for the murderous Salamanca cousins is likewise intriguing. The narrative offers no information as to whether or not they are Catholic, but they do pay homage to a local death deity. Despite their depravity, the Salamancas are thus humanized in that they do not conform to the typical stereotypes of Latino identity usually displayed on American television. Other characters round out the broad-based depiction. Despite holding a job in law enforcement, Steve Gomez is quiet and nurturing, not exhibiting any of the machismo often associated with powerful Latino characters. The swagger and braggadoccio are instead brought by his partner, the Anglo Hank Schrader. The small-time drug dealer nicknamed Combo appears Anglo; indeed, the audience only learns of his Latino background following his death, when his real name is revealed. And the boy Brock Cantillo undergoes an identity crisis. His mother gives him an English name and recognizes that education is the key to leaving the barrio, although he is at risk of falling into the drug culture that claims so many of the poverty-stricken youth that share his background. This chapter will offer close analyses of these characters and others, exploring the manner in which they engage with the landscape of political, economic, social, and cultural variability in depicting Latinos.

Despite popular and critical success, by the debut of the fifth and final season in July 2012, there had yet to be a major collection of cultural criticism examining the series in real depth.[2] There are, however, a number of essays and books exploring the representation of Latinos in film and television, particularly by academics since the 1980s. These academics focused upon the manner in which mainstream artistic expression evidenced a fascination with the cultural 'Other,' and focused upon how the patterns or portrayal that evolved evidenced certain cultural fears or attitudes. Ever since Thomas Edison's 1894 kinetograph short *Chinese Opium Den*, film has provided a rich medium for an audience's fascination with the Other. Due to American manifest destiny serving as the controlling metaphor for the spread of the European colonizer across the North American continent,[3] notions of "the west" provided a narrative obsession throughout much of the twentieth century. It was only after the terrible losses sustained during Vietnam, both military and political in nature, that the western genre as a celebration to nation-building began to lose its appeal for American audiences. Ironically, it was during this moment that the political outgrowth of the American Civil Rights Movement began to seep into both the arts and academia, resulting in critics such as Chon Noriega who began to write powerfully and effectively about depictions of Latinos. Such critics noted the stereotypes that were rampant in American cinema and television, from the *The Treasure of Sierra Madre* (1948) and the image of the uncouth bandito ("We don't need no badges!") to the fiery, hyper-sexualized spitfire, made famous by Hollywood's typecasting of Lupe Velez in the 1930s. As Stephanie Larson (2006) notes, despite existing in more politically enlightened times the representation of Latino males in contemporary television is no less troubling, as criminal elements are often invested in such characters: "Villainous representations of Hispanic men include sexually threatening males, criminals, gang members, drug dealers, and illegal aliens." (58). José E. Limón (1992) cites the stereotypically aggressive and vicious qualities that contribute to the above depictions, but also notes that the Latino "also often appears as cowardly, apathetic, and dormant" (3).

One of the key reasons behind such crass stereotyping involves the dominant culture's perceptions of the threat posed by a large and, following the Civil Rights Movement, increasingly energized minority. As Clara E. Rodriguez (1997) notes:

Hollywood's history with each group has also been in part a reflection of larger political and economic relationships between the United States and other countries. Political and economic factors have clearly influenced how groups came to occupy or leave the position of negativized "Other" in the media. . . changes in the images of Latinos resulting from changing political conditions, geopolitical considerations, market factors, and protests from Latin America. (8)

Although in this passage Rodriguez discusses how the United States' relationship with Mexico and other Latin American nations impacts representation in American film and television, clearly *domestic* events/ movements such as the Zoot Suit riots of 1943, the United Farm Workers of America strikes of the 1960s, California's Proposition 187 in 1994, and ongoing construction of the U.S.-Mexico Border Fence affect media portrayals of Latinos. Among other critics, Chon Noriega and Rosa Linda Fregoso have noted that stereotypes must be met with opposition in all aspects of the filmmaking process. As Fregoso (1993) notes, "the project of Chicano cinema may succinctly be summed up as the documentation of social reality through oppositional forms of knowledge about Chicanos" (xv). During a time of complex empowerment for Latin Americans living in the United States, where citizens wield greater economic and political power than ever before but illegal immigrants continue to struggle, *Breaking Bad* and other forms of popular media are reflecting the complex times in which we live. In so doing, the series undermines many of the stereotypes that have long been perpetuated in American film and television, although there are a few negative associations that are affirmed.

Breaking Bad is a narrative about the drug business, and despite the fact that the two primary characters—Walter White (Bryan Cranston) and Jesse Pinkman[4] (Aaron Paul)—are Anglo drug manufacturers, there is no shortage of Latino characters in this series' depiction of the industry. Some of these Latino characters operate north of the border, some south of the border. A character who represents the fluidity of the U.S.-Mexico border is Tuco Salamanca (Raymond Cruz), a character who lives in New Mexico but has ties to the Mexican drug cartel.[5] One of the first major Latino figures to enter the narrative, Tuco fits pre-existing stereotypes of Latin American drug dealers. He is violent, paranoid, and perhaps even psychopathic; furthermore, he is given to wild outbursts, both oratorical and physical in nature, and appears constantly on the edge of giving over to his base emotions. The first time Pinkman meets him in "A Crazy Handful of Nothin" (3/2/08), Tuco compliments the methamphetamine he is given by saying that it "kicks like a mule with his balls wrapped in duct tape," but then proceeds to physically assault Pinkman when the latter asks for payment. Tuco's actions when White arrives to demand payment are no less volatile—he puts a cigarette out on his own tongue and threatens to rob him as well—although he does come to admire

White after the former demonstrates his strength by nearly blowing up the building with fulminated mercury. In the cliffhanger to season one, "A No-Rough-Stuff-Type Deal" (3/9/08), Tuco beats one of his own henchmen to death because the man speaks out of turn. In this scene, he is reminiscent of Joe Pesci's characters in both *GoodFellas* and *Casino*. His propensity toward violence is definitely linked to his emotional volatility, but it does serve the purpose of sending a message to those with whom he does business. Indeed, as he beats his employee senseless, a look of shock but also awareness appears on the faces of both White and Pinkman, who finally realize the bind in which they now find themselves: they have thrown in with and now work for a maniac. Tuco's violent outbursts are fueled by his addiction to the product he sells. He thus fits into a tradition of cinematic drug dealers whose downfall comes when they allow their addictive personalties to overwhelm reason and dominate their lives. Although there are some well known examples that involve Anglo characters (notably George Jung in *Blow* (2001), which is based on a true story), the prototype for this trope comes from Brian De Palma's *Scarface* (1983),[6] which updates Howard Hawks 1932 original by moving the narrative to Miami and centering the story upon Cuban immigration and cocaine. Although he is Italian-American, Al Pacino's portrayal of Tony Montana solidified the cinematic stereotype of the wild-eyed, unstable Latin American drug dealer addicted to his own product. Tuco Salamanca is most definitely a cultural inheritor of that fairly young albeit nonetheless powerful stereotype.

Tuco's role in the series, although notable, lasts for only four episodes before he is tracked down by, and killed in a gunfight with, Hank Schrader (Dean Norris) of the Drug Enforcement Agency (DEA). Tuco's scenes are brief, but memorable, although the latter is arguably due to the over-the-top manner in which they play to certain stereotypes. Other Latino characters largely avoid such stereotyping, however. It is almost as if Vince Gilligan set the baseline with the most outrageous character possible in order to demonstrate the sheer distance from which the series was about to diverge. After a period during which White attempts to set up his own methamphetamine distribution network, he is introduced to businessman Gustavo Fring (Giancarlo Esposito). In one of only a few examples of non-geographically appropriate casting in *Breaking Bad*,[7] the Italian/African-American Esposito was chosen to depict Fring, who would become one of the narrative's primary and most interesting characters in seasons three and four. Early on in season three, Fring defies easy character analysis. In addition to being the notional drug kingpin of the American Southwest, he is a shrewd businessman who owns a chain of successful fast food restaurants called "Los Pollos Hermanos" (translated as "The Chicken Brothers"). Other than the color of his skin, Fring is generally portrayed as a sort of mainstream white character. He dresses fastidiously, driving carefully to and from work, making sure not to exceed the speed limit. He has close ties to the Albuquerque community, donating money to charitable causes and even partnering with the DEA in fundraising. Fring is meticulous and controlled as a character, both in his daily life as the owner/manager of his restaurants and also as a drug distributor. Despite his secrecy, it is quickly evident that he is Latin American in origin and has connections within the Mexican drug cartels. As his importance within the narrative increases, the series reveals a bit more about his past. Fring is in fact not originally from Mexico, but instead Chile. Due to his business acumen, he has become the American contact for at least one of the cartels. He is not just the brains behind the operation, however, and can be moved to violent proaction. In "Box Cutter" (7/17/11), one of the most chilling episodes of the entire series, Fring violently dispatches his own henchman Victor (Jeremiah Bitsui) after the latter was seen near a crime scene. He arrives at the underground meth lab constructed for White and Pinkman, methodically takes off his clothes, neatly folds and hangs them without saying a word, dons a protective work suit, and then savagely cuts Victor's throat with a box cutter.

Despite his occasional use of violence, Fring is nothing like Tuco. He is not capricious: nothing he does is without a significant amount of risk assessment. He is not addicted to meth: indeed, he has real reservations in working with Pinkman, as he views that even being associated with addicts is risky business. He is humanized; we learn a bit about his philosophy when White is invited to dine at his house. And finally, he is given a background in a key flashback in "Hermanos" (9/4/11), the audience is given insight into Fring's complicated relationship with Don Eladio (Steven Bauer), boss of one of the Mexican cartels. Fring and his partner Max (James Martinez), with whom Fring has begun making methamphetamine, are brought to meet Don Eladio. After bantering with them for a bit, Eladio has Max shot, forcing Fring to watch as his friend bleeds out. This traumatic episode provides a clue about Fring's background, one that is never fully explored. There are several hints throughout the series, one mentioned by Eladio in this scene, that Fring was involved in some aspect with the violent excesses that occurred during and immediately following Augusto Pinochet's 1973 military coup in Chile.[8] An additional indication comes in the episode "One Minute" (5/2/10) when Hector Salamanca (Mark Margolis) refers to Fring as "Generalissimo," suggesting that the latter held some power or authority within Pinochet's military junta. During this bloody episode in Chilean history, various tactics such as torture and assassination were employed by Pinochet's agents against Marxists and other political dissidents. Although the series never makes clear Fring's specific involvement or even which side he supported, hints dropped by both Eladio and Hector suggest that he played a role in the bloodshed, in fact a significant enough one that he was forced to change his name upon immigrating to Mexico to begin a new life.

By the time of his death in the episode "Face Off" (10/9/11), Fring is a well-rounded character with interesting and complex motivations. He is not at all the addicted, violent, shallow stereotype of an over-the-top Latin American drug kingpin *a la* Tony Montana or Tuco Salamanca. The fact that Fring is black also establishes an interesting aspect of Latino identity not often referenced in popular culture. During the sixteenth through the nineteenth centuries, the Middle Passage brought African slaves not only to the eastern shores of North America, but also to Brazil and the Caribbean, as well as a few Central American nations such as Panama. The "Black Hispanic" is rarely portrayed in American depictions of Latinos, and the choice of Esposito for the role of Fring introduced complexity to the series' racial depictions. Furthermore, in deciding that a Chilean character would play a lead role in serving as conduit between the Mexican drug cartels and U.S. market, Vince Gilligan signaled the complexity of border politics, where not only Mexicans seek to create a new life by crossing from south to north.

Much as Fring and Tuco establish that, north of the border, *Breaking Bad* is as adept at obliterating as it is employing Latino stereotypes, so too does the series do the same with the cartel south of the border. In the episode "Salud" (9/18/11), Don Eladio instructs Fring to bring him the maker of the blue meth. Not wanting to identify White as the mastermind behind the drug, but knowing that he cannot ignore Eladio's summons, Fring flies to Mexico and brings Pinkman with him. He passes Pinkman off as the genius behind the blue meth and, in a tense cook overseen by a Mexican chemist, Pinkman produces a batch with a purity index above 95 percent, almost as pure as White's. Getting a glimpse into the machinations of a Mexican drug lab, replete with a university-trained biochemist, is not the type of scene that would usually find its way into a drug narrative, where the product simply shows up on the street in the United States or is seen mid-transport. What happens next, however, fits a stereotype commonly associated with portrayals of Latin American drug cartels. Fring and Pinkman are taken to Eladio's villa and, after some preliminary business talk and a toast of friendship, are treated to a party with liberal amounts of alcohol and scantily-clad women. Such scenes are commonplace in drug narratives that shine a light on the cartels, particularly those involving depictions of the Colombian cartels. Pablo Escobar, long-time chieftain of the Medellin Drug Cartel, was well known for throwing such parties,[9] and they have become staples in depicting powerful drug lords (*Blow, Scarface*, and the television series *Kingpin*). *Breaking Bad*, however, subverts this genre plot point. Although Eladio's party begins in a predictable fashion, it soon devolves into utter chaos. Having poisoned the tequila with which he, Eladio, and Eladio's capos had toasted, Fring excuses himself to the bathroom to force vomit. All around

the complex, Eladio's henchmen begin dying; the party reaches an igno-
minious end as the scantily-clad women run off, taking with them some
of Eladio's possessions and handfuls of cash and even stealing a few of
his cars. After beginning true to form in pure debauchery, the party ends
as Eladio dies while his empire crumbles around him, foreshadowing
what will happen to Fring a few episodes later and perhaps what will
happen to White by the end of the series.

Perhaps the most astonishing figures in the narrative, however, are
the "Salamanca cousins" as they are referred to in the *Breaking Bad* lexi-
con. These characters, Leonel and Marco (Daniel and Luis Moncada), are
hit men associated with one of the cartels. They are, in fact, brothers to
each other and cousins of Tuco Salamanca. From their introduction in the
first scene of season three in the episode "No Mas" (3/2/10), the Salamanca cousins do not conform to any stereotype traditionally associated with
Mexicans in American popular culture: they are intelligent, dedicated,
contemplative, and logical. They first appear in a small desert town driving a Mercedes, after which they get out and join a group of people
crawling on their hands and knees up a hill toward a shack. Inside the
shack sits a grim-reaper like figure, a skull dressed up with clothes and
holding a scythe. Although it is never stated overtly in the narrative, this
figure almost certainly pertains to the Santa Muerte cult.[10] In that it is a
hybridized collection of beliefs and rituals deriving from both European
and non-European origins, Santa Muerte is not unlike Voodoo or Sante-
ria. However, the combination here is Catholic and Meso-American, and
the focus is very much upon death. Mexican culture exhibits a fascination
with death, from minutiae such as the common practice of wearing skull
masks to soccer matches to national holidays such as the Day of the Dead
(November 1), a decidedly morbid celebration of deceased ancestors.
Most narratives would not provide such insight into antagonists destined
to inhabit only half a season, but Vince Gilligan complicates the depiction
of the Salamanca cousins by doing just this. He humanizes them by displaying an interesting character quirk, simultaneously shedding light
upon another aspect of border culture. It is interesting to note that in
Santa Muerte a supplicant can ask for the death of another, so long as that
death is in the greater service of justice. Leonel and Marco Salamanca
believe that Walter White killed their cousin Tuco, and thus they are
justified in asking for and even causing his death. It is also instructive to
note that Santa Muerte also tends to be more highly patronized among
the poorer sections of Mexican society, perhaps suggesting a bit of back-
story for the Salamanca cousins. They are successful hit men, driving a
Mercedes and dressing in fancy suits; however, they may have come
from humble origins.

Even before they reach the shack and pin their drawing of White to
the wall, it is clear that the Salamanca cousins will be key antagonists.
The death's head figurines on the tips of their boots and the manner in

which they menacingly crawl directly toward the camera are suggestive, as is the fact that they rarely speak (indeed, between the two of them the cousins utter only about forty words over the course of seven episodes). More specifically, showing up in a dusty town driving a Mercedes and dressed in expensive suits indicates that the Salamanca cousins are somehow associated with one of the cartels. The character convention of the dapper hit man dressed in a suit is nothing new in cinema,[11] although it is not often associated with narratives involving the Mexican drug cartel. The manner in which the Salamanca cousins enter the United States is interesting, also serving to undermine normative stereotypes. In American television and cinema, the process of illegal entry into the United States is portrayed in a fairly narrow way. Films such as *Lone Star* (1996) present the crossing as traumatic, often with families making the difficult decision to leave home due to economic privation. As the crossing is often dangerous, it is usually depicted as a solemn affair, with any villainy coming in the form of profit-mongering 'coyotes' (those who charge money to take people across the border) or crooked members of law enforcement. The Salamanca cousins find themselves in the back of a fake hay truck, sitting across from an incredibly chatty individual. This character is a body shop worker who once painted cars for gangsters in Michoacán, theoretically members of one of the area's cartels. Whatever the affiliation, this character recognizes that the Salamanca cousins are gangsters, and in response they not only kill him but also the other nine passengers as well as the driver of the truck.

The complexity of border crossings is also manifest in a very brief scene that takes place after the Salamanca cousins cross the U.S.-Mexico border. As it turns out, there are other physical borders that exist. Numerous indigenous tribes, all of them situated on land contained within but separate and distinct from the United States, populate the desert portions of the American southwest, a fact that most border narratives ignore. In the brief scene that opens the episode "Sunset" (4/25/10), a tribal police officer on an unnamed reservation investigates why a woman has not been answering her phone. The reason is that the Salamanca cousins have killed her and taken over her house as their base of operations. This short scene, which only represents about three minutes of screen time, introduces yet another layer to the geopolitical complexity of this narrative. On reservation land, the rules and regulations of the United States do not apply, and state and federal law enforcement officials such as Hank Schrader do not have jurisdiction. In many ways, due to its rural setting and lack of federal oversight, the Salamanca cousins have found a good place to hide out, one where even the intense scrutiny focused upon other areas of the border region is not a given. Although it does not appear to be the case in this situation, tribal surnames in such areas are often Spanish instead of English. Just as Fring establishes the fact that not all Latin Americans who pass from Mexico to the United

States are Mexican in origin, so too does the reservation complicate the notion of 'borders' within the American southwest.

There are a few minor characters that also contribute to the series' complex and highly variable portrayal of the Mexican drug cartels. Hector Salamanca is wonderfully layered as a character; formerly a major capo for Don Eladio, he is now confined to a wheelchair following a stroke. In his heyday, he was quite powerful and was the capo who killed Fring's partner Max. However, he is now reduced to communicating by ringing a bell. When he is first introduced, Hector succeeds in keeping White from killing Tuco after he notices the former putting poison in Tuco's food. Later, after Tuco is killed by Schrader, Hector refuses to give up White as the drug manufacturer though they have become enemies, even going so far as to release his bowels so that the police will stop interrogating him. The only reason Hector saves White is so that he can have his nephews, the Salamanca cousins, track down and kill him. At the end of season four, however, in the episode "Face Off" (10/9/11), Hector allows White to strap a bomb to his wheelchair, identifying Fring as a greater villain and realizing this will be his only chance to once again become proactive and kill one of his enemies (he does so by triggering the bomb's switch with his bell). Hector may be violent, but he is also intelligent and, in the end, sacrificial. Another member of the cartel that does not fit the profile of a drug gangster is Tortuga (Danny Trejo). Instead of a mindless killer, Tortuga is an alcoholic, self-styled philosopher who has agreed to pass information along to the DEA. His decapitation in the episode "Negro y Azul" (4/19/09) definitely pushed the boundaries of television violence, but it also brought a moment of sobering reality to what is otherwise a fictional narrative. During the Mexican Drug War, which has raged since late 2006 through this book's delivery to press, tens of thousands of Mexicans have been killed as various cartels fight not only the Mexican military and police but also each other over trafficking corridors to the United States (O'Reilly 2012).[12] Many of these killings involved beheadings, a signature used by the cartels to humiliate the victims while simultaneously threatening their families and friends.

Several other minor characters illustrate the fact that not all criminals of Latin origin are involved with the cartels. Hugo Archilleya (Pierre Barrera), the janitor where White teaches high school, is initially suspected of stealing meth-producing equipment from the stock room because he has a prior history with marijuana possession. He is not given the benefit of the doubt in the distinction between drug user and drug dealer, and is led away in handcuffs after the DEA finds a small amount of marijuana in his possession. Although he is, in fact, a dealer, Combo (Rodney Rush) is very much a minor player and not at all piped into the cartel. He is a small-time, street-level meth dealer associated with Pinkman. Even though he has the least screen time of Pinkman's cronies due to his premature death, Combo is perhaps the most important. He sells his mother's RV to Pinkman who, along with White, uses the vehicle as a mobile drug lab. The fact that Combo steals the RV in order to sell it later allows Schrader to conclude that Pinkman is connected to the blue meth. It is following Combo's death, however, that the audience learns that he is Latino. During Schrader's investigation, it is revealed that Combo's name is actually Christian Ortega. Combo is light-skinned, light-haired, and has blue eyes, appearing every much as Anglo as Pinkman and their mutual friends Brandon "Badger" Mayhew (Matt L. Jones) and Skinny Pete (Charles Baker). It is thus a surprise when it is revealed that Combo is at least part Latino, as Hollywood typically casts actors with darker hair, eyes, and skin for such characters.[13] And finally, Tomas Cantillo's (Angelo Martinez) appearance in the narrative is not at all standard. Heart wrenchingly, the eleven-year-old brother of Pinkman's girlfriend becomes involved with some rival meth dealers, serving as a lookout and drug dispenser. In the episode "Mandala" (5/17/09), Tomas even shoots Combo after being ordered to by his bosses. The boy's murder a short time later indicates the vicious cycle that exists, where young men of Latino descent growing up in poverty fall victim to a drug subculture that perhaps offers financial security in the short term, but often ends in death. Tomas' nephew, Brock Cantillo (Ian Posada), who is only a few years younger, is the next potential victim of this cycle, although his mother, Andrea (Emily Rios), and Pinkman are determined that he will not get involved with this subculture, pushing him to succeed in school.

Although the majority of the Latino characters in *Breaking Bad* are involved with drug production, transportation, or distribution, there are a few who exist on the other side of the spectrum. Schrader's partner in the DEA, Steve Gomez (Steven Michael Quezada), does not at all conform to typical stereotypes of Latino males who hold power. He is pacific and nurturing, often sublimating his own career to the needs of those around him. Although they are partners, he takes his lead from Schrader, a tendency that is formalized following the latter's promotion. Indeed, the only times Gomez seems to take the initiative are when he leads a gang of DEA agents as well as White to gloat over the grievous wounds suffered by the surviving Salamanca cousin, and when he accepts a promotion to the El Paso office. However, these moments have less to do with his character development and more to do with, respectively, getting White into the same room with Salamanca and developing a wedge between him and Schrader. It is the latter, in many ways, who most closely matches the traditional notion of Latino machismo during the course of the series. Although he is an Anglo character, Schrader swaggers through the narrative (at least in the first two seasons), taking immediate charge of every single encounter, bragging about his own abilities, and dispensing ribald and even racially-tinged insults to his co-workers. He is the alpha male of the Albuquerque DEA and is portrayed as a stereotypical machismo Latino character.[14] Although Schrader is a dedicated husband, he is all about competition and even social dominance. Indeed, Schrader's machismo takes his character in interesting directions and asserts him as one of the narrative's most interesting characters. Although he is Anglo, his is the character that best elucidates the complexities of border machismo throughout the narrative.

Agent Schrader's machismo attitude is first challenged when he is damaged psychologically in the episode "Negro y Azul" (4/19/09), and later when he is physically devastated in the episode "One Minute" (5/2/10). In the former episode, Hank joins a rowdy group of El Paso DEA agents in a cross-border task force set to monitor Tortuga as he gains information about the drug cartel. Schrader is out of his element in that he is a newcomer to a team of alpha males with an already established pecking order. Furthermore, he does not speak Spanish, making it difficult for him to communicate with the Mexican cops assigned to the task force. He knows that other members of the team are making fun of him in Spanish but finds himself unable to retort. Things go from embarrassing to traumatic, however, when Tortuga's decapitated head is found attached to a tortoise. Schrader walks off to vomit, enduring the scorn of both DEA agents and Mexican police alike but ironically saving his life when a grenade hidden within Tortuga's head explodes. As Schrader runs past several dead bodies to use his belt as a tourniquet for a fellow agent whose leg has been severed, the scene cuts away to a photograph of an atomic explosion at the National Museum of Nuclear Science and History, where Pinkman is meeting with his dealers. Indeed, this episode does have an explosive effect within Schrader's consciousness; for the rest of the season and into the next, he suffers from Post Traumatic Stress Disorder and no longer acts the macho alpha male to quite the same degree. He is still recovering from this episode and beginning to re-assert his dominance in the Albuquerque office when he is exposed to an even more severe event in "One Minute." In order to protect White from the Salamanca cousins, Fring reveals to them that it was Schrader who killed their cousin Tuco. In order to give Schrader the advantage, Fring makes an anonymous phone call to the DEA agent just before the attack. What he does not realize, however, is that Schrader had just been put on administrative leave and thus does not have a firearm. What transpires is a battle during which one Salamanca brother is killed, another badly injured, and Schrader shot four times. As one of the bullets lodges near his spine, for the rest of season three and throughout much of season four, Schrader is bed-ridden and must rely upon his wife, Marie (Betsy Brandt), for even the most simple tasks. For a man of his confidence and braggadocio, having to learn how to walk again and needing assistance to go to the bathroom is devastating, and his convalescence is as much psychological as it is physical. The traumas that attend a border culture predicated upon the drug trade make it difficult to maintain the machismo typically associated with this region. *Breaking Bad* finds an additional avenue of destroying Latino stereotypes in having an Anglo character so obviously manifest one of the overarching ones.

There was a time when, in the United States, Asia was viewed as the source of illicit drugs. Although opium had long since peaked by the transition from the nineteenth to the twentieth centuries, it was not until after World War II that Latin America had firmly replaced Asia in the American consciousness as the source of drugs. The finality of this shift came at a time when the rise of a youth culture brought with it unprecedented divisions between generations, a distinction that would manifest itself most fully in the 1960s. Distrust of the youth and concern over the growing volume of Latino immigration combined following World War II in a renewed fear of marijuana and several decades later in a fear of Colombian cocaine. Not surprisingly, media portrayals of Latinos, which had long been tinged with racism, now began embracing specific stereotypes associated with the drug culture. Patterns of stereotypical portrayal have often been accompanied by political engagement among those combatting these patterns. Certain projects in film and television began to avoid conforming to normative and simplistic representations of Latino identity. Charles Ramirez Berg (1992) notes that there are positive and negative ways of going about this, but that representations that aim for complexity allow for a greater awareness among audiences (40-46). In *Breaking Bad*, Gilligan offers up portrayals of Latino identity across a very wide spectrum. It is important to note that, with the exception of Gustavo Fring, the majority of the Latino characters that populate his narrative are secondary in nature; indeed, the two main characters are Anglo. Gilligan's project of portrayal is thus not oppositional filmmaking as noted by Chon Noriega, but instead one of cultural complexity. In other words, instead of Mexican-American filmmakers such as Luis Valdez and Cheech Marin, and Mexican filmmakers such as Alejandro Iñárritu, directors who have purposely shone a light on multi-faceted aspects of Latino identity, Gilligan has been more about investing his narrative with as much complexity as possible. In doing so, the series has undermined numerous Latino stereotypes, making the characters who populate *Breaking Bad* anything but average.

NOTES

1. Terminologies can be difficult to utilize with precision, particularly as a wide range of variable usage exists. For instance, both "Latino" and "Hispanic" are used to denote those of Latin American origin, although people from Spain can also be implicated with these terms. Although "Tejano" is usually specific to Mexican-Americans living in Texas, it is occasionally used to denote Texans originating from other Latin American countries. The same is true for "Chicano," although this term sometimes denotes Mexican-Americans living only in California, and sometimes across the border states. The common denominator with this term is that the individual has an identity stake with at least two geopolitical entities. In *The Chicano-Studies Reader*,

Fernando Peñalosa (2010) notes the multiple factors—cultural, political, ethnic, and biological—that inform such discussion (16-27). As this essay is a character study, and the characters analyzed derive from a variety of backgrounds, no singular term will be employed. However, in service of consistency when discussing the series' overall project of portrayal, the term "Latino" will be employed, as it most precisely indicates a general background shared by the various characters, nearly all of whom are male.

2. The only full-length work of criticism thus far published is *Breaking Bad and Philosophy: Badder Living Through Chemistry*, edited by David R. Koepsell and Robert Arp. Although it contains some interesting essays, this collection is part of the "Popular Culture and Philosophy" series that often trades in-depth analysis for speed in hitting the marketplace quickly after a film or television series' success.

3. It is interesting to note that the American frontier was declared closed by Frederick Jackson Turner in 1893, right in the middle of the two moments often given for the beginning of cinema: Thomas Edison's invention of the kinetoscope in 1891, and the Lumiere Brothers' invention of the cinematographe in 1895. In other words, Americans were beginning to reflect upon the frontier and its contributions to the formation of the national character at a moment when new technologies allowed for visual and thus highly powerful visions of the past, many of which would quickly become rooted in notions of racial superiority.

4. Even the names of these two characters—White and Pinkman (pink + man)—perform their Anglo-ness, and at no time during the narrative are either of them imbued with any of the stereotypical traits or qualities associated with Latinos. The only moment White is portrayed as a Latino figure is when Heisenberg appears as a character in a narcocorrido at the beginning of "Negro Y Azul" (4/19/09). Narcocorridos are Mexican folk ballads that portray border culture and are generally favorable toward drug smuggling and other criminal activity.

5. Due to the continually shifting nature of cartel alliances during the Mexican Drug War (2006 to the present), as well as the fact that *Breaking Bad* avoids giving specifics as to which cartel Don Eladio controls, it is difficult to know to whom Tuco owes his allegiance. Theoretically, due to the narrative's setting in Albuquerque, which although 250 miles to the north of El Paso is still part of the border drug zone and a shipping hub to various parts of the American Southwest, the cartel referenced is most likely either the powerful Sinaloa cartel, which controls much of the western part of Mexico, or the Juarez cartel, which controls much of the area immediately surrounding Ciudad Juarez/El Paso. According to Héctor Dominquez-Ruvalcaba and Igancio Corona (2010), this part of northern Mexico constitutes the biggest drug corridor in the world, with three of the five largest Mexican cartels vying for control of delivery and distribution to the North American drug market (3). Certainly, the areas in the series portrayed south of the border, including the land around Don Eladio's villa, appear to be a good match for the Chihuahuan Desert of north-central Mexico. The appearance of the Salamanca cousins in season three, however, complicates this hypothesis. The body shop worker being smuggled across the border, who worked for "some of the biggest gangsters in Michoacán," recognizes the shoes worn by the hit men, suggesting that they at one point worked for either the La Familia Michoacán group or the Knights Templar cartel. So, there is no way of knowing for sure to which cartel Eladio or any of the Salamancas belong, and it is certainly possible due to the shifting alliances that multiple cartels are involved in the narrative. For a wealth of information about the Mexican Drug War, see the *Los Angeles Times* website "Mexico Under Siege" (2012), a clearing house of articles, photographs, and videos from over a four year period.

6. It should be noted that although the figure of the over-the-top Latino drug kingpin became entrenched in the popular media after the rise of the Columbian cartels, links between Latin America and drug culture preceded *Scarface* by decades. The Opium Exclusion Act of 1909 made that drug illegal, leading to addicts looking for other avenues for a fix. Marijuana proved to be inexpensive and easy to obtain, leading to a growing concern over its hold over young people during the inter-war

period and culminating with highly sensationalized "educational" films such as *Reefer Madness* (1936) and *Assassin of Youth* (1937). However, it wasn't until Raymond Chandler and the Beat poets during and immediately after World War II that this association was made more firmly in popular culture. Set in the criminal underbelly of Los Angeles, Chandler's short stories and novels often involved drug plots, and one section of Jack Kerouac's *On the Road* (written in 1951, published in 1957) depicts the ease in which marijuana can be obtained in a Texas border town. As they were subject to a censoring body, mainstream films were a bit slower than novels to explore this terrain, although certainly one of the directors who began to push the boundaries on this subject, Orson Welles, made the connection between drugs and Latin America in *Touch of Evil* (1958). By the late 1960s with films such as *Easy Rider* (1969), the link was firmly established, although the character of the kingpin did not become solidified in popular culture until later.

7. Many border narratives in American film and television have been criticized for employing Carribean [Benicio del Toro in *Traffic* (2000)], South American, and even Spanish actors [Javier Bardem in *No Country for Old Men* (2007)] to depict Mexican or Chicano characters.

8. In overthrowing the democratically-elected government of Socialist Salvador Allende, Pinochet had not only the support of the right-wing army but also of the American Central Intelligence Agency (CIA). Some members of the Chilean military and police involved in the program of torture and assassination were CIA assets, as a memo from the National Intelligence Council made evident following the declassification of materials in 2000: "Many of Pinochet's officers were involved in systematic and widespread human rights abuses following Allende's ouster. Some of these were contacts or agents of the CIA or U.S. military" (2). In the episode "Hermanos," Agent Schrader notes that no information exists for Gustavo Fring prior to his application for Mexican citizenship in 1986. He wonders if Fring's identity is assumed but expresses surprise that he could have received American citizenship in 1989 without a thorough background check. The possibility exists that Fring had help from the CIA in establishing his new identity, although this hypothesis is unlikely given Fring's move into narcotics. Regardless of how he entered the country, a Pinochet loyalist becoming instrumental in the U.S. drug trade is a minor example of "Blowback," whereby American support of a foreign entity empowers that organization or individual to later engage in actions deleterious to American interests.

9. According to the Associated Press (1992), Pablo Escobar routinely arranged orgies for himself and his henchman, even while "behind bars" in a prison he had ordered built to house him after deciding to turn himself in!

10. For images depicting Santa Muerte, including some featuring its supplicants, see the photo essay "Santa Muerte" (2012) in *Time*'s online magazine.

11. In its most famous iteration, Hong Kong filmmaker John Woo and actor Chow Yun-Fat teamed together in *A Better Tomorrow* (1986) and *The Killer* (1989) to present a professional hit man whose sartorial formality is matched only by his facility with a gun.

12. Although by late 2012 the total number of fatalities in the war had usually been set at just over 50,000, a recent study by Molly Molloy at New Mexico State University puts the number at closer to 100,000 (O'Reilly).

13. Case in point—Although Cameron Diaz grew up speaking Spanish while Jessica Alba did not, it is the darker-complected Alba who is more often cast in Latina roles.

14. Hank's quest for social dominance in the DEA office reflects the structuring of the Mexican patriarchal order. In *Modernity and the Nation in Mexican Representations of Masculinity* (2007), Hector Domínguez-Ruvalcaba notes that Mexican machismo is an outgrowth of the class system in Spanish colonialism. In a nation where skin color and surname no longer carry the meaning they once did under Spanish rule, aggression and dominance are tools of establishing and preserving the social order. As Domínguez-Ruvalcaba states: "Mexican masculinity is an invention of modern coloni-

alism, in which sensualizing means disempowerment" (3). He also notes the homosocial nature of Mexican culture, linking it specifically to machismo. In Mexico, during male-male intercourse the passive recipient is the only partner to be considered homosexual. As actor Gael Garcia Bernal noted while promoting *Y tu mamá también* (2001) in 2002: "It's a Mexican idiosyncrasy . . . you're more macho if you fuck men" (quoted in de la Mora, 12). Hank uses jokes, taunts, and nicknames to objectify those around them and re-inscribe their place below him in the hierarchy. In so doing he typifies the specific flavor of machismo described by Domínguez-Ruvalcaba and other critics.

WORKS CITED

A Better Tomorrow. Directed by John Woo. Troy: Anchor Bay Entertainment, 1986. DVD.

Assassin of Youth. Directed by Elmer Clifton. Narberth: Alpha Video, 2004. DVD.

Associated Press. "Escobar Had Ritzy Prison." *The Register Guard*. 4 August 1992.

Berg, Charles Ramirez. "Bordertown: The Assimilation Narrative and the Chicano Social Problem Film." In *Chicanos and Film: Essays on Chicano Representation and Resistance*, edited by Chon Noriega. 29-46. New York: Garland, 1992.

Blow. Directed by Ted Demme. New York: New Line Cinema, 2001. DVD.

Casino. Directed by Martin Scorcese. Universal City: Universal Pictures, 1995. DVD.

Central Intelligence Agency. "CIA Activies in Chile." 19 September 2000. http://www.gwu.edu/~nsarchiv/news/20000919/01-01.htm.

de la Mora, Sergio. *Cinemachismo: Masculinities and Sexuality in Mexican Film*. Austin: University of Texas, 2006.

Easy Rider. Directed by Dennis Hopper. Culver City: Sony Pictures, 1999. DVD.

Frogoso, Rosa Linda. *The Bronze Screen*. Minneapolis: University of Minnesota Press, 1993.

GoodFellas. Directed by Martin Scorcese. Burbank: Warner Brothers, 1990. DVD.

Dominguez-Ruvalcaba, Héctor and Ignacio Corona. *Gender Violence at the U.S.-Mexico Border: Media Representation and Public Response*, edited by Hector Dominguez-Ruvalcaba and Ignacio Corona. Tucson: University of Arizona Press, 2010.

———. *Modernity and the Nation in Mexican Representations of Masculinity: From Sensuality to Bloodshed*. New York: Palgrave, 2007.

Kingpin. Created by David Mills. National Broadcasting Company, 2003. Television.

Koepsell, David R. and Robert Arp, eds. *Breaking Bad and Philosophy: Badder Living Through Chemistry*. Chicago: Open Court, 2012.

Larson, Stephanie Greco. *Media and Minorities: The Politics of Race in News and Entertainment*. Lanham: Rowman & Littlefield, 2006.

Limón, José E. "Stereotyping and Chicano Resistance: An Historical Dimension (1973)." In *Chicanos and Film: Essays on Chicano Representation and Resistance*, edited by Chon Noriega. 3-17. New York: Garland, 1992.

Lone Star. Directed by John Sayles. Burbank: Warner Brothers, 1995. DVD.

"Mexico Under Siege: The Drug War at our Doorstep." *Los Angeles Times*. 9 October, 2012. http://projects.latimes.com/mexico-drug-war/#/its-a-war.

No Country for Old Men. Directed by Joel Coen and Ethan Coen. New York: Miramax, 2007. DVD.

O'Reilly, Andrew. "Mexico's Drug Death Toll Double What Reported, Expert Argues." August 10, 2012. http://latino.foxnews.com/latino/news/2012/08/10/mexico-drug-death-toll- double-what-reported-expert-argues/.

Peñalosa, Fernando. "Towards an Operational Definition of the Mexican American." In *The Chicano-Studies Reader: An Anthology of Aztlan 1920-2010*, edited by Chon Noriega et al. 16-27. Los Angeles: University of California Press, 2010.

Reefer Madness. Directed by Louis Gasnier. Beverly Hills: Walking Shadows, 2010. DVD.

Rodriguez, Clara E. *Latin Looks: Images of Latinas and Latinos in the United States Media.*
    Ed. Clara E. Rodriguez. Oxford: Westview, 1997.
"Santa Muerte." *Time.* October 12, 2012. http://www.time.com/time/photogallery/
    0,29307,1676932_1474285,00.html.
Scarface. Directed by Brian De Palma. Universal City: Universal Pictures, 1983. DVD.
The Killer. Directed by John Woo. New York: Fox Lorber Films, 1989. DVD.
The Treasure of Sierra Madre. Directed by John Huston. Burbank: Warner Brothers, 1948.
    DVD.
Touch of Evil. Directed by Orson Welles. Universal City: Universal Pictures, 2000. DVD.
Traffic. Directed by Steven Soderbergh. New York: USA Films, 2001. DVD.
Turner, Frederick Jackson. *History, Frontier, and Section.* Albuquerque: University of
    New Mexico Press, 1993.
Y tu mamá también. 2001. Directed by Alfonso Cuarón. Beverly Hills: MGM. DVD.

SIX

A Life Not Worth Living

Jami L. Anderson

What is so striking about *Breaking Bad* is how centrally impairment and disability feature in the lives of the characters of this series. It is unusual for a television series to cast characters with visible or invisible impairments.[1] On the rare occasions that television shows do have characters with impairments, these characters serve no purpose other than to contribute to their 'Otherness.'[2] *Breaking Bad* not only centralizes impairment, but impairment also drives and sustains the story lines.

In the pilot episode, Walter White is diagnosed with inoperable lung cancer. From that moment on, Walter's cancer becomes the driving force of the entire series: it is ultimately the explanation of every event affecting every character in every episode. After being blind-sided with the morbid announcement that the main character is terminal, viewers may expect to see Walter become reconciled to his new identity as cancer patient or to see him delivered the miraculous news that he has beaten cancer and is cured. Both story lines would give viewers "feel good" television. Instead, Walter angrily, violently blazes a third path, one which sees him both deny his status as cancer patient while at the same time bitterly insisting on the inevitability of his imminent death. During both the first and second season, Walter's body makes vivid that Walter is seriously ill. Walter shrinks in size, develops a debilitating hacking cough, loses consciousness, and becomes increasingly frail. Seemingly against his wishes, Walter undergoes treatment. Then, after being told that the cancer has shrunk by eighty percent, Walter submits to, and survives, surgery. And although told that his cancer is then in remission, Walter nonetheless insists that he knows that it is just a matter of time before his doctors will give him unwelcomed news.

Walter is not the only character in *Breaking Bad* who struggles with having a body that is, to use language found in disabilities scholarship, "undisciplined" or "unruly" (Terry and Urla 1995; Siebers 2008). Indeed, each of the main characters struggle to maintain control over his or her body while presenting a public pretense of normalcy. Skyler, Walter's wife, regards herself as a good mother—indeed the moral compass for the family—especially when accusing Walter of being deceitful or when discussing his meth-making activities. Yet, on several occasions she seemingly cannot stop herself from smoking while pregnant, drinking, or from having an adulterous affair. Marie, Skyler's sister, cannot control her kleptomania. Although Hank suffers from post-traumatic stress disorder after witnessing the bombing in Juarez, his later, self-aggrandized version of events is completely false. Later still, after being shot, Hank becomes a hostile paraplegic, fearful that he will no longer be able to function as an officer of the law, or even as a man. Yet, he publically presents himself as confident as ever. Walter Jr., whose cerebral palsy renders his physical impairments most visible, voices the frustrations of a son who cannot understand the disappearance and reappearance of his father in the family home, or the cold war going on between his parents. The stammering speech of Walter Jr. perfectly expresses the slurred rage of a character who wants to, but cannot, fully understand or take control of the situation he is in. As *Breaking Bad* progresses, each of these characters becomes somewhat, though perhaps not wholly, reconciled with their impairments. Skyler smokes and drinks in front of Walter, rather than secretly in the bathroom, and tearfully acknowledges her flaws as a parent and her frailties as a person. Marie acknowledges her need, and the benefits she has received, from seeing a therapist for her emotional and psychological problems. And Hank, though he initially repeatedly, and rudely, refused offers of assistance from others, came to graciously ask for and accept his longtime (and long-suffering) friend Gomie's supporting arm to help him walk while at work.

Jesse, Walter's meth-making partner, starts the series as a drug dealer and drug dependent. Jesse's life lacks direction; his 'business' is sloppily run; he has had many run-ins with the DEA and the local police; and, his knowledge of meth cooking (though he refers to it as an 'art') is crude. Although Jesse has a large circle of associates, and a tight circle of friends he can rely on for small favors, he has no one to whom he can turn for real emotional support. While Jesse has moments of sobriety, whenever confronted with trauma (such as the lethal overdose of his girlfriend Jane or the murder of Gale), he spirals into cycle of self-abuse.

In stark contrast to Jesse's chaotic self-doubt and self-abuse, Walter remains astonishingly unwavering in purpose and unaffected by his experiences. At no point does Walter become reconciled to his cancer status. He neither regards himself as someone living with cancer nor as someone having survived cancer. Indeed, he exhibits an astonishingly level of cognitive dissonance about his cancer, stating on several occasions that his cancer has disappeared and that he is good, but also that he is "dying— we're all dying." But this last claim is an empty rationalization, for, although it is true that we are all dying in the sense that we are all *mortal*, such a claim does not explain anything. And it certainly fails to justify any of the actions that Walter has undertaken since his diagnosis of cancer. Moreover, Walter insists that he is in charge of his life and that cancer does not rule him. This declaration jars in stark contrast with Walter's frail body, the body that lost consciousness, shriveled in size and coughed up blood. And Walter's means of maintaining control requires engaging in lies and acts of violence: murder, assault, and repeatedly deceiving his family members about his business. These efforts do not leave Walter unmarked. Walter is seen with bruised ribs, blackened eyes, and a bandaged and bloodied face. Nonetheless, Walter insists that, despite all evidence to the contrary, he is in complete control.

Walter is not terrified of dying, but he is absolutely unwilling to leave his family financially destitute. As a high school teacher, Walter is a rather inadequate provider for his family; they struggle to make ends meet and their financial future is uncertain. Were he to die, though, he would utterly fail to provide for them, making their already precarious situation profoundly worse.[3] To die is to fail, both as a father and a husband. And so, when confronted with the fact of his almost imminent death, Walter assumes a double life and becomes complicit in a series of lies and unspeakably violent crimes. When he begins this double life, Walter does not believe he is going to cheat death, but he does believe he is going to cheat failure. He believes he has found a winning move in a very bizarre game. But the longer Walter plays this game, the higher the stakes become: the longer he keeps up this double life, the more lies he must tell, and the more utterly depraved and immoral he becomes. Ultimately, the harder Walter works to ensure that he *becomes* the good father and husband he so desperately wants to be, the worse a father and husband he *is*.

I use three interrelated themes from disability scholarship to analyze *Breaking Bad*. The first theme, *Bodily Control*, is that good bodies are controlled bodies and that uncontrolled, messy bodies are frightening, bad bodies. Indeed, the messiness of impairment and disability is so bad, that impaired and disabled individuals are excluded or shut out from many areas of public life.[4] The second theme, *Normalcy*, is that the effect of hiding away impairment, of attempting to conceal disability, is that society becomes defined by, and structured around, the concept of normalcy. Normalcy, being normal, attaining and maintaining normalcy, is the preoccupation of most in society. To fail to be normal, or to fall from what is considered to be normal, is a source of tremendous anxiety for most people. These two themes, Bodily Control and Normalcy are conceptually connected: impairment, disease, and dying are so feared because they are socially invisible and, therefore unknown and unknowable. They are the undiscussable taboos. The third theme, *Bodily Realism*, is that having a realistic view of the body, which would at minimum require accepting the fact that human bodies are fragile things, prone to disease and accident and are ultimately destined to die, makes one more at ease in the world, and able to live better lives and live as a better person. Indeed, so the argument goes, our lives would be richer, more rewarding—emotionally and morally—if we cared less about normalcy because of a dread of abnormalcy, but instead learned to accept if not positively value the physical variability of human existence.

CONTROL . . . NORMAL . . . REAL—CONTROLLED AND UNCONTROLLED

We have decidedly contradictory beliefs about our bodies. On the one hand, since Descartes, we regard ourselves as essentially thinking beings. Therefore, as thinking things our bodies are of secondary importance to our sense of self. After all, bodies are mutable: they grow, age, get injured, bits may be surgically removed, but it is one's mind through which a person attains a stable sense of identity. Yet at the same time, we are anxious about our bodies. Bodies certainly seem relevant to one's sense of identity when it comes to one's gender, sex and race identity. And one's state of health, well-being, and physicality are surely of central importance to one's sense of self and one's identity.[5] So it is not too surprising that, although we may not want to define ourselves in terms of our bodies, we are nonetheless very concerned, if not anxious, about the health and well-being of our bodies.

Given the intense ambivalence we feel about our bodies, it should not be surprising that a powerful set of ideological beliefs about bodies is embraced by many in our society. Susan Wendell (1996) explains what she refers to as the "Myth of Control." She claims that the essence of this myth is that we can have the bodies we want; if we simply work hard enough, we can avoid illness, disability and even death. Wendell points out that, because there is an element of truth to the myth, we can work to *reduce* risk of disease, and act cautiously to avoid many physical risks. But the myth states more than that; it states that the body can be controlled. Despite the implausibility of the idea of total control, people insist of the truth of this myth even when presented with evidence of its falseness (93-94). When people are blamed or made to feel responsible for having non-ideal bodies despite their reasonable care, when unproveable theories are generated to explain how someone could have avoided becoming ill, when people with disabilities are seen as having their psychological, moral, or spiritual failures written upon their bodies, and when every death is regarded as a defeat of human efforts, the myth of control is as work.

Wendell refers to the "full reality of bodily life." This reality presents us with a cluster of very unpleasant but nonetheless undeniable facts. Among these facts are that we are born with fragile, vulnerable, disease-prone (perhaps even diseased) bodies. Another undeniable, yet equally unpleasant, fact is that each and every one of us is mortal. Because of this "reality of bodily life," or, speaking more carefully, because of the unpleasantness of bodily reality, the myth of control is widespread in our culture. The key idea of this myth is that if we exert sufficient control over our bodies, if we maintain adequate perfect health and thereby stave off disease, then we could thereby defer our own death. The myth of control is absurd, of course. We are surrounded by people who become ill, have impairments, have disease, and have died—each and every one of us has certainly become ill even if only temporarily at some time during our lives, and many of these people have worked hard to protect their health. Yet the myth of control persists. And, paradoxically, with the advance of medical technology it grows stronger for medicine does not prove to us that we are mortal and that we must suffer illness, but promises us an escape from disease or the suffering caused by impairment or injury. The more medicine advances the more inexplicable disease, impairment and death becomes.

Despite the overwhelming evidence that humans are not immortal and that each of us will experience disease or impairment (unless we die very quickly while we are very healthy), the myth of control serves its ideological function very well. This myth tell us that if we work hard enough, exercise enough, eat right, take the right pills, go to the right physicians, and are very, very disciplined—in other words, do not live badly or take risks, do not make any mistakes with our body—then we will remain healthy and disease free. The reward of normalcy is, according to Wendell, to escape having a "rejected body." In so far as we fail to control our bodies, in so far as we fail to be normal, we will be ill, diseased, abnormal and bad. It is our fear of abnormality, disease, deformity and deviancy that drives us to control our bodies and strive for normalcy.

Initially, Walter would not tell his family about his diagnosis. The terribleness of this disease, of being terminal, is too awful to discuss. The only person he does tell is Krazy-8, a young man he holds hostage in Jesse's basement, locked to a basement ceiling support with a bicycle lock. Since Walter has determined that he must kill Krazy-8, telling him about his cancer is only revealing his terrible secret temporarily. Once Krazy-8 is dead, Walter's secret will die with him.

Because of the complexity of his double life, and Skyler's suspicions of his lengthy absences, Walter is ultimately unable to keep his cancer secret from his family and begrudgingly tells them of his diagnosis. He also tells them that he does not intend to get medical treatment. Alarmed by this decision, Skyler, in the episode "Gray Matter" (2/4/08), gathers the family together for an "intervention" to change Walter's mind. Skyler starts the conversation by reassuring Walter that, though money is tight, because of the offer to pay for treatments made by his former partner Elliot and his wife Gretchen, there is no reason to not get the treatments. Hank speaks next and both agrees with Skyler that the offer of money should not be rebuffed but also adds that, though Walter was given a poor set of cards, since he wants to remain playing life's game, he should simply make the best of it while fighting. Walter Jr. follows next and accuses his father of not fighting and being scared of the cancer treatments. Marie then argues that Walter should do what he wants to do. She claims that treatment for terminal conditions can be tough for most patients, but those people go through with it merely to make their family members happy, not because they genuinely want to. After hearing Marie, Hank chimes in that he now agrees with Marie, adding that were Walter to refuse treatment he could die on his own accord.

After hearing all their opinions and suffering the heated argument that ensues, Walter finally offers an explanation of his choice. He claims he is refusing treatment not because of the concerns for the cost, not because he is afraid of the treatment, or the thought of the treatment itself as being unpleasant, but because what he needs is to control his life. For his whole life, he has never made a choice for himself and this time, he wants to make a choice for himself. He then describes how he envisions his future if he chooses treatment: thirty to forty pills every single day, loss of his hair, days spent too tired or nauseous to move or even turn his head, a person just marking time till he dies. But worse, according to Walter, is the thought that forever after his death that he would be remembered as a sickly, weak, dying man.

It seems just so obvious to Skyler that the reasonable option is to get medical treatment because that would, she believes, ensure that Walter would live longer and thus allow him to be with his family for more time. Likewise, Walt Jr. cannot fathom why anyone would refuse treatment. Even if the treatment is unpleasant, as medical treatment usually is, in his mind it cannot be any more unpleasant than any other medical treatment that people have undergone and survived. In his mind, his father's behavior is simply dumb.

But Walter is well aware that his chances of surviving lung cancer are practically nonexistent. He simply has, as far as he is concerned, too few choices and the only future that medical treatments will provide is one of debility, dependence and weakness. This imagined future self, though having a *longer* life, is living a life so repulsive to him, that he would rather die sooner than to live as a "dead man." Walter's greatest anxiety is the nature of the legacy he will leave his family: he is desperate that his legacy be financially and emotionally sound. He does not want to leave his family financially vulnerable or with tainted memories of him, memories of him sickly and repulsive. The idea that they would remember him ill is so abhorrent that he would rather forgo anything medicine has to offer.

Without explanation, Walter does agree to receive medical treatment. Yet his attitude toward cancer and being in control does not change, as revealed in this conversation in the episode "Cancer Man" (2/17/08), which takes place about a year later after his surgery and his cancer is in remission, with a fellow cancer patient while they both wait for a PET/CT scan. The other patient explains to Walter that getting cancer has changed his life and has taught him to give up control of his life. Walter scoffs at this mealy-mouth advice referring to it as crap. In response, he offers his own insights, which is that one should never lose control of one's life. The other patient immediately sees the flaw in Walter's logic, after all, "cancer is cancer." Some people survive cancer and some people do not. That is just the way it is and there is not anything we can do about it. Not Walter. He tells cancer it can go to hell. Strong words, indeed. But *believing* one is in control does not mean one *is* in control. And there is little evidence, other than Walter's words, that Walter is in control of his life.[6]

NORMAL AND ABNORMAL

The concept of normalcy pervades our society (Dudley-Marling and Gurn 2010; Snyder and Mitchell 2006). Every aspect of our bodily experience is analyzed in terms of normalcy and abnormalcy. Given the ubiquity of normalcy, it may seem surprising that this term did not appear in English language until 1840 (Davis 2010). It was the French scholar Adolphe Quetelet who first applied the mathematical concept "norm," which was then used by astronomers, to people, and developed the notion of *l'homme moyen*, "the average man." Quetelet hypothesized that *l'homme* was also *l'homme moyen morale* ("the moral man") and set out to with his measuring tapes, calipers and scales to prove it (Davis 2010, 5). Quetelet did not see the average man's body as something mediocre, but as the perfect ideal. He wrote, "an individual who in himself, at a given time, all the given qualities of the average man, would represent at once all the greatness, beauty and goodness of that being" (Porter 1986, 102). The ideal to be attained was a nation entirely comprised of average men, for then we would have a bourgeois paradise. Quetelet was confident that because of the "error curve," a term he coined, all bodily "defects and monstrosities" as well as "vice in morals" would eventually disappear, just as "errors" in mathematics "average out" (Davis 2010, 4-9).

Quetelet's ideas were extremely popular in his day, not only in France but also throughout Europe and the United States. The use of statistics to study humans spawned the birth of many eugenicist societies, each created for the purpose of researching the improvement of the human species and human societies.[7] Eugenicists assumed that most physical defects and "mental defects" (which included traits such as laziness, criminality, drunkenness, and "imbecility") were hereditary. It was also assumed that, just as with many diseases, some people were carriers of what were considered social diseases (Hubbard 2010). Cleansing society of such individuals became a national preoccupation.[8]

Being normal in such an environment is no minor matter; it is everything. To fail to be normal is not merely to be ill or naughty or mischievous. Rather, you are a burden to your family, a scourge of the city, a source of ruin in the whole society.[9] A physician cuts off a gangrenous leg to curtail the deadly threat to the patient and so, too, reasons the eugenicist, should we curtail the deadly effects that diseased and defective people have on the body politic. In the words of Supreme Court Justice Oliver Wendell Holmes, "Three generations of imbeciles are enough."[10] Tolerating social defectives is comparable to committing medical negligence.[11] Yet, as Hubbard (2010) claims, "health and physical prowess are poor criteria for human worth" (187). There is very little reason to believe that so-called normal people are morally good people and there is very little reason to believe that persons with deviant bodies are the worst citizens.

Jesse is regarded by many as not much more than a fucked up junkie, with little moral or social worth. He has a well-established criminal record and his parents have long ago given up on him. When Jesse announces that he wants out of the meth business, Walter tells Jesse he does not have anything in his life and asks him when they can start back cooking again. Yet, unlike Walter, who can whistle contentedly minutes after hearing a news report about the missing boy they just liquefied in a jug of acid because he witnessed them robbing a train, Jesse is tormented with guilt by the deeds he has committed. Although Jesse knows that there is right and there is wrong, he is repeatedly overwhelmed with self-doubts about his ability to navigate moral terrain.

Jesse first begins attending rehab to manage his drug use and to deal with his feelings of guilt regarding the death of his girlfriend Jane. Later, unable to handle his guilt for killing Gale, Jesse once again lapses from sobriety and starts using crystal meth. Only after Mike forcibly takes Jesse from his home and keeps him clear of all drugs and alcohol is Jesse able to become sober. Still unable to come to terms with the murder of Gale, Jesse, in the episode "Problem Dog" (8/28/11), heads back to rehab for moral support.

Rehab is a place for abnormals: addicts, deviants, and society's outsiders. Yet, the rules of this space make clear that, no matter how horrific their actions, they are rebranded as acceptable because, within that space, nothing is judged. Within that rehab space, abnormality is normality. The discussion leader tells everyone attending that they cannot change the past. Yet, Jesse finds himself so troubled by the gravity of the immoral actions he is directly responsible for, the latest being his murder of Gale, that he cannot even speak of them directly. Instead he tells the group he is pained because he has recently killed a dog, a "problem dog."

Another person in rehab explains that meth is to blame for this action since using the drug can cause a person to go right back to a dark spot in life where he or she has no control over his or her actions. But Jesse rejects this pat explanation. He did not kill the problem dog because meth made him act rather he chose to do it. Moreover, he had options: he could have put an ad in the paper, dropped "the dog" off at the pound. He did not *have to* kill Gale. There are always choices. To this the discussion leader reminds Jesse that the group is not in a position to render moral judgments. But Jesse is not consoled with these words. Rather, he finds them deeply disturbing. He argues that even if you do nothing about it, this whole process is about self-acceptance and there is really no point to one's actions. To further drive home his point, he mentions that he only came to rehab sessions to sell meth. Only at this point does the rehab discussion leader revise his policy about rendering moral judgments and acknowledge that such behavior is unacceptable.

Rather than seek comfort from such familiar platitudes as 'it all happens for a reason,' or 'what's done is done,'[12] Jesse insists on the acknowledgement of right and wrong. But in doing so, he must acknowledge, both to himself and others, that he has committed acts that are profoundly wrong, acts that cannot be undone. Moreover, the guilt he will feel for what he has done will, in all likelihood, never abate. But in taking full responsibility for his actions he will gain a sense of self as a moral person, as someone who has not only committed profoundly immoral actions, but also of someone capable of tender, loving relationships and doing good deeds, such as taking care of his aunt in her final days while she died of cancer, his love for Jane, financially securing Andrea and Brock, and his loyalty to Walter and Mike. Jesse, despite being nothing more than a socially deviant user, nonetheless demanded and obtained moral agency along with full moral accountability as well as the privilege to make moral judgments.

REAL AND UNREAL

Tobin Siebers (2008) elaborates on how people perceive their lives,

> Most people do not want to consider that life's passage will lead them from ability to disability. The prospect is too frightening, the disabled body, too disturbing. In fact, even this picture is too optimistic. The cycle of life runs in actuality from disability to temporary ability back to disability, and that only if you are among the most fortunate, among those who do not fall ill or suffer a severe accident. (60)

Able-bodied people like to think of themselves as essentially able-bodied: once able-bodied, *always* able-bodied. We grow and work and play within a culture that markets immortality with creams, pills, and surgeries. If we accept the myth of control, we are accepting the idea that we can stave off illnesses, even our own death. Yet we know that cannot possibly be true. But, as Siebers claims,

> [T]hat we embrace these contradictions without interrogating them reveals that our thinking is steeped in ideology. Ideology . . . sutures together opposites, turning them into apparent complements of each other, smoothing over contradictions, and making almost unrecognizable any perspective that would offer a critique of it. (8)

We cling to these contradictory thoughts about our bodies, about sickness and health, because we do not want to face the reality of bodies.

Because the truth of the matter is that impaired, diseased or dying bodies sometimes seem to have plans of their own, independent of what we wish them to do. Cheryl Marie Wade (1994) defends what is referred to as a bodily realism, an approach advocated by some disability studies scholars. Wade asserts that only the use of blunt language, shockingly detailed, completely frank and uncensored descriptions of bodily functions and bodily dependence are the way to end our collective fear of disease and disability. Because so long as we refuse to acknowledge the reality of bodily needs, so long as we are ignorant of disabled bodily reality, we will live in fear of those realities. Wade argues that the only way we will ever "be really at home in the world" is if we first use "real language" to discuss these "crude realities" (88-90).

Sick, diseased and impaired bodies can so terrify the able-bodied that they will refuse to even consider the possibility that such bodies exist, or that one day they could have a body like that. But the more disabled are treated as the Other, the more the able-bodied avoid confronting those blunt, crude realities, the more terrifying disability looms in the imagination of ability ideology. It is for that reason that Wade insists that we should talk about these realities. But why should we confront these horrors? Why not just shut them away? Because, according to Wade, this is our world, our home and the way we live in it and if we are to have any hope to *be at home* in it, then we must confront the truths, not only that some bodies are "not normal," but that what is now able-bodied may someday become "not normal." Perhaps the most fortuitous effect of "saying these things out loud" is that the able-bodied will come to realize that most disabled people do not regard their lives as not worth living. Many disabled regard their disability as part of their identity and as a source of pride (Siebers 2008; Wendell 1996).

Walter exerts tremendous effort to conceal not only his criminal life from his family, but also the effects of his sickness from his family. He withholds the diagnosis of cancer for as long as he can. He is saccharinely false about his illness, lying to them about his coughing fits, his weakness, loss of consciousness and his frailty. Even after his surgery is successful and he is going in for his follow up chemo treatments, he omits to tell his family the results of the tests; if they want to know, they have to ask him about the tests and it is not clear that he is being completely forthright given that he has rarely been truthful with them in the past, ostensibly to spare their feelings.

Walter has missed out on numerous family events in the previous months since he began making crystal meth. And, after Walter moved out of the house, he is only tangentially involved with the family. But completely missing his son's birthday party is even more negligent than usual. Walter Jr., in the episode, "Salud" (9/18/11), arrives at his father's condo for an explanation. Walt Jr. rings the doorbell, but the rings go unanswered. He calls, but the call goes through to the answering machine, and we can hear the answering machine message, with Walter's detached voice identifying himself and asking the caller to leave a message. Walter Jr. asks if he is alright and informs him that he knows he is home because his car is parked in the driveway. Walter listens to his son's pleas as he lays in bed, clutching bloodied sheets, evidence of his most recent fight. Walter Junior continues telling Walt that he missed his son's party and he knows something is wrong so he will call for help. When Walt Jr. speaks of contacting 9-1-1, Walter is sufficiently motivated to admit Walt Jr. into his house. Alarmed by his father's appearance, Walt Jr. asks him what happened and Walt responds that he was in a fight. Alarmed, Walter Jr. starts to call his mother on his cell phone but Walter begs him not to. Then, crying, he confesses to his son that he made a huge blunder and he paid for his mistake. Walter Jr., completely misunderstands this conversation, and believes that they are talking about his father's (non-existent) gambling addiction. He consoles his father, and then leads the distraught Walter to bed, to sleep off the effects of the pain pills and distress.

The next morning, Walter wakes up to find the apartment clean and Walter Jr. asleep on his couch. Embarrassed, Walter apologizes to his son for missing his birthday. Refusing to accept Walter Jr.'s forgiveness, he takes complete responsibility for any misunderstanding between them. Seeing Walter Jr.'s inability to fully understand this apology, Walter tells him that his own father died of Huntington's Disease when Walter was quite young. Worse, the disease caused his father to end his days in a hospital needing full care because of the neurological damage caused by the disease. Despite wanting to know his father, what he was like as a person, Walter confesses that he has only one real memory of his father lying in bed, dying and gasping his last breath of air. This memory so disturbs him that Walter tell his son that, more than anything, he does not want his memory of him to be one of a sick, weak man. Walter Jr.

dismisses his father's worries and tells him that such a memory would not be bad because it would be better than missing him for the past year.

Walter's main concern, as with the Talking Pillow conversation, is the legacy he will leave his family. He is terrified that after he is dead his family will remember nothing more than the smell of him while he is ill, or of him crying and bloodied, wearing nothing but his underwear while clinging to his paraplegic son for support. Walter insists to Walter Jr. that he is his father, as if declaring a biological fact bolsters his credibility. But it does not. In the past year, Walter has been the worst sort of absentee father desperately accumulating millions all so that he can escape being the sickly dead man who needs his family for physical or emotional support.

But to Walter Jr., far worse than dirty sheets or a future with adult diapers is an absentee father, inadequate explanations and false bonhomie which is what life has been for the past year. Even worse is a father that moves in and out of the house and parents who are not on speaking terms with no explanation. In comparison to the controlled deceptions Walter has constructed, the bodily realism of tears and weakness is refreshing indeed.

WALTER WINS AN EMPIRE . . . AND LOSES EVERYTHING THAT MAKES A LIFE WORTH LIVING

After killing Gus Fring, Walter calls Skyler to let her know that he is safe and that he has won. Walter did not set out, first and foremost, to topple Gus Fring, to beat cancer, or even to cheat death. Walter wanted to cheat failure. Walter did not want to die smelly and weak, laying in a hospital bed, stinking and frail, with tubes and needles poking into him, the object of pity and a financial burden to his family. He did not like his choices life had handed him so he created his own. After just about a year later, he has more money than he could spend in several lifetimes and is running the highest grade meth operation ever organized, with a territory reaching throughout the entire southwest of the United States and expanding interests in the Czech Republic. So, Walter has won, it would seem. But what has he lost? The love and respect of his wife,[13] the trust and loyalty of Jesse,[14] and, of course, the opportunities to spend time with his two children. Walter was not driven by a naked desire for cash, nor did he have a lifelong desire to make meth. Instead, it was his terror of confronting his illness that prompted everything. But rather than reconcile his parental responsibilities with whatever inevitable, and perfectly natural, physical weaknesses he would experience, he instead chose to abandon his family and his moral values. In effect, Walter's fear that cancer would make his life not worth living propelled him to make terrible choices such that much of what makes life worth living is gone or so thoroughly damaged, that his life *is* not worth living.

NOTES

1. Throughout this chapter, I will follow Susan Wendell's usage of the terms *impairment, disability,* and *handicap*. Wendell is in turn borrowing the United Nations definitions, though with a reasonable degree of caution. An *impairment* is "[a]ny loss or abnormality of psychological, physiological, or anatomical structure or function." A *disability* is "[a]ny restriction of lack (resulting from an impairment) of ability to perform an activity in the manner or within the range considered normal for a human being." Handicap is "[a] disadvantage for a given individual, resulting from an impairment or disability, that limits or prevents the fulfillment of a role that is normal, depending of age, sex, social and cultural factors, for that individual." See Wendell's careful and intelligent critique of both the value and limits of the U.N. definitions (Wendell 1996, chap. 1 [especially 13-19]; U.N. 1983). By "visible impairment" I mean any impairment that a non-familiar can become aware of with relatively little or no personal knowledge of that person. Examples of a visible impairment may include paraplegia, cerebral palsy or Down Syndrome. By "invisible impairment" I mean any impairment that a non-familiar could not become aware of by looking at or listening to someone or, perhaps, even working with someone, even for quite some time. Awareness or a person's invisible impairments requires more personal and intimate knowledge of them. Examples of invisible impairments may include partial or perhaps even severe hearing impairment, Autism Spectrum Condition, or myalgic encephalomyelitis (ME) to name a few.

2. Wendell (1996) states that, "Stereotypes of disabled people as dependent, morally depraved, superhumanly heroic, asexual, and/or pitiful are still the most common cultural portrayals of people with disabilities" (46).

> If disability appears in a novel, it is rarely centrally represented. It is unusual for a main character to be a person with disabilities, although minor characters like Tiny Tim, can be deformed in ways that arouse pity. In the case of Esther Summerson, who is scarred by smallpox, her scars are made virtually to disappear through the agency of love. On the other hand, as sufficient research has shown, more often than not villains tend to be physically abnormal: scarred, deformed, or mutilated (Davis 2010)

Please see also Kent's chapter on the images of women with disabilities in fiction and drama, Dahl's article on the role of media in promoting images of disability, Harnett's article on images of disability in popular television, and Gartner and Joe's book on images of the disabled.

3. To make matters worse, Walter's medical treatments are extremely expensive, hopelessly beyond his family's financial means. Thus, not only would his death be leaving a wife and two children without a provider, but if he seeks treatment for his (probably terminal) disease, he will leave his family hopelessly destitute, likely homeless.

4. For example, images of impairment and disability are omitted from most forms of advertising unless the advertisements are for charity advertisements or health service magazines. And those images are more negative than positive. Please see Hevey's chapter on the enfreakment of photography, and Gartner and Joe's 1998 book on images of the disabled. Public housing rarely accommodates the needs of disabled and employers underemployed individuals with disabilities (Siebers 2008). Public schools still regularly fail to accommodate the needs of students with disabilities. School districts throughout the United States have renamed special education schools as programs. Once so relabeled, test scores from such programs can be excluded from state

assessment tabulations and schools districts can then report that students in their schools are meeting federal mandates. As to whether or not the children in educational programs are flourishing, since those test scores are junked, parents have no way to assess either the progress of their own child or compare the merits of one program with another. Despite the fact that a primary purpose of the No Child Left Behind Education Act was to provide parents with the assessment information necessary to ensure that their disabled child's education was progressing as optimally as possible, administrators around the country have excluded test scores of children with disabilities to ensure those scores will not harm the financial futures of the schools—the effect, however, is that children with disabilities, and their accomplishments, are effectively being erased (*New York Times* as quoted in Siebers 2008, 137). Please also see Silver, Wasserman, and Mahowald's book on disability, difference and discrimination.

5. I am speaking in general terms about health and well-being, impairment and disability. How particular conditions and bodily symptoms affect particular people can vary, but I believe persuasive arguments have been made for accepting the claim that Deafness and Autism, say, are conditions that can affect a person's body and their relationship with the able-bodied community so thoroughly that it makes sense to speak of a person's Deaf identity or a person's Autistic identity. Please also see Padden and Humphries chapter on deaf people, Edwards' chapter on technology and the deaf world, and Staus's chapter on autism as culture all in Lennard Davis's *The Disability Studies Reader*, a 2010 edited collection.

6. Mike refers to Walt as a ticking time bomb. Walter promises Jesse that there will be no more killing. But Walter's promise of no more killings is as patently absurd as his proclamation against cancer—bold words, but implausible in running a successful meth business. And there are more dead bodies, a lot of them. Walter orders the deaths of Fring's men because they could lead the DEA to him. Walter also kills Mike because Mike would not give him the names of those men. As Mike bleeds to death, Walter has an uncharacteristic, albeit brief, moment of regret. He admits that he could have forced Lydia to give him the names of the men. Mike interrupts him asking him to let him die alone. Not only does Walter kill, he kills people he does not even need to kill.

7. Francis Galton is usually credited with creating the first eugenicist scientific society in England. However, it was years later, in the United States, that large scale governmentally financed eugenics programs really got underway in earnest. President Theodore Roosevelt created the Heredity Commission. It was charged to investigate the genetic heritage of the citizens and to "(encourage) the increase of families of good blood and (discourage) the vicious elements in the cross-bred American civilization" (Bruinius 2006; Black 2003). The United States was the first country to past sterilization laws. Starting in 1907, Indiana was the first state to pass sterilization legislation. The states that sterilized the highest percentage of their residents were: Michigan, Wisconsin, Minnesota, and California. California had by far the highest number of sterilizations in the United States (one third of all sterilizations nationwide). By the 1960s, over 20,000 patients per year in that state were being sterilized; almost 60 percent were considered mentally ill, just over 35 percent were considered "mentally deficient" ("California Eugenics.").

8. Although referred to eugenicist ("good birth") societies in the United States and Britain, the term "racial hygiene" (*Rassenhygiene*) was used in Germany but the idea is the same: preserving the good people and eliminating the diseased and defective individuals who are a corrupting influence on society.

9. Early in the twentieth century, statewide contests were established throughout the United States, funded by the Eugenics Records Office, such as the Better Baby Contest and Fitter Family for the Future. The purpose of these contests was to measure and rank babies and families for "fitness" (idealness) and to determine which ones were perfect models for future citizens. Winners won free medical treatment. Though one would think the losers would need medical treatment more, rewarding sickly

individuals with medicine is exactly contrary to eugenicist logic. These contests lasted several decades, until the late 1940s (Selden 2005, 199-225).

10. Giving the majority opinion in *Buck v Bell*, the U.S. Supreme Court case that decided that states can sterilize "imbeciles" against their will and without their knowledge, Holmes writes,

> We have seen more than once that the public welfare may call upon the best citizens for their lives. It would be strange if it could not call upon those who already *sap the strength* of the State for these lesser sacrifices, often not felt to be such by those concerned, to prevent our being *swamped with incompetence*. It is better for all the world, if instead of waiting to execute degenerate offspring for crime, or to let them starve for their imbecility, society can prevent those who are manifestly unfit from continuing their kind. The principle that sustains compulsory vaccination is broad enough to cover cutting the Fallopian tubes. [*emphasis added*] (*Buck v. Bell* 1927)

11. Some eugenicists were not satisfied with sterilization measures and instead lobbied for euthanasia. A 1911 Carnegie Institute report recommended euthanasia as a solution to the problem of unfit individuals. An institute in Lincoln Illinois fed cognitively impaired patients milk laced with tuberculosis, obtaining an annual death rate of 30-40 percent per year. In 1931, The Illinois Homeopathic Medicine Association began lobbying for the "right to euthanize" "imbeciles" (Black 2003).

12. When Skyler lamented the guilt she felt for her role in Ted Beneke's injuries, Walter tried to comfort her by saying that she made a misstep and lost control over the situation. He explained to her that such actions did not make her a bad person, but instead made her "human." She immediately dismisses such words as flawed rationalizing. The implication is clear: Walter has learned to rationalize moral horrors.

13. At one point, Skyler tells Walter that her best move is to wait for the cancer to return to him. Not a good sign for a marriage, and a stark contrast to her feelings for him just a short year ago.

14. Throughout most of their "odd couple" adventures, Jesse remained loyal to Walter, always deferentially referring to him as Mr. White. Yet, enough seemed to be enough for, once Jesse was aware that Walter had ordered Mike's men killed and then showed up at his house, Jesse answered the door armed. Jesse seemed to consider the possibility that Walter might kill him for knowing too much about the operation.

WORKS CITED

Black, Edwin. *War on the Weak: Eugenic and America's Campaign to Create a Master Race.* New York: Four Walls Eight Windows, 2003.

Bruinius, Harry. *Better For All the World: The Secret History of Forced Sterilization and America's Quest for Racial Purity.* New York: A. A. Knopf, 2006.

Buck v. Bell. 1927. 274 U.S. 200. "California Eugenics," http://www.uvm.edu/~lkaelber/eugenics/CA/CA.html.

Dahl, Marilyn. "The Role of the Media in Promoting Images of Disability—Disability as Metaphor: The Evil Crip." *Canadian Journal of Communication.* 18. (1993): 75-80.

Davis, Lennard. "Constructing Normalcy." In *The Disability Studies Reader*, 3rd. ed, edited by Lennard J. Davis. 4: 28. New York: Routledge, 2010.

Dudley-Marling, Curt and Alex Gurn, eds. *The Myth of the Normal Curve.* New York: Peter Lang, 2010.

Edwards, R.A.R. "Hearing Aids Are Not Deaf: A Historical Perspective on Technology in the Deaf World." In *The Disability Studies Reader*, 3rd ed., edited by Lennard J. Davis. 403-417. New York: Routledge, 2010.

Harnett, Alison. "Escaping the 'Evil Avenger' and the 'Supercrip': Images of Disability in Popular Television." *The Irish Communications Review.* 8. (2000): 21-29.

Gartner, Alan and Tom Joe, eds. *Images of the Disabled, Disabling Images*. New York: Praeger, 1987.

Hevey, David. "The Enfreakment of Photography." In *The Disability Studies Reader*, 3rd ed., edited by Lennard J. Davis. 507-521. New York: Routledge, 2010.

Hubbard, Ruth. "Abortion and Disability: Who Should and Should Not Inhabit the World?." In *The Disability Studies Reader*, 3rd ed., edited by Lennard J. Davis. 187-202. New York: Routledge, 2010.

Kent, Deborah. "In Search of a Heroine: Images of Women with Disabilities in Fiction and Drama." In *Women with Disabilities: Essay in Psychology, Culture, and Politics*, edited by Michelle Fine and Adrienne Asch. 229-244. Philadelphia: Temple University Press, 1988.

Padden, Carol and Tom Humphries. "Deaf People: A Different Center." In *The Disability Studies Reader*, 3rd ed., edited by Lennard J. Davis. 393-402. New York: Routledge, 2010.

Porter, Theodore M. *The Rise of Statistical Thinking 1820-1900*. Princeton: Princeton University Press, 1986.

Selden, Steven. "Transforming Better Babies into Fitter Families: Archival Resources and the History of the American Eugenics Movement, 1908-1930." *American Philosophical Society*. 149:2. (2005): 199-225.

Siebers, Tobin. *Disability Theory*. Ann Arbor: The University of Michigan Press, 2008.

Silvers, Anita and David Wasserman and Mary B. Mahowald, eds. *Disability, Difference, Discrimination: Perspectives on Justice in Bioethics and Public Policy*. Lanham, MD: Rowman & Littlefield, 1998.

Snyder, Sharon and David T. Mitchell, eds. *Cultural Locations of Disability*. Chicago: University of Chicago Press, 2006.

Straus, Joseph N. "Autism as Culture." In *The Disability Studies Reader*, 3rd ed., edited by Lennard J. Davis. 535-559. New York: Routledge, 2010.

Terry, Jennifer and Jacqueline Urla, eds. *Deviant Bodies*. Bloomington: Indiana University Press, 1995.

U.N. "World Programme of Action Concerning Disabled Persons." New York: United Nations, 1983.

Wade, Cheryl Marie. "It Ain't Exactly Sexy." In *The Ragged Edge: The Disability Experience from the Pages of the First Fifteen Years of the Disability Ra*, edited by Barrett Shaw. 88-90. Louisville, KY: Advocado Press, 1994.

Wendell, Susan. *The Rejected Body*. New York: Routledge, 1996.

III

The Style and Reception of *Breaking Bad*

Breaking Bad (AMC). Season 2 Episode 16: "4 Days Out." Airdate: 3 May 2009.
Shown: Aaron Paul, Bryan Cranston.
AMC/Photofest © AMC. Reprinted by permission of Photofest.

SEVEN

Breaking the Waves

Pierre Barrette and Yves Picard

Vince Gilligan (2011), the creator of *Breaking Bad*, during the *Séries Mania* festival in Paris in 2011 explained his work to a French audience clearly locating his series as belonging to the kind of recent American television fiction that draws on cinema rather than on television, or even in some cases on radio, for its aesthetic paradigm:

> Chris Carter, the creator of *The X-Files*, his philosophy was that we are using moving pictures, we should therefore be telling a story visually, as visually as possible. That was, at the time, 1993, a bit, somewhat radical for an American television, the idea that showing rather than telling. In other words, a lot of television has been historically dialogue dependant, because series television has often not much time to shoot an episode and have to tell rather than show. But he was about showing rather than telling, whenever possible. And that is the philosophy I have very much taking heart, very much incorporated into the creation of *Breaking Bad*. (Gilligan, 2011)

Like the series *Mad Men*, which is also broadcast on the AMC network and which, as Jeremy Butler (2012) has demonstrated, has a visual aesthetic whose mise en scène references 1960s cinema more than it does television of the same period, *Breaking Bad* is part of a phenomenon that one scholar, following *Variety*, has described as the "cinematization of the small screen" (Buxton 1999, 69). That being the case, is the *cinematization* of American television fiction only a technological moment (the advent of high-definition television), or also a new degree of aesthetics? *Breaking Bad* provides an enlightening answer. Since the advent of the new millennium American television fiction, along with that found elsewhere, including Quebec (Picard 2011), has entered a "third Golden Age" (Perez-

Gomez 2011), which we believe is also an age of second-degree style. This is what we set out to explain in the present text. In essence, we will argue that the television series created by Gilligan has attained a new degree of expression, one that Christian Metz (1991) described, following other scholars but in a distinct sense, as "enunciation," or in a few words the meta-discursive expressive figures disseminated in the text. In the present discussion we will examine only a sampling of the series *Breaking Bad*'s second season. Beyond the wink, the reader will find here an invitation to compare our results with the other seasons, afterward examining the final season in particular, which was not yet completed at the time these lines were written. This text thus has a scholarly quality that Walter White would undoubtedly not have disdained at the outset of his quest: if the results of the experiment can be transferred, it is because the demonstration was conclusive.

To attain this end, we will proceed in three stages, according to a common scientific method: hypothesis, results and interpretation. First, we will discuss the hypothesis of the second degree of television through a path that leads from zero-degree style (Barthes 1977) to second-degree style (Genette 1997), situating them on an aesthetic spectrum in keeping with Jeremy Butler's (2012) proposals. For reasons of space, we will not discuss first-degree style. Second, as we described above, we will apply the concept second-degree style to the second season of *Breaking Bad*, taking examples from two episodes, the first[1] and the last. In each case, we will analyze three exemplary sequences in order to bring out the variety of expressive techniques used and the coherent vision they create. Finally, we will discuss the results and consider the paths that our theoretical model opens up.

FROM ZERO-DEGREE STYLE TO SECOND-DEGREE STYLE

Roland Barthes' (1977) concept zero-degree style of writing is not unfamiliar in television studies. John Thorton Caldwell (1995), for example, used it to shine light on the sitcom aesthetic. Elsewhere, Butler (2012) used the concept to cast into relief the aesthetic of the soap opera. These two scholars' bodies of work complement each other like masks in the theatre. What is more, their ideas converge. Basically, their results show that, because they are recorded in studio, these two genres of American television fiction have in many respects a restricted visual style to the point that it could be argued that we are in the presence of a "non-style." The absence of clear subjectivity gives the (false) impression that the result is objective. Naturally, as journalism shows us, complete objectivity is a myth. When events seem to tell themselves, journalists have taken a passive attitude towards reality and limited themselves to observing from without and to showing us raw fragments, the so-called facts, without interpreting them. This is similar to the aesthetic of sitcoms and soap operas: here we are shown a televised fiction from the point of view of a spectator watching a stage performance taking place before him, recording it without interruption to preserve these pieces of life. As Butler remarks, the result "seems live." Clearly, zero-degree style unfolds in the present.

Zero-degree style in television is the sign of a passive act of creation whose aim is to best show what is taking place before it and which often takes the form of a high degree of theatricality. For a film studies scholar, these remarks recall the work carried out on early cinema. There, as Tom Gunning (1986) remarks, *attraction* is so vivid that the work engages in *monstration* (Gaudreault 2009). Watching Lumieres' *Arrival of a Train at La Ciotat* (1895), the content is so interesting that the point of view is incapacitated. The motion pictures then indeed *seem live*. That said, we must emphasize a crucial difference between film and television. While zero-degree style applies to the silent cinema period, in television, as Caldwell and Butler realized, it applies to "dialogue-driven worlds." In other words, to employ the theoretical model proposed by one of the present authors in his doctoral dissertation (Picard 2013), in television, *visuality* is subjected to *orality*. In other words, the image conveys speech and shows the verbal attraction. Within the zero-degree style, gaze monstrates the voice.[2] The zero-degree style of televised fiction was archaic when it began and rudimentary today; it is when the image, at one extreme or the other of the temporal spectrum, shows the spoken word. In zero-degree, style becomes impersonal and interchangeable, not because of a lack of knowledge or ambition but because of the conditions under which the work is made: the steelmaker has to record a performance based on talk; she or he has to make a fictional talk show. Indeed, it is difficult to create a personal visual style when the goal is to bring out the spoken word. And the audience knows this, because it demands that the style in such cases not overshadow the theatre of life. Indeed as Butler (2012) demonstrates, there were many complaints online about the overly stylized look imposed by the network on *Guiding Light* (1952-2009) to bring new life to the genre: viewers complained that they didn't want "stylish images." In other words, they said aloud what the usual audience thinks all along: that speech should be transmitted by a zero-degree style or by means of what the scholars Jay David Bolter and Richard Grusin (1999) aptly call "transparent mediacy"—by means of a deformed form.

However, Jeremy Butler (2012) advances that the aesthetic continuum of the televisual fiction is made of two ends or polarities. He writes with acumen: "One hand of the spectrum is a play that is recorded from a single point with no editing—the camera positioned at the "best seat in the house." On the other end of the spectrum is a wholly abstract animation or wholly processed image, one that could not exist without the medium itself " (Butler 2012, 216). More precisely , he argues that the last style is "aggressive, roughened, and opaque, not smooth and transparent. It carries meaning. It makes jokes. It might call attention to itself. It can even make familiar things seem strange, creating art as technique" (2012, 197). This style, which until now has not been named in television studies, is clearly that employed by *Breaking Bad*, as Jason Mittell (2011) has observed:

> In short, *The Wire* embraces a "zero degree style" that strives to render its televisual storytelling techniques invisible, whereas *Breaking Bad* foregrounds a "maximum degree style" through kinetic visuals, bold sounds, and unpredictable storytelling form—it is hard to imagine two programs within the general norms of crime drama that take such different approaches to narrative, visual and sonic style.

In our view, this "maximum degree style" has been identified in literary studies, and in particular in the work of Gérard Genette (1997), by the expression "literature in the second degree." In cinema studies, the concept has been explored in greater depth, in particular by Christian Metz (1991).[3] Second-degree style is a meta-cognitive style, which is aptly adapted to a meta-television era that some Spanish scholars call the Third Golden Age of TV (Carlon 2006, Tous Rovirosa 2009). The style is constructed of meta-discursive expressive figures disseminated within the television text. To put it bluntly: instead of the formless form of the zero-degree style, the second-degree style offers a form-filled structure that becomes the focus of attention directed toward a subjective.[4]

To grasp this concept we must, as Genette argued, see texts as deriving from each other, directly or indirectly, and also realize the ways in which films, as Metz observed, implicitly or explicitly *stand apart* from one another. The same intellectual operation is involved in the present case: one must compare an object to its system in order to understand how meaning is produced. Second-degree style is the opposite of zero-degree style: while the latter requires little effort on the part of the audience, the former requires a maximum level of effort. When watching a second-degree-style television fiction, the audience must go toward the work and evaluate the relative originality of its artistic expression. They must carry out a dual reading: identify how it differs from the norm and gauge its interest. They must *recognize* the style. As part of a meta-cognitive logic, second-degree style is clearly meta-discursive: it reflects its presence through meta-textual devices. In simple terms, second-degree style is a form of double meaning: a style, which demonstrates its subjectivity and thereby reflects its creator's mastery. Second-degree style is even more *enunciative*, when it mocks conventions, fails to deliver on expectations and destabilizes; when it is opaque, hermetic, or even abstract. In journalistic terms, second-degree style takes the form of a commentary, editorial, or critique: a point of view that stands out, evaluates and judges and thus contributes to public debate. In cinematic terms, it is an individual perspective, if one likes, which interposes a gaze between reality and the audience in order to change both attitudes and form. In TV fiction, the second-degree style is no different; the metacognitive process is in fact, in this case, both enunciative and trans-textual: meta-discursive expressive figures disseminated in the televisual text derive from the cinematic text. In other words, which indicate the gulf created with the zero-degree style, the second-degree is first, the point of view that reflects its presence in the visual field by self-reflexive constructions; second, the image that bends toward less orality or even silence; third, the montage that tends toward a temporality that is the object of telescoping or a time narrative; and fourthly the work that engages in the aesthetic journey of the televisual fiction, which is tied to the emergence of auteur television in the cinematic sense — the triumph of style (Butler 2010, Ames 2012).

Seven Thirty-Seven

Three sequences in the episode, "Seven Thirty-Seven" (3/8/09) of *Breaking Bad* demonstrate a forceful second-degree style. The first is an exterior sequence whose expressiveness is a product of the filming or the image; the second is an interior family sequence whose expressiveness is a product of the shot breakdown or of the *decoupage*[5]; and the third is a work sequence whose expressiveness is a product of the editing or of the montage. At the beginning of the episode, a long daytime sequence takes place in an auto junkyard showing Walter and Jesse meeting with Tuco and his men. From the start, the importance of the visual style is signaled by a reflexive gesture that appears unremarkable on a first viewing but is emblematic of our argument: Walter White removes his sunglasses and puts on his regular glasses. His gaze is thus situated by the mise en scène from the outset as being a structuring force. We are far from television fiction in which telephone calls are a privileged way of producing meaning. Then, a very high-angle medium-long shot recalls the opening sequences of films, especially westerns, and a superimposed credit informs us that the episode was directed by Bryan Cranston (Walter White), who chose this visual context for the appearance of his name, telling us a lot about his ambition.[6] The rest of the sequence demonstrates the director's concern for setting the second season of *Breaking Bad* apart from the usual television fiction. We note, for example, accentuated low-angle shots, shots taken at ground level, centered and decentered compositions, staging in depth and leader blocking the field of vision. None of these techniques would betray the presence of subjectivity on their own, but their cumulative effect is to suggest that the mise en scène is trying to beexpressively stylistic and seeks to set itself apart from the norm in a significant way and to reflect an individual vision that interposes itself between the world and the public and imposes its point of view. We might say that these different shots, which take pleasure in showing us an otherwise conventional situation from more meaningful perspectives, form a treatise on second-degree style, right from the start. The mise en scene is keen to set out the terms of the contract in the opening sequence. This episode, the first episode of the second season, is designed to stand out from the norm to reflect the director's view and to offer a second-degree style. Next, two shots confirm the desire to create reflexive structures that are certainly used to create meaning but which are also used to create presence. In the first, a corpse is slipped beneath an automobile. The position and mobility of the camera indicate that this is a point-of-view shot, while there is no one. In the second, Tuco continues his work in a very high-angle shot. The resulting view from on high gives his activity a futile character, but also gives the image a strong visual style. The aftermaths of the crime are thus shown from the most unusual angles possible in a broken up, if not to say distanced manner, as Brecht would describe it. Here the director has adopted an *aesthethic* posture—a distance from the action is created, as if to indicate its obscene nature, emphasizing that the point of view of the omniscient narrator is that of the *auteur* in the cinematic sense of the term: the author of the mise en scène. These two final shots, which Alfred Hitchcock would undoubtedly not have disdained, show that a formal reflexivity is also a human sensibility. Or, if one prefers, that the sequence ends on a point of view which editorializes on the situation and takes a position on it through visual style in order to touch the audience's private thoughts.

Let's turn now to the indoor sequence; studying it will enable us to dissipate any doubts. The director succeeded in achieving a second-degree style not only outdoors, where this is facilitated by being on a set without walls, but also indoors, in a studio, where the task is more difficult and television's aesthetic is often zero-degree. This indoor sequence takes place in the home of a couple who are friends of the Whites, the Schraders. It opens on a slow tracking shot in extreme close-up, a kind of dynamic insert shot showing packages of sugar, and then comes upon a coffee cup upon which we can read an X-ray clinic's advertising slogan: "We see right through you." This opening shot is disconcerting in that it takes away our bearings and adds a touch of humor through the reference to Marie Schrader's work. It forms a declaration of aesthetic principles. On the one hand, it imposes a point of view, which interprets the visible to the point of being opaque. On the other hand, it winks at the audience, who must carry out a second-degree reading for the reference to make sense. The second shot confirms this expressive ambition. Rather than showing a person speaking in a seated position facing the camera, as is usually the case in indoor scenes in soap operas and sitcoms, thereby limiting the scene's expressiveness and centering our attention on the spoken word, it shows us Marie to the left in the background, shot from behind and in out of focus, and thus quite indistinct, calling the Whites by telephone, where the object is being in sharp focus to the edge of the frame in the foreground to the right. The shot thus becomes an exemplary illustration of second-degree style.

Following Western reading order, the usual *orality* is indeed obscured in favor of a *visuality*, which imposes the presence of subjectivity. In other words, the mise en scène shifts our interest in the character's voice towards the gaze of the director and self-reflects its role as an orchestrator of meaning. What comes after this first part of the sequence enables the audience to see clearly, finally, while at the same time driving the point home. On the one hand, a shot of Marie handling the packages of sugar and a medium close-up of her speaking on the telephone from behind and to the side give viewers the information needed to fully grasp what is happening: Marie is simply calling Skyler and leaving her a message. On the other hand, we realize that everything was a skillful manipulation of the meaning orchestrated by the mise en scène. What might have been shown in the common zero-degree television style as a talk show here is shown in a second-degree as a visual show.

From an aesthetic point of view, the second part of the sequence is the opposite of the first. While the earlier part shows us disparate pieces, which must be pieced together to make sense, the later part consists of a deep-focus and immobile sequence shot that Welles would have approved. Here the mise en scène shows Marie, from behind, bustling about in the background; Hank, also seen from behind, enters from the right-hand foreground. Marie comes towards the camera and then turns to speak to Hank before leaving the frame facing the viewer. The mise en scène has given us another conversation without any shot isolating the character facing the camera while speaking. Of course the effect appears stylized, but we must admit that the angularity of the camera position, the characters' positions in the space, Hank's entry and movements, and Marie's movements and exit, as well as the fact that most of the conversation takes place in the background, reminds us that we are far from a "white telephone" zero-degree style mise en scène. We thereby grasp the aesthetic strategy of this seemingly banal indoor scene: by being by turns too close to and then too far from the narrative situation, the mise en scène makes us think about its power to interpose its gaze and to impose its presence however it wishes. In this episode, the auteur-in-the-text gives itself a ticket to impose his presence at will.

Having examined the interest of the image in an outdoor sequence and the shot breakdown of an indoor sequence, and remarked that a second-degree style is abundantly apparent in each, let's now look at a sequence in which the editing manipulates time. The sequence takes place in the clandestine lab where Walter and Jesse produce their crystal meth. It unfolds without a word being spoken and shows the precise gestures they make and their concentration as they work. This kind of sequence is not new in recent American television fiction. It can be found in particular in the *CSI* series (*CSI, CSI Miami, CSI New York*), in which forensic medical experts silently and professionally ply their trade in police laboratories. Extra-diegetic music takes the place of dialogue, provides continuity and gives the whole scene the appearance of a mini video clip whose images follow after one another in arbitrary order, making it possible to short-circuit the rules and offer up repeated jump cuts, accelerating the passage of time. Nevertheless, the sequence in *Breaking Bad* stands apart for its interiorization. It opens on Jesse's focused eye in close-up as he looks at a container seen in a matched cut-away. The mise en scène makes his gaze forceful, as it did above, and offers up a matched cut. The fact that the scene is silent, in combination with the attention paid to the character's gaze, leads us to realize that the director has created, to paraphrase Jeremy Butler (2012), a "visual driven world." There follows a series of short shots of Walter reiterating this aesthetic strategy and taking it a step further. Walt, with his glasses in his hand, looks at a container to the right that then lights up; next, concentrated through his mask, he looks left at another container. This segment calls to mind the beginning of the episode, when Walt changed his glasses, and highlights once again the structuring role of the gaze in the mise en scène while establishing a visual continuity that differentiates White from his context, making him a subject, in the sense of the programming of the gaze, as discussed by Nick Browne (1975) and Daniel Dayan (1983) with respect to the film *Stagecoach* (1939). In essence, Jesse's gaze is directed, while Walter's is orchestrated. It is present before and after the object and thus becomes the subject of the discourse. It is the center of our attention. Afterwards, the series of shots is edited in such a way as to create successive jump cuts and ellipses thereby providing both an outer summary of the two chemists' work and an inner plunge into the psyche of a character (Walt) who is as tortured as *Dexter* (Showtime, 2006-present). Like Dexter, Walt uses his scientific knowledge to further his deviant interests. Walt's successive gestures are those of both a professional and a criminal. This may be true of the gestures of Jesse, but for the viewer, whose reading of the scene has been "programmed" by the "play of images," it is especially true of those of Walt (Dayan 1983). The overexposed shot which follows synthesizes Walt's inner conflict. The mise en scène takes us inside Walt's mind through what we might call, not a flashback or a flash forward, but a flash-in, so that we grasp temporality by means of the visual style in a form with a coefficient of subjectivity, creating an inner time, that of thought. Walt's synapses create short-circuits; indeed, they fry. Finally, a shot showing Walt's eyes holds our attention, confirming the importance of the gaze and reasserting the primacy of the visuality. Although his eyes are clearly visible behind his mask, his lips are overtly hidden from view. The image is a synecdoche of this first part of our chapter: while zero-degree style is that of the voice of the other, second-degree style is that of one's own gaze.

ABQ

Three sequences in the episode "ABQ" (5/31/09) also forcefully demonstrate the work of enunciation and contribute to identifying the series with second-degree style. The first sequence comes before the credits and consists of a series of visually very expressive exterior shots almost entirely in black and white; the second sequence is sandwiched between the other two and, through the editing, creates a series of connections which undeniably form a discourse; and the third uses the mise en scène of a television news crew, a critique of television and its relation to reality—a sequence not without meta-discursive resonance.

The first sequence of "ABQ" appears before the credits and is a recurring element in season two; beginning with the first episode ("Seven Thirty-Seven"), the same sequence—varying in length and its elements in different order—is used as an "enigmatic" prologue to the story that begins after it.[7] It is made up of twenty-five shots, almost entirely in black and white (we will return to this subject below), made up for the most part of inserts but none of a human face, and accompanied by ambient noise which contributes to the mysterious quality of this highly stylized opening sequence. It begins with a few shots that set the scene (a leaking garden hose, a Chinese lantern, a low stone wall across which a snail is crawling, a swimming pool in the backyard of a private residence) and create a persistent impression that time is "suspended." The sequence continues with a shot of the water's surface in the swimming pool. In this shot, at first empty, we soon see a small sphere strongly resembling an eye which quickly crosses the screen from right to left before running up against the pool's skimmer and disappearing. We hear the sound of a siren, at first far off and then closer. The camera then goes underwater where a fuchsia-colored teddy bear (the only colored element of the sequence) suddenly appears drifting toward the surface. Following a series of dissolves, there is a change in the point of view of the camera—still underwater—and, half-blinded by the sun, we see a silhouette leaning over the pool. The next shot returns to the shadow and then the content of a dip net, in which the teddy bear is seen. A man in a white suit then places the teddy bear in a plastic bin. The camera's point of view changes again and we see, in slow motion and through the cracked window of an automobile, two men carrying the bin to a service vehicle. A crane shot takes the camera over top of the banged-up car; on the other side, we discover two dead bodies in plastic body bags. The rest of the sequence is made up of several close-up shots of a disparate collection of objects scattered about the garden (a burnt shoe, a dog-eared book, a necktie hanging from the branch of a tree and a small flag stating evidence, please do not remove) and then of a series of shots showing us men in one-piece suits busily cleaning the scene. The sequence concludes with a high-angle crane shot which provides an establishing shot of the entire neighborhood in which the scene is taking place. In the distance, as the image changes from black and white to color, we see two columns of black smoke rising to the sky.

This sequence is significant for at least two reasons. First, aesthetically, it stands out from the rest of the series by its very peculiar use of black and white, in which one object in color creates a striking contrast; what we might call the excessive mobility of the camera creates an exaggerated aesthetic of the content and the image. The world we are shown is thus in no way natural; on the contrary, these elements work together to disconnect the image from the narrative, in a sense, the images take on value on its own right. Second, on the level of enunciation, the camera positions and visual perspectives contribute to the shots' high degree of subjectivity strongly rooted in a gaze and yet detached from any human body, unless the body and the eye of the teddy bear are proposing we see them as the sequence's organizing principle. In this sense, it is as if the viewer were looking at the world through the anthropomorphized eye of a child's toy fallen from the sky (in fact at the end of the episode we learn that the teddy bear landed in the pool when an airplane crashed), an ambiguous symbol of shattered innocence and the Almighty. The eye floating on the water's surface at the beginning of the sequence, separated from the body of the teddy bear, and the broken-up, overcharged vision it produces thus take on the task of reminding us reflexively of the constructed and subjective nature of the world we are being shown.

The second sequence in the final episode we would like to discuss here is not, strictly speaking, a sequence, but rather a series of images sandwiched between two sequences. These images are connected in such a way that the work of enunciation becomes perfectly legible and clearly inscribed in the editing joining two scenes constructed to be isomorphic. The sequence begins in Jane's apartment (she is shown to have died of an overdose at the beginning of the episode), where her father is trying to find a dress to put on her for the funeral. Through a series of shot-reverse shots, we follow the gaze of the crushed man as he discovers his daughter's drawings and then a mural she painted herself, showing a young woman caught in a network of colorful arms high in the sky, a teddy bear floating by her side. Then, an apparently subjective point of view—the camera is at the back of the closet—shows him on the telephone, facing his daughter's clothes hanging in the closet, looking for the right kind of dress. The man is complaining to his interlocutor that there are only black dresses, nothing colorful or gay. When he finds what he is looking for, the camera changes angle and we see the man place the dress on the bed and smooth the sleeves with his fingers to get out the wrinkles. In the final shot of the sequence we see the man in a low-angle shot leaning over the dress, its arms crossed, overcome with emotion, but the "reverse shot" takes us to a completely different location to the White residence and the matching shot is Walter's baby, her father leaning over her preparing to change her diaper. The rest of the sequence shows us Walter interacting with Walter Jr., his adolescent son, who he reproaches for making too much noise. Although all Walter Jr. has done was to express his joy when he learned that his website to raise money for his father had met with great success. Here the work of enunciation is revealed through the promiscuity between two places, two characters and two attitudes made possible by the editing, confronting viewers with the highly constructed nature of a syntagm which, surprised or amused, they discover to be less subject to the rules around the transparency of reality than to the rules of a particularly eloquent discourse. Many factors contribute to this effect and are not limited to the matched cut mentioned above. In fact a comparison of the two scenes reveals a number of similarities. In each case, the world of childhood is evoked, in one scene through the presence of a teddy bear in Jane's painting and in the other by the little polka-dot pajamas worn by Walt's daughter; both men reproach their offspring for things which in fact are the symptoms of their own guilt; the two articles of clothing appear empty, one because it is and the other because it is too large for the baby wrapped up in it. Of course, there is a radical difference between the two scenes in the sense that Walt's actions are motivated by this wriggling new creature which depends on him, while Jane's father's actions are motivated, on the contrary, by the attentions required by his daughter's cruel death. When joined in this way, the two scenes shine light on each other: although the two men are carrying out the tasks required of an affectionate and attentive father, their respective positions are completely antagonistic. In addition, it is even possible to imagine that the drugs produced by Walt were in part, or indirectly, responsible for Jane's death, rendering the intrication of the enunciation in the *énoncé* even more apparent.

In the episode's final sequence we will discuss here renders the enunciative work visible in two ways: one obvious and the other much more subtle. The sequence begins when Walt comes home to find a television crew there, waiting for him to begin shooting a news story on the money his son has raised through his website. Walt is not at all pleased about being in the spotlight, given the extent of his criminal activities. His sister-in-law planned the interview and she is brimming with self-satisfaction. The journalist invites Walt to sit on the living room couch with the son in the center and the parents on each side. A series of shot-reverse shots taken from the TV camera's perspective alternates with shots of the journalist asking Walter Jr. questions, along with Walt's family composed together in a traditional family portrait pose, a falsely idyllic image of a unified and supportive home. Then, without any real justification, the camera suddenly focuses exclusively on Walt and begins an insistent zoom in while we listen to his son's off-screen voice discussing how much he respects his dad as a father, a teacher, and a hero. With each word spoken by the young man, the camera frames Walt's face tighter and tighter, revealing his palpable discomfort. When the zoom is complete, the camera lingers for a few long seconds on his face while we can almost hear the veins in his forehead throb and sense the growing redness in his face. Far from showing the dialogue (in this case an interview) in a transparent and classical manner, the scene works openly to isolate each person producing a powerful counterpoint effect. Here it is mostly the mise en scène that contributes to creating a reflexive tone by bringing out the medium's strategy. The living room of the White family is literally overrun with television equipment for at most a few minutes of filming illustrating the boorish and disagreeable manners of TV crews. This reality is in addition overdone, deliberately hackneyed, like an overly flattering portrait of a family which in fact is in the process of falling apart. The contrast between the "TV image" (glimpsed through the video monitor) and the "cinema" image is thus a clear indication of the gap between these two kinds of filming opening up a reflexive reading of the scene: the truth of the latter is even better revealed through the way in which everything tallies to show the falsity of the former. On a more properly discursive level, it is interesting to note how each word spoken by Walter Jr. is carefully chosen to refer to precise elements of the script which, the viewer knows, contradict these remarks or can be understood in a quite different sense. Thus, when he says that Walt is a good father and a good teacher that he's "patient and always there for you," it is hard not to think how he has been quite absent from his son's life for past few months, and to remember a quite recent sequence in which he illustrates these qualities with Jesse, but not with his own son. The last few seconds of this sequence showing us Walt completely paralyzed, frozen with discomfort and remorse, thus helps show the other side of a completely televisual mise en scène, which is seen as untruthful. The last few words spoken by Walter Jr. are about is father being his personal hero also serve as a direct reference to the empathy some audience members may feel for Walt as the series' protagonist.

CONCLUSION

It would appear necessary at this point in our discussion of these two episodes of *Breaking Bad* to demonstrate the implications of our analysis for an understanding of contemporary American television series and the role they play in the contemporary media landscape. For if it is possible to speak of a revolution in quality (Feuer 2007) in an initial 1950s and later 1990s period of television, the transformation of the drama series illustrated by programs such as *Breaking Bad* and a few others—for the most part associated with the HBO phenomenon—may be the sign of a kind of "permanent revolution," a state of affairs that is becoming stabilized and through which commercial TV programming is not only improving in quality but is now assuming an aesthetic role generally associated with the cinema. Institutionally and economically, it is apparent that the efforts of cable television networks to position themselves in the market, as they have gradually abandoned programming centered on off-network series and second-run theatrical releases to produce original TV series, have contributed to the establishment of a new paradigm. Nevertheless, these new television programs available on new platforms will fulfill this role only very marginally if they do not succeed in meeting public demand in terms of quality and, by extension, of aesthetics. It is precisely this demand, we believe, that the openly meta-discursive function of the case studies we have analyzed here highlights and deserves the critical and audience reaction to the series, which has been both enthusiastic and unanimous. For what exactly is this device, the "enunciation that enunciates itself," which we have seen pretty much everywhere in the visual narrative of *Breaking Bad*? Metz (1991) is quite eloquent on this point:

> Many *énoncés* have a more general ability to fold in on themselves in places, to appear here and there, as if in relief, to peel off a fine film of themselves on which is engraved a few indications of another nature (or of another level) having to do with production and not the product. . . . Enunciation is the semiological act by which some parts of the text speak to us of this text as an action. (20)

This enunciation *speaks to us*, it signals to us, it stands out in a world which tends to conceal itself; it is constituted through address, and as such it supposes, even abstractly, even textually or "filmically," an addressee, who will mould his or her gaze to it and recognize in the process a collusion effect, a wink, an invitation to depart from his or her traditional role. Here, in our view, we can see the primordial function of second-degree style: the recognition, on the level of the enunciated material itself, of a target, a destination. When the camera gradually slips out of its role to express a given situation and the characters' interactions, when it "forgets" to follow visually an action which was nevertheless until that moment determinative in order to frame Walt's face, and when this face is obviously a mask of pain and guilt that the off-screen words spoken by his son aggravate, it is difficult not to feel that some instance is speaking directly to us through the effects produced by the *énoncé*. This thing that concerns "production and not the product," which refuses to let it be carried along by a diegesis enclosed within the narrow boundaries of narrative, is the surest marker of *Breaking Bad*'s modernity, its inimitable belonging to the discursive mode.

To say that these stylistic devices are new to television would clearly be incorrect. On the one hand, as soon as one departs from a fictional mode to take up news, variety, and reality programming, "visible" enunciation ceases to be the exception and becomes the norm. On the other hand, there are many historical examples, even fictional ones, of such self-referential pirouettes, winks to the viewer and breaks by turns subtle and coarse between the diegetic world and the act that makes it what it is. Yet, systematically, these have been the work of television programs whose dominant pragmatic mode is humor: one thinks of *M.A.S.H*, or more clearly still of *Monty Python*. In the category of more traditional sitcoms, a program such as *Seinfeld* in the 1990s ushered in a new era with an offbeat style of humor that was not without a degree of self-deprecation; more recently entire series such as *The Office*, *Extras*, and *Curb Your Enthusiasm* have opened up an explicitly reflexive tone using by turns transtextuality and the use of cameos, but also through their use of formal experiments which undeniably draw the viewer's attention to their "produced" quality. These programs, however, all share a humorous approach.

More effort is required to find examples of dramatic series that reveal their process of enunciation and no program seems to truly appear on the horizon before the advent of "quality TV" in the 1990s. The examples given are almost always the same: *E.R.*, whose authors even pushed their formal boldness to the point of creating entirely live shows (with the consequences one can imagine on the level of enunciation); *Ally McBeal*, which blended realism with "fantastic effects" that were incompatible with the transparency we are accustomed to in American TV series; and a few others (*NYPD Blue* and *Northern Exposure*). These remain exceptional examples, however, and very often involved situations going awry in ways which, while not strictly speaking comedic, tended toward that vein. *Breaking Bad*, on the contrary, is part of a quite different pragmatic mode whose corollary can be found in recent contemporary series, such as *Six Feet Under*, *The Sopranos*, *Entourage*, *Unscripted*, and *The Walking Dead*. These are the category of programs most similar to *Breaking Bad*. The mutations under way are thus profound, and concern what Pierre Bourdieu (1971) would have termed the "symbolic and cultural capital" of television series. In this context, we must avoid treating the work on enunciation discussed in the present article in isolation and place it within a broader but no less coherent ensemble of strategies which share an ability to create a correlative position with respect to an aesthetic tradition which tends to accord greater value to cinematic practices than to those more specifically associated with television. What does a program such as *Six Feet Under*, for example, propose to do if it is not to "[reach] out to an entire tradition in modernist cinema that thematizes life and death, dream and reality"? (Feuer 2007, 151). What do *The Sopranos*, *The Walking Dead*, and *Deadwood* do if not exploit in television the trend toward the revision of genres in a certain kind of recent auteur cinema?

Naturally, this question engages with the entire phenomenon of one's interpretative community, which Stanley Fish (2005) defines as "a professional community whose norms, ideals and methods determine an interpretation's validity." What Fish calls "interpretation" also holds for judgments of the quality of a work or a given group of works, as Feuer (2007) points out:

> The judgment of quality is always situated. That is to say, somebody makes the judgment from some aesthetic or political or moral position. . . . Reception theory teaches us that there can never be a judgment of quality in an absolute sense but that there are always judgments of quality relative to one's interpretative community. (145-46)

In support of this position, it would be easy to find many reactions to *Breaking Bad* which are completely the opposite of our own. The reactions of critics, for example, who single out in order to denounce the moral lapses, exaggerated expressions of a pernicious violence and complacent view of drug trafficking. It is essential to acknowledge that the interpretive community to which we belong (which to simplify we could call that of television studies scholars) tends to prefer formal readings to thematic ones and "modernist" strategies to the strategies of transparency typically found in the televisual tradition. And to the extent that this is precisely what the new wave of post-HBO quality television tends to offer, the phenomenon as a whole can be interpreted as an aesthetic and strategic position of cable networks. Let's look at this state of affairs with respect to the AMC Network on which *Breaking Bad* is broadcast. AMC is a little less well known than HBO but is offered in most of the basic cable packages in the United States. AMC has been around since 1984. Initially, its mandate was to show classic Hollywood films (for the most part from before 1950) in their original "uncut" and not colorized version. But, by 2000, under pressure from its advertisers, the network began showing more recent films and since 2003, has begun producing its own original fictional series, such as *Mad Men*. These mutations in AMC's programming are typical, we believe, of the changing role of cinema on TV: at first sufficiently popular to make up the bulk of a specialized network's programming, repertory films gradually lost ground in favor of contemporary films, which have increasingly been replaced in turn by original series. This is perhaps easy to understand: the role of these original series in today's landscape is the same, in terms of cultural prestige and aura, as that of films from the 1970s to 2000, and because they are original and exclusive content they contribute better than films to the network's brand identity.

In the end, this approach on the part of certain cable networks should be seen as part of a broader mutation in American television today, and especially in light of the rise and popularity of reality shows. Faced with the major networks' style of programming, which increasingly tends towards programming that is inexpensive to produce with broad appeal to a mass audience, the "It's not TV" strategy of HBO and other networks intent on producing original quality programming is a strategy which benefits in addition from the growth in platforms for disseminating their products, in particular the growth in the DVD market where boxed-set series compete head-on with feature films. The particular aesthetic of *Breaking Bad*, its commitment to a second-degree aesthetic and the way in which it bases part of its spectatorial contract on a meta-discursive register are all parts of the battle to achieve artistic legitimacy in the eyes of a growing audience through an appeal to cinephiles. It should be noted that our analysis, which has been deliberately limited to the aesthetic and formal aspects of the series, could easily be extended to other types of televisual content. In fact it appears that *Breaking Bad*'s story and characters provide another advantage, in this case symbolic, to its viewers. As François Jost (2011) mentions in the short volume he has recently devoted to American TV series, "through the expert hero, the average viewer gets his revenge on the institutions which rule over him" (60). Indeed, there is no other explanation for the countless contemporary series (*House*, *The Sopranos*, *Mad Men*, *The Mentalist*, *Lie to Me*, *24*) featuring an "expert" with special knowledge—which may be obscure or even esoteric—that is used against official power (or despite it, which boils down to the same thing in the end). Against a system deemed abusive or not transparent enough, against institutional reason, which is synonymous with death (literally or figuratively), an individual tries to recover his or her full identity. This is certainly the case of Walter H. White, an upstanding man if ever there was one, whom the system has crushed, brought to the brink of an unjust death (from lung cancer, when he doesn't even smoke) and to whom crime offers a final chance to live. In the end, the fictional protagonist is not that different from some regular Joe or Jane on a reality show transformed into the star of the day in that they both offer a mirage where we can act out our seemingly unshakable desire to escape the anonymity we suffer more distressfully each day.

NOTES

1. We examine here the second season of *Breaking Bad* and in particular its first episode also because of the production circumstances which make this season and this episode especially interesting. The scriptwriters' strike had a significant effect on the first season, to the extent that we can think of the second season as better expressing the ambitions of the people behind the show. In this sense the first episode of this series might constitute the series' pilot.

2. We can't fail to remark that an actual TV show, which displays throughout a zero-degree style, is aptly named *The Voice* (NBC 2011-present).

3. While the volumes by Roland Barthes and Gérard Genette we cite have been translated into English, one volume by Christian Metz remains to be translated: *L'Énonciation impersonnelle ou le site du film*. We wonder whether the fact that the concept of second-degree style has not until now been defined by Anglo-American television studies scholars is the reason that Metz's volume on enunciation, which makes it possible to define the concept in cinema and consequently in television, is the reason that it is still not available in English.

4. The reasoning implies three degree-styles: zero-degree, first-degree and second-degree. We will discuss in the chapter the two polarities of the spectrum aesthetics of

TV fiction: the zero-degree style in general and the second-degree style in particular in *Breaking Bad*. However, we won't discuss the first degree-style, which could be called the *normative form* or the *consensual form*, due to space constraints. It will be the focus of future works.

5. The French notion of *découpage* is different from filming (*tournage*) and editing (*montage*). It is the equivalent of storyboarding in its abstract form: to cut the filming in its pieces. In clear, the *découpage* is to the preview of the filming, what the editing is to its review: the first phase in the production process. For a detailed discussion of the notion see the translation notes of the work of Andre Bazin, *What is cinema?* by Timothy Barnard (2009). We would also like to thank Timothy for his translation work on this chapter.

6. We should point out that because the series is directed by the lead actor adds to the interest of our initial remarks. In fact we discuss how the mise en scène, by having Walter White take off his sunglasses and put on his regular glasses at the very beginning, restores the gaze as the structuring force. Here, precisely, the actor is the director. The gaze is also, we should doubtless note, a structuring force *behind* the camera.

7. As the Wikipedia site notes, the titles of four episodes in which the black-and-white enigmatic sequence appears, when put together in order, form a sentence, which gives the clue, "Seven Thirty-Seven," "Down," "Over," and "ABQ."

WORKS CITED

Ames, Melissa. *Time in Television Narrative: Exploring Temporality in Twenty-First Century Programming.* Jackson, MS: University Press of Mississippi, 2012.

Barnard, Timothy. "Translator's Notes." In Andre Bazin's *What is Cinema?* Montreal: Caboose, 2009. 251-312.

Barthes, Roland. *Writing Zero-Degree.* New York: Hill and Wang, 1977.

Bolter, Jay David and Richard Grusin. *Remediation. Understanding New Media.* Cambridge: MIT Press, 1999.

Bourdieu, Pierre. "Le marché des biens symboliques," *L'année sociologique.* vol. 22. (1971): 49- 126.

Browne, Nick. "Rhétorique du texte spéculaire." *Communications.* 23. (1975): 202-211.

Butler, Jeremy. *Television Style.* Londres & New York: Routledge, 2012.

Buxton, David. "De «Bonanza» à «Miami Vice.»" *Formes et idéologie dans les séries télévisées.* Nantes: Chlorofeuilles, 1990.

Caldwell, John Thorton. *Televisuality: Style, Crisis and Authority in American Television.* New Brunswick: Rutgers University Press, 1995.

Carlon, Maro. *De lo cinematografico a lo televisivo. Metatelevision, lenguaje y temporalidad.* Buenos Aires: La Crujia ediciones, 2006.

Dayan, Daniel. *Western Graffiti. Jeux d'images et programmation du spectateur dans La Chevauchée fantastique de John Ford.* Paris: Clancier-Guenaud, 1983.

Fish, Stanley. "There is No Textualist Position." *San Diego Law Review.* 42:1. (2005): 1-22.

Feuer, Jane. "HBO and the Concept of Quality TV." In *Quality TV: Contemporary American Television and Beyond,* edited by Janet McCabe and Kim Akass. 145-157. London, New York: I.B. Tauris, 2007.

Gaudreault, André. *From Plato to Lumière: Narration and Monstration in Literature and Cinema.* Toronto: University of Toronto Press, 2009.

Genette, Gérard. *Palimpsests: Literature in the Second Degree.* Lincoln: University of Nebraska Press, 1997.

Gilligan, Vince. "Interview with Vince Gilligan." Hosted by Pierre Langlais. Master Class sponsored by *Séries Mania.* Paris, France. 16 April 2011. Interview available in French and English at *Forum of Images.* http://www.forumdesimages.fr/fdi/Videos/Les-Master-class-et-les-rencontres/Toutes-les-Master-class-et-les-Rencontres/Rencontre-avec-Vince-Gilligan.

Gunning, Tom. 1986. "The Cinema of Attraction: Early Films, its Spectator and the Avant-Garde." *Wide Angle.* 7: 3/4. (1986): 63-70.

Jost, François. *De quoi les séries américaines sont-elles le symptôme?* Paris: CNRS Éditions, 2011.

Metz, Christian. *L'énonciation impersonnelle ou le site du film.* Paris: Méridiens Klincksieck, 1991.

Mittell, Jason. "The Qualities of Complexity: Aesthetic Evaluation in Contemporary Television." 2011. http://mediacommons.futureofthebook.org/content/qualiteis-complexity-aesthetic- evaluation-contemporary-television.

Perez-Gomez, Miguel. *Previously on Interdisciplinary Studies on TV Series in the Third Golden Age of Television.* Sevilla: Frame, 2011.

Picard, Yves. De la télé-oralité à la télé-visualité. Évolution de la fiction télévisuelle québécoise du *téléroman* à la *sérietélé* (1953-2012). Thèse de doctorat. Montréal. Université de Montréal, 2013.

———. "From Téléroman to série télévisée québécoise: The (Coming of) Golden Age of Quebec TV." In *Previously on Interdisciplinary Studies on TV Series in the Third Golden Age of Television,* edited by Miguel Perez-Gomez. 181-195. Sevilla: Frame, 2011.

Tous Rovirosa, Anna. "Paleotelevisión, neotelevisión y metatelevisión en las series dramáticas estadounidenses." *Comunicar.* 17:33. (2009): 175-183.

EIGHT

Uncertain Beginnings: *Breaking Bad*'s Episodic Openings

Rossend Sánchez-Baró

Breaking Bad is a series written with the classic four-act structure of American television drama. Although, in recent years, most dramas have seen how their structure have evolved from four acts to six, most one-hour shows produced by AMC channel— for example, *Rubicon* (2010), *The Walking Dead* (2010-present), *The Killing* (2011-2013), *Hell On Wheels* (2011-present)—maintain the classic four-act structure. The only exception on this point seems to be the show *Mad Men*, originally conceived for the premium cable network HBO[1] and, therefore, written without heeding commercial breaks. Thus far, *Mad Men* still remains as the only original series on AMC with neither cold opens nor an act structure. This classic structure that AMC imposes on its productions also include an allegation of the *teaser*—or *cold open*—as the short initial segment of the episode before the first interruption of the narrative and the first act. Although some shows from the 1960s, like *Star Trek* (NBC, 1966-1969), have employed it, it was not until the 1990s that the teaser was popularized in commercial television as a sort of mini-act operating as a hook for the viewer.

Many contemporary series, especially those on the basic cable system, ignore the cold open with the intention of having more narration time before the first break. Consequently, those dramas have more time for the setting out of the plots and conflicts of the episode. Nevertheless, in the case of AMC dramas, the initial presence of a teaser, which in most cases does not exceed four minutes in length, imposes the need for a beginning capable of interesting and intriguing the viewer with almost no time for

139

exposition. As Pamela Douglas (2007) pointed out, the cold open "exists to grab viewers faster than the enemy, which is the remote. The notion is to open the hour with an action, image, situation or character that provokes enough anticipation to keep viewers through the title sequence and into the first act" (78). "It's intended to pull you in," argues Alex Epstein (2006, 66).

Among all AMC series, *Breaking Bad* claimed itself early on as the most imaginative in its conception of the cold open or teaser. Thereby, it is easy to find fan-made videos on the Internet[2] devoted to collecting these cold openings as unique narrative pieces. Consequently, it is not surprising that David Lavery (2009) defines these teasers as "minisodes." Following Lavery's idea, I conduct an analysis of *Breaking Bad*'s teasers as minisodes within the episodes of the show, along with how they represent the series' main narrative strategies in a concentrated dramatic form. The analysis of these teasers is conducted under the terms of the concept of *beginning* in contemporary television. This study's intention is to consider the resources that *Breaking Bad* uses from the cold open segment in order to generate expectations and interest in the audience.

THE BEGINNING OF THE BEGINNING

The pilot episode of a television series introduces the story and at the same time, as is common in serial narrative, establishes the principles and rules of that fiction. While it was historically common for audiences to begin viewing an episodic TV series already in the middle of its run, current television consumption is increasingly predicated on the significance of the idea of a beginning. The emergence of video-on-demand, DVR systems, and the proliferation of DVD box sets gathering all the episodes of a television show have made television pilots more accessible. Therefore, the viewers are generally reluctant to start watching a series with another episode other than the first one. The pilot is recognized as the intended beginning of the story, thus it appears to be the right place to start watching a show.

Beyond television, in the world of comics, publishers Marvel and DC have recently restarted their flagship series with the aim of restoring their beginnings to attract new readers. With each revision of the origins of a superhero, publishers not only adapt the story to modern times but propose a new "possible world" (Eco 1994, 64-80). The same possible world established by the pilot episode in television fiction.

In the U.S. television industry pilot episodes are used by broadcasters to assess the potential of a series. If the result of this episode is satisfactory, the network will order more episodes of the series. The same goes for the viewer. As the first chapter of a book is used as an invitation to the reader to continue the story, the first episode of a series not only invites the viewer to return the following week for the continuation of the story. Besides the conflict that will be used as the driving premise of the plot, the pilot also sets the time, the place, the social status of the characters and the narrative rules governing the world they inhabit. But pilots, especially those with serial elements attached to them, involve an implicit commitment; they represent a pact between the series and the audience. As Epstein points out (2006), "If your pilot looks much different from your series, it will draw a different audience than your series. It may draw people who will walk away from the later episodes . . . That's why you have to do everything in your pilot that you're going to want to do in the show" (257). Therefore, a pilot is a promise of repetition. It warns the viewers of what might happen again in later episodes establishing a pattern. From that moment on, the remaining episodes of a series will be judged based on that foundational pilot. In the case of *Breaking Bad*, the first episode introduces the original premise of the series: Walter White, a chemistry teacher who is diagnosed with cancer, decides to cook crystal methamphetamine (meth) to financially secure his family's future. In addition, the episode presents the other main characters of the series: Walter's wife and son, Skyler and Walter Jr.; Hank, Walter's brother-in-law; Marie, Walter's sister-in-law; and Jesse Pinkman, the co-protagonist of the story and Walter's business partner. Thereafter, the audience will expect a development of the premise in the two spheres of conflict presented: family and illegal business.

It is obvious that, at the moment of watching a television show, the viewer rarely is at a position of complete ignorance about what is available to see. Synopsis, trailers, promotional materials, reviews—all are multiple paratexts that act prior to the premiere of a television program conditioning its reception. As Jonathan Gray (2010) points out: "We may in time resist the meanings proposed by promotional materials, but they tell us what to expect, direct our excitement and/or apprehension, and begin to tell us what a text is all about, calling for our identification with and interpretation of that text before we have even seemingly arrived at it." (48). Even if a viewer had stayed away from all these contents, the very title itself is also another paratext providing information prior to the series. It is what James Phelan (2008) calls "exposition," the first starting point of every narrative and "everything, including the paratexts of the front matter (illustrations, epigraphs, preludes, notices, author's or editor's introductions, etc.), that provides information about the narrative, the characters (listings of traits, past history, etc.), the setting (time and place), and events of the narrative" (197).

It is possible that *Breaking Bad*'s plot was known by a large number of viewers even before its premiere. The pilot episode, however, establishes from the teaser, the aesthetic and narrative form of the whole series. Beyond that, the start of this first episode is proposed as a canonical cold open model. Therefore, from that time, the rest of the episodes' teasers will establish a dialogue with the viewer based on the variation or the repetition of that inaugural teaser. *Breaking Bad*'s pilot episode opens with images of the desert of New Mexico to immediately showing pants flying in slow motion contrasting with the appearance of an RV moving at high speed. We then discover the driver of the vehicle, a man wearing only underpants and a gas mask. Due to the high speed, the driver loses control of the RV and it ends up ditched on one side of the road. We hear sirens in the background. Afterward, the man leaves the RV and puts on a shirt to record a message for his family on a video camera. At that point we discover the man's name is Walter White. Then, Walter wields a gun and points it toward the horizon as the sound of sirens becomes more and more intense. With that image, the teaser ends and the opening credits of the series are introduced. After the credits, the first act of the episode opens with the shot of a house with the caption: "Three weeks earlier."

As we see, this opening offers the viewer a large amount of information. From the outset, the cold open provides strangeness and disorientation. The decontextualized image of a pair of pants flying in the desert suggests unpredictability as a narrative device. Then, the surrealist image of Walter White, introduced in his underwear and with a gas mask, exhibits an absurd humor that contrasts with the gun violence and sirens announced. The explicit mark of temporality "Three weeks earlier" tells the viewer that he or she is confronted with a start in media res that corresponded to a cold open prolepsis or flash-forward. From that time on, the pilot's teaser prepares the viewer to find more examples of decontextualized images, absurd humor and temporal disordered narrative throughout the series. The concentration of all these elements in the teaser announces to the audience that they should expect more beginnings of this kind. Finally, at the same time, this initial sequence acts as an enigma to be solved and tells the viewers they are watching a drama committed to formal experimentation.

DECONTEXTUALIZED IMAGES

Throughout the whole series, *Breaking Bad* shows a pronounced tendency toward the use of extreme close-up shots. This inclination for revealing extreme detail is not a purely aesthetic decision but part of a narrative intention as seen by looking at the original scripts of the series.[3] For example, on the script of the episode "No Mas" (03/21/10), when the characters of The Cousins are introduced, the text says: "As we TRACK LOW with The Cousins, we note their distinctive, hand-tooled COWBOY BOOTS. We watch as their SILVER TOE-CAPS press into the dried mud, leaving IMPRINTS" (2). As seen from the writing of the show, the series gives special attention to detail

In most cases, we can see extreme close-ups on individual objects that contrast with the open wide shots of the desert of New Mexico, another aesthetic brand of the show that seems to be an homage to Sergio Leone's spaghetti westerns, especially *The Good, The Bad, and The Ugly* (1966), and *Once Upon a Time in the West* (1968). In fact, Leone's visual style is a reference for the directors of the series as Vince Gilligan[4] and Michael Slovis,[5] *Breaking Bad's* director of photography, have confirmed on many occasions. Slovis has admitted that Gilligan and him tried to convince AMC and Sony Entertainment, the production company, to shoot the series in widescreen, like a Leone movie. Both the open wide shots and the extreme close-ups in *Breaking Bad* have the same purpose creating images out of context, along with constructing undefined and ultimately ambiguous frames. The wide shots serve to contextualize the action but they make it impossible to distinguish the details in the small size of the television screen. This lack of information generates in the viewer the uncertainty of not knowing what is happening in the frame. The same occurs in the opposite situation, the excess detail of the extreme close-up accurately identifies the object but makes understanding the context impossible so the information becomes, in the same way, incomplete.

The disorientation of the viewer is a recurrent strategy in contemporary narrative television, as Jason Mittell (2006, 2010) has observed. The creation of intentionally vague images, difficult to contextualize in the parameters of space and time, has proliferated in the last decade in American television producing more complex narratives. These strategies, which Mittell (2006) calls "narrative special effects, " not only arrests the audience's attention, but serve to make visible the mechanics of narration. Despite the fact that classic TV series were also familiar with temporal and spatial alterations, these narrative devices were introduced to the viewers by means of an obvious exposition. In contemporary complex TV drama, however, orienting clues are obviated in order to produce images of ambiguity. Series such as *Lost* (ABC, 2004-2010), *24* (Fox, 2001-2010), or *Battlestar Galactica* (Sci-Fi, 2003-2009) have frequently produced such complex images. For that reason, as Mittell (2006) points out, "narratively complex programming invites audiences to engage actively at the level of form" (38). These kinds of fictions present their narration as a complex puzzle and audiences receive pleasure to trying to solve it.

In the case of *Breaking Bad* complexity is revealed through the ambiguity of decontextualized images, most of which are concentrated in the cold open sequences. The series uses the episode beginnings to generate confusing images through extreme close-ups. There are clear examples of this narrative practice in a number of episodes from the series' second season. An example of this practice is the series of episodes of the second season, "Seven Thirty-Seven" (03/08/09), "Down" (03/29/09), "Over" (05/10/09) and "ABQ" (05/31/09). Each of these episodes begins with images corresponding to a black and white sequence which the viewer may not make sense of until the end of the season. The episode "Seven Thirty-Seven" opens with a close-up of a hose dripping, which is followed by the shot of a light and a snail crawling on a wall. The opening then reveals an eye floating in a pool and then a pink teddy bear—the only object with color in all the sequence—slightly battered and with one eye missing. With that image of the teddy bear under water the narration is interrupted to give way to the opening credits of the series and, after them, the story continues where we had left it at the end of the first season, with Tuco doing business with Walt and Jesse at an auto junkyard.

The confusion for the viewer is formidable. From the images previously shown it becomes impossible to determine where and when that sequence occurs. Both could be a flashback and a flash-forward, or even a dream sequence. The succession of decontextualized close-ups increase the audience's interest in what they are seeing, so they look for immediate answers. The episode, however, concludes without offering any guide and in the two following episodes there is no reference to those strange images. During that wait, expectations and uncertainty escalates. Not until the fourth episode of the season, "Down," will the series return to the black and white sequence. In this case, returning to the previous image of the pink teddy bear the teaser adding the silhouette of a human figure pulling the stuffed toy out of the water and places it in a plastic bag. The opening sequence ends with a close-up of glasses similar to those used by the character of Walter White. In the episode "Over," six episodes later, the sequence reappears again. This time the above information is followed by a shot of the entrance to Walter's home where we can see his car. At this point we can confirm that the objects previously seen were located in Walter's backyard. This time, the latest image of the teaser shows two corpses in a bag. As we can see, new information is being added gradually with each teaser, however, the sequence remains ambiguous, indefinite.

The last episode of the season, "ABQ," includes more details of that sequence, including a sign reading "Evidence. Do not remove," which confirms that we actually are at the scene of an incident under investigation. It is not until the end of the episode, however, that the main story finally connects with these decontextualized images and it is revealed that it was a flash-forward focused on the consequences of a crash. Only now, with the complete information, the viewer is able to restore the meaning of each image seen in previous episodes. The use of the close-up shot encourages a conscious strategy of concealment. Instead of showing the general scenario of waste and damage caused by the crash, the series pays attention to the slightest detail creating a vast and unreachable off scene. This *mise-en-scène* presumes, eventually, a space fragmentation. The previous teasers offer a succession of images juxtaposed, between which there is not a connecting thread. This strategy of juxtaposition and fragmentation is a common occurrence throughout the entire series, as discussed below.

It should be noted that the titles of the episodes including these teasers: "Seven Thirty-Seven," "Down," "Over" and "ABQ," represent a paratextual clue. All the titles together form the phrase "737 (Boeing) down over (ABQ)." It is true, then, that for the viewer who knows this information, the first two episodes would be enough to unravel the mystery of the crash. However, even with this knowledge, images are confusing enough to maintain their status of ambiguity. In the same categorization we can include the teasers of the episodes "Grilled" (03/15/09), "Fly" (05/23/10), and "Bug" (09/11/11). All of them are designed under a similar structure based on the fragmentation of the extreme close-up as a strategy of disorientation. The case of "Fly" is probably the most extreme example of disorientation by fragmentation. This bottle episode[6] opens with a series of extreme and blurry close-ups impossible to identify while we hear the voice of Skyler singing a lullaby in the background. Then, these close-ups become more explicit, showing insect legs, eyes, until finally there appears the image of a fly. As in the case of the plane crash sequence, this cold open alludes again to disorientation and confusion. At first, just for a moment, the viewer does not know what he is seeing on the screen. Once the fly is identified, it is impossible to place these images in the space-time context of the series. As the episode progresses the image makes sense when we realize that the main plot show us Walter obsessed with killing a fly. At the end of the episode, the image of another fly on a smoke detector in Walter's home suggests that the cold open was actually a flash-forward spatially located in the house, with Skyler singing the lullaby to their daughter Holly. But, that is just a guess. The images are so fragmented that it is impossible to place them accurately in a context and a precise time.

On the other hand, the episode "Grilled" starts with extreme close-ups of a worm, some bullet shells, a few bottles of beer and broken glass before moving on to a series of fragmented shots of a car bouncing to reveal, in a wider shot, an unidentified body lying on the floor. At the end of the episode we will discover that it actually is a flash-forward teaser and that the dead body is Tuco's. Until you reach that point, the teaser of "Grilled" moves into the realm of uncertainty. Moreover, in this case, the teaser launches a strategy of suspense through the juxtaposition of close-ups. This opening is similar to the classic final duel of *Once Upon a Time in the West* (1968). The beginning of the episode "Grilled" artificially slows the time down by stringing a series of close-up shots as we can see at the end of the episode. The sequence lengthens the duration of these shots in order to give the impression of suspended time. When the main story connects with the teaser it becomes apparent that the sequence of violent events has taken place more quickly than the teaser shows with its succession of extreme close-up shots.

Breaking Bad's teasers frequently employ the suspense device of extending the temporal duration of shots in their narrative sequences. This reference seems to be, once more, the first episode of the series with the slow motion picture of Walter's pants flying in the desert, but there are more examples. At the start of the episode "No Mas" a succession of decontextualized shots delays the introduction of The Cousins and the sanctuary of Santa Muerte. In *Breaking Bad*, each opening episode seems to have the implicit objective of generating an uncomfortable image for the audience. Instead of recurrently coming back to a well-known and recognizable place, as dictated by the canons of seriality, the series appears to promote and foster the abyss of strangeness. Each episode can begin anywhere and in any way, to major confusion of the viewer. These openings question the idea of unlimited potentiality of each concept of beginning in literature and, by extension, by any narrative exercise.

TEMPORAL COMPLEXITY: WHAT IS THE PATTERN?

Breaking Bad, as much of contemporary TV series, frequently uses narrative structures that involve complex temporal disorder. As in the case of extreme close-ups, the fact of playing with temporality aims to capture the viewer's attention by means of disorientation. Teasers seem to be the most predisposed examples of temporal dislocation and disorientation in the series. The *Breaking Bad* teaser combines, in the terminology of Gérard Genette (1983) "analepsis" (flashbacks), "prolepsis" (flash-forwards), and even ellipsis in order to create uncertain beginnings following the idea that "everything is possible." The alternation of different temporary strategies in teasers appeals to serial repetition to play with the expectations of the audience. Once again, the first episode of the series will become a pattern for the rest.

As described above, the pilot of the series starts in medias res with a sequence that, after the opening credits, the audience is able to place in the near future. "Three weeks later" says a caption on screen. It is a beginning that immediately "How did we got here?"[7] and encourages the viewers to fill in the gap between that teaser and the beginning of the first act. Thus, the viewer understands that there is missing information to be discovered, as the story progresses, in order to interpret this beginning. For the audience, the story presents itself as a narration based on the search for clues in the same way it occurs in detective stories. But that is not all. Furthermore, the teaser of the pilot closes with a cliffhanger that maintains the action in suspense. Consequently, it creates another gap and, at the same time, another question is added to the previous one: "What happens next?." This feature is typical of in media res beginnings as Sternberg (1978) points out, "the reader is eager to have this withheld material not only in order to disambiguate and reconstitute the narrative past or even the present state of affairs per se but also to acquire the premises necessary for forming warrantable expectations as to the probable developments of the action in the narrative future" (54). If the viewer wants to disambiguate this beginning, she will have to wait until the end of the pilot. It is true, however, that the caption detailing the passing of three weeks has already offered the viewer some clues for interpreting this teaser.

At the start of the second season, in the episode "Seven Thirty-Seven," the strategy seems the same. The episode begins with a succession of ambiguous images placed temporarily in a more distant future than the three weeks from the pilot. In this case, however, the series offers no interpretation guides to the viewer. From its second season, *Breaking Bad* ignores explicit timing marks reinforcing its commitment to the confusion. The viewer knows from the experience of the first season that he can expect temporary disorientation. Beyond the pilot, the episodes "Cat's in the Bag . . ." (1/27/08) and ". . . And the Bag's in the River" (2/10/08) include a flashback in their teasers, while the episode "Crazy Handful of Nothin" (3/2/08) incorporates a flash-forward. In all cases, however, temporal disorder remains explicit. In the episode "Cat's in the Bag . . ." there is a textual temporary mark on screen which reads: "Twelve hours earlier." In the episode ". . . And the Bag's in the River," Walter's physical presence indicates that we are in a flashback. The same occurs in the teaser of the episode "Crazy Handful of Nothin" where Walter appears with his head shaved indicating a flash-forward.

In "Seven Thirty-Seven," however, the series ignores any temporary indicator. It is true that watching previous episodes has taught viewers to expect temporary games but with a succession of close-up shots on decontextualized objects, the disorientation becomes absolute. The presence of a black and white image, a common resource in film and television history for flashback sequences,[8] makes even more puzzling a teaser that actually happens in the future. At that time, due to past experience, the viewer expects the main story to connect with teaser images at the end of the episode as has happened in previous examples. In this example, the prolepsis has a larger extent in Genette's terminology and will not connect to the main story until the last episode of the season, "ABQ." The audience's feeling of disorientation increases. The viewers expected that at the end of the episode the gaps would be filled, but the series postponed this information increasing their curiosity. *Breaking Bad* begins its second season with what Sternberg (1978) refers to as a "retardatory structure," which deliberately reserves expository information till the end and thereby follows a narrative strategy of sustaining "curosity and suspense" (182).

The series also has the ability to distribute the cold opens that refer to that outcome offering new information for speculation every time, so that the viewer will be more intrigued as the season advance toward its end.

From that moment on, each season beginning establishes a dialogue with the past season playing with the expectations of the audience. When the third season begins with the ambiguous image of people crawling on a dirt road the viewer wonders if he is watching a flash-forward, as in the previous season starts. Over the episode and the season, we will finally understand that this sequence takes place in the present and has to do with the Mexican ritual of Santa Muerte. In the same way the series *Lost* did during its six seasons, *Breaking Bad* plays in a self-conscious way with the audience's knowledge so as to offer variations or repetitions regarding previous structures. Using images of spatial and temporal ambiguity, the series delays the introduction of key information as much as possible. The show does that at the micro, within the teasers, and at the macro-levels over the course of a season. Thus, the viewer tries to fill in the gaps and so he uses past episodes looking for a pattern. Conscious of this process, the series plays with the audience by offering similarities and variations creating the idea of a pattern that, in the end, is not there. After that, the only certainty the viewer can hold is unpredictability. The audience knows that facing a new episode of *Breaking Bad* means facing uncertainty.

At the start of the fourth season this self-conscious dialogue between the series and the viewer becomes even more evident. "Box Cutter" (7/17/11) begins, as the title makes explicit, with a close-up of a hand wielding a box cutter to reveal, then, Gale Boetticher. The third season had ended with Jesse Pinkman shooting Gale at his apartment door, thereby the audience experience a feeling of evident bewilderment looking back at a character they believed dead. As the teaser goes on, we discover that, in fact, it is a flash-forward. The narration plays with confusion during the initial instants, given that the series so far has not offered us any image to confirm that Gale died in the shooting.

At the start of the fifth season, the episode "Live Free or Die" (7/15/12) refers back to the teaser's pilot episode of the series but in this case the flash-forward takes place a year in the future from the present time of the narrative. In this start, we see Walter White using a false identity and having breakfast. The fact that the character draws, using bacon, the number 52 on the plate, an image that takes us back to the pilot episode, announces to the viewer that the sequence is set in a very distant future. As in previous cases, this teaser is presented sufficiently vaguely and ambivalently to suggest without offering specific information. After the first eight episodes of the season, the series does not make any other reference to that start. At this point, however, the audience accepts the game of confusion because their past experience has taught them that in the end they will be rewarded.

Apart from the beginnings of the season and the examples cited above, *Breaking Bad* uses the strategy of temporary disorientation in several teaser sequences throughout all seasons. The episodes "Grilled,"

"Breakage" (4/5/2009), "Bug," and "Dead Freight" (08/12/12) begin in medias res with a flash-forward. In "Breakage," we see two unknown men crossing a river. Upon reaching the shore, one of them finds a dental grill encased in an acrylic cube that turns out to be Hank's souvenir from his encounter with Tuco. When, after the opening credits, the series shows the cube on Hank's desk, the audience wonders how the cube will end up in the river, A question that will be answered at the end of the episode. The start of "Bug," by contrast, is more ambiguous. The episode opens with an extreme close-up of a pair of glasses, which apparently seem to be Walter's, lying on the ground. The image of a few drops of blood on the floor and on a shoe follows these initial shots. At the end of the episode, all these images are revealed as a flash-forward but until this moment they remain ambiguous and open to speculation. The same thing happens in the case of "Grilled" and "Dead Freight." Both the image of a bouncing car in the desert and the image of a kid riding a bike in the desert form quite an indeterminate cold open, so that the viewer cannot fill the gaps until the episode advances. In the end, the viewers will understand that they were flash-forward sequences.

In addition, the series also uses often, as in the episode "Box Cutter," teasers set in the past with the intention of restoring some events previously elided by the story. This is the case of "I. F. T." (4/4/10), which shows the death of Tortuga, "Mas" (04/18/10), which tells the story of how Jesse got the RV to cook meth, "Cat's in the Bag . . ." which shows what happened in the desert before Walter came home at the end of the pilot and "Abiquiu" (05/30/10) which shows a scene of Jesse and Jane visiting a Georgia O'Keeffe exhibit. In this sense, the teasers have the function of filling some gaps in the story that will provide useful information for the present of the narrative.

Finally, there is also another type of recurring flashback in the teasers of the series. In this case, those flashbacks delve into the past of the characters, just as was the case with Walter in the episode ". . . And the Bag's in the River." In this second type are the beginnings of the episodes "One Minute" (05/02/10), "Full Measure" (06/13/10) and "Hermanos" (09/04/11). The first case delves into the past of The Cousins, while "Full Measure" is situated more than fifteen years ago to show Walter and Skyler just before buying their house. In the case of "Brothers," the episode starts with a flashback that takes us back to last season, just after Hank's shooting. At the end of the teaser, still in flashback, we see Gus Fring talking to Don Hector Salamanca and just before the opening credits, after Gus utters the words "blood for blood," the disorienting image of a bloodstain on water appears. At the end of the episode, in another flashback sequence, the viewer will discover the bloodstain was caused by the former partner of Gus, Max Arciniega, killed by Salamanca years ago. This time the teaser anticipates the revelation promoting an image of curiosity.

GENRE AND HYBRIDITY

As Jason Mittell (2004) has analyzed on several occasions, generic hybridization is a distinctive feature of contemporary television fiction. In the case of *Breaking Bad*, the series is presented, from the start, as a drama with tragic overtones. Vince Gilligan has defined the series on several occasions as a falling story—"From Mr. Chips to Scarface." Also, AMC's series often uses scenery close to the film or TV western, a staging that openly pays tribute to Sergio Leone or the Coen brothers filmography, and a touch of black comedy, which makes contrast with the violence generated by its dramatic conflicts.

From this point of view, the beginnings of *Breaking Bad*'s episodes act as a perfect metonymy from the series, showing its generic hybridization. Beyond what has been mentioned before, *Breaking Bad* contributes from the cold opening to expand this concept of generic hybridization. A clear example of this practice can be found in "Negro y Azul" (04/19/09). The teaser of this episode is made up completely of the video clip of the song "Negro y Azul" sung by the band Los Cuates de Sinaloa. In this case, the television drama genre meets the video musical genre, a genre also spawned from television. Written by the creator of *Breaking Bad*, Vince Gilligan, and the Mexican composer Pepe Garza, the song joins the musical subgenre of narcocorrido. A narcocorrido is a version from the Mexican corrido addressed to the exaltation of drug dealers and to the account of real events which recently occurred in the drug trafficking world. In this particular case, the song praises Walter-Heisenberg figure, while extoling the fame that its blue meth has obtained beyond the American border. The musical video is used to report to the audience the progress Walter has made inside the trafficking world and, at the same time, brings forward the threat of the Mexican cartel and the inability of ever escaping its retribution. Throughout the series, the song "Negro y Azul" is not even mentioned again. However, since the moment the episode was aired, the song started to be part of the Los Cuates de Sinaloa usual repertory. At the end of 2009, the band published the song for the first time in the record *En Vivo con la Plebada* (Sony Music) and it has recently been republished in the compilation record *Mis favoritas* (Sony Music, 2012). Also, a teaser of the series has developed into the musical field creating a kind of transmedia narrative.

Another similar example can be found in the episode "Kafkaesque" (05/16/10), which starts with a commercial of the restaurant chain Los Pollos Hermanos. In order to simulate the aesthetics of food advertising, the teaser shows extreme close-up shots of spices, peppers and roast chickens while a voice-over narration describes the goodness of Los Pollos Hermanos. At this point, the episode appropriates the usual rhetoric of fast food advertising to show, afterward, the mass production process and distribution of blue meth by Fring's organization.

In the examples mentioned before, we come across teasers that, throughout the emulation of other audiovisual genres, act themselves independently from the rest of the series. A similar case takes place during the episode "Better Call Saul" (04/26/09), which starts with an auto-conclusive cold open that reflects Lavery's notion of minisode perfectly. The opening sequence of the episode, which is settled in two shots, Badger is waiting at a bus stop when an undercover policeman approaches him to buy blue meth. Although at the beginning Badger is suspicious, eventually he agrees to sell him the drug and so the policeman arrests him. In this case, the teaser works as a short film perfectly understandable to anybody who is unfamiliar with the show. It is true that the regular audience of *Breaking Bad* recognizes Badger in that sequence and knows that the blue meth he is selling has something to do with Walter and Jesse. This teaser, however, functions as a stand-alone, closed narrative; a micro-story. The game of appearances established between the two characters has a beginning, with Badger suspecting the buyer and even making fun of him, a development, with the policeman denying Badger's accusations and making him change his mind, and an ending, with the policeman arresting Badger, proving ironically that his initial suspicions were right. The episode "Problem Dog" (8/28/2011) includes in its teaser the image of a videogame Jesse is playing in his living room. It is the first-person shooter *Rage* and the infographic image of the videogame that comprises most of that cold open.

The series *Breaking Bad* uses disorientation as a narrative asset to create uncertainty and promoting viewer's curiosity toward the story. Above all, the show executes this practice through teaser sequences, which are always a fertile ground for narrative and aesthetics experimentation. By using these openings, the series created by Vince Gilligan manages to generate a permanent sensation of unpredictability that immediately catches the attention of the audience. *Breaking Bad* obtains a sense of disorientation based on the application of two main strategies: the use of extreme close-ups and the implement of a non-linear narrative that often draws in media res beginnings alternating flashbacks and flash-forwards. The utilization of close-ups, beyond being an aesthetic decision, becomes a narrative device used in most cases to produce disorientation through space fragmentation. As a consequence, viewers are alert to the narrative with the objective of filling the gaps. Furthermore, the fragmented images provided by the close-up shots are often used to generate time dilation and, therefore, as a strategy for suspense. *Breaking Bad* also uses generic hybridization as another device for unpredictability in its teasers. Drawing on music video, video games or the language of advertising, the series incorporates all kind of resources into a real mixture of genres. The cold openings serve as the grounds for aesthetic and generic experimentation through the course of the whole series.

NOTES

1. See Bloomer, "Why *Mad Men* isn't on HBO?" on the website *Paste: Signs of Life in Music, Film & Culture.*
2. There are several videos on YouTube dedicated to *Breaking Bad*'s cold opens. For example, here is a compilation of all season one opening scenes http://www.youtube.com/watch?v=N2Anq0zHQK0. More teaser compilations can be found at http://blogs.indiewire.com/pressplay/sheila-omalley-breaking-bad (seasons one and two) and http://blogs.indiewire.com/pressplay/sheila-omalley-breaking-bad-part-2 (seasons three and four).
3. Scripts available on www.scriptcity.com.
4. Please see the interview at http://blogs.amctv.com/breaking-bad/2011/10/vince-gilligan-interview.php.
5. Please see the interview at Indiewire.com. http://www.indiewire.com/article/television/michael-slovis-interview-breaking-bad-director-of-photography.
6. A bottle episode is an episode of a television series produced with the smallest budget possible. For that reason, usually these kind of episodes are set in a single location and employ only part of the regular cast of the show. For more information see "Bottle episode," *TV Tropes.* http://tvtropes.org/pmwiki/pmwiki.php/Main/BottleEpisode.
7. See "How we got here," *TV Tropes.* http://tvtropes.org/pmwiki/pmwiki.php/Main/HowWeGotHere.
8. Examples in this area are multiple. The use of black and white images or other post-production effects is common in contemporary television to distinguish flashback scenes and make them explicit to the audience. For example, that is the case of *Babylon 5* (PTEN/TNT, 1994-1998) or the series *Veronica Mars* (UPN/The CW, 2004-2007) that used sepia-toned images for its flashback sequences.

WORKS CITED

Bloomer, Jeffrey. "Why *Mad Men* isn't on HBO?" *Paste: Signs of Life in Music, Film & Culture.* 2009. http://www.pastemagazine.com/articles/2009/08/why-mad-men-isnt-on-hbo.html.

Douglas, Pamela. *Writing the TV Drama Series: How to Succeed as a Professional Writer in TV.* Studio City, CA: Michael Wiese Productions, 2007.

Eco, Umberto. *The Limits of Interpretation.* Bloomington, IN: Indiana University Press, 1994.

Epstein, Alex. *Crafty TV Writing: Thinking Inside the Box.* New York: Holt Paperback, 2006.

Genette, Gérard. *Narrative Discourse: An Essay in Method.* Translated by Jane E. Lewin. New York: Cornell University Press, 1983.

Gray, Jonathan. *Show Sold Separately: Promos, Spoilers, and Other Media Paratexts.* New York: New York University Press, 2010.

Lavery, David. "Bad Quality: *Breaking Bad* as Basic Cable Quality TV." *Critical Studies in Television.* 2009. http://www.criticalstudiesintelevision.com/index.php?siid=13805.

Mittell, Jason. *Genre and Television: From Cop Shows to Cartoons in American Culture.* New York, London: Routledge, 2004.

———. "Narrative Complexity in Contemporary American Television." *The Velvet Light Trap.* 58. (2006): 29-40.

———. "Previously On: Prime Time Serials and the Mechanics of Memory." In *Intermediality and Storytelling,* edited by M. Grishakova and M.L. Ryan. 78-98. Berlin, New York: Walter de Gruyter, 2010.

Phelan, James. "The Beginning of *Beloved*: A Rhetorical Approach." In *Narrative Beginnings: Theories and Practices,* edited by B. Richardson. 195-212. Lincoln, NE: University of Nebraska Press, 2008.

Sternberg, Meir. *Expositional Modes & Temporal Ordering in Fiction.* Baltimore & London: The Johns Hopkins University Press, 1978.

Weinman, Jaime."Should We Watch TV Shows From the Beginning?." *TV Guidance.* 2011.   http://www2.macleans.ca/2011/03/07/should-we-watch-tv-shows-from-the-beginning/.

NINE

Buying the House: Place in *Breaking Bad*

Ensley F. Guffey

In the past five years, AMC's critically acclaimed series *Breaking Bad* has become known for its compelling storytelling. Relying heavily on its diegetic history to develop its plot, *Breaking Bad* uses one of the most fundamental of human experiences to provide a framework of narrative memory: the ability to intentionally create meaningful places. This use of place contributes significantly to the emotional realism of the series by drawing on the viewer's own phenomenological experience of the world. This essay will examine the homes of Jesse Pinkman and the White family; the three labs used in the show by Walt and Jesse to produce crystal meth; and the desert landscape seen throughout the series to demonstrate the manner in which *Breaking Bad* uses experiences of place and space to create a more fully realized diegetic world.

The concepts of "place" and "space" as used here draw upon theories of humanist geography. As developed in the mid-1970s, humanist geography was in part driven by the need to redefine place as something more than mere location or an ideographic space of concern only to a particular place, time, or people. Instead, humanist geographers sought to realize an idea of place which was "a universal and transhistorical part of the human condition" (Cresswell 2004, 20). To do so, scholars turned toward phenomenological and existential philosophy to develop a theory which depends upon subjective human experiences to give places meaning. As Edward Relph (1976) writes, "a place is not just the 'where' of something; it is the location plus everything that occupies that location seen as an integrated and meaningful phenomenon" (3). This intentional process of imbuing a given place with meaning is seen as an inherent part of the human experience of the world, and this relationship between human experience and place is encapsulated by such common sentiments as "making a house a home "or "this is where I grew up."

Humanist geographers consider the concepts of place and space as being closely related yet partaking of different experiences. According to Yi-Fu Tuan (1977) "the ideas 'space' and 'place' require each other for definition: From the security and stability of place we are aware of the openness, freedom, and threat of space, and vice versa" (6). In *Place and Placelessness*, Relph (1976) links the two ideas even more closely arguing that "however we feel or know or explain space, there is nearly always some associated sense or concept of place. In general it seems that space provides the context for places but derives its meaning from particular places" (8). Both agree, however, that space is the more abstract of the two ideas, and is far more suggestive of the unknown and undifferentiated. Tim Cresswell (2004) sums up the essential difference as one where space is "a realm without meaning. When humans invest meaning in a portion of space and then become attached to it in some way . . . it becomes a place" (10). For example, when we rent a new, unfurnished apartment, we often view it as an empty space, full of potential, perhaps, but still unrealized. As we move in, decorate, cook, spill drinks, argue, make love, get sick, become well, celebrate, mourn, eat, sleep, eliminate, and perform all the other ordinaries of human existence, the empty space becomes *our* space, our *place*. Our experiences within the space give it a meaning, importance, and significance which, while admittedly subjective, are all central to our sense of place.

9809 MARGO STREET: JESSE PINKMAN'S HOME

Of all the places experienced by human beings, home is perhaps the most meaningful. Relph (1976) states that "home is the foundation of our identity as individuals and as members of a community, the dwelling place of being. . . . Home is . . . an irreplaceable centre [sic] of significance" (39). In season one of *Breaking Bad*, Jesse's home is a place imbued with the personal history of his Aunt Jenny, her struggle with cancer, and her relationship with Jesse, whom she apparently took in when his parents kicked him out of their house for using drugs. Although in seasons one and two Jesse considers the house to be his place, in reality, it is his aunt's memory and history which predominate. The décor is dark, feminine, and floral; there are delicate knick-knacks on the shelves, and doilies on the furniture. Though Jesse undoubtedly inhabits more of the house than when his aunt was alive, even in his upstairs bedroom Jesse's presence remains minimal, and is largely confined to a few possessions strewn atop his aunt's lingering order. The house is therefore in a transitional state. Jesse lives there as he did while his Aunt Jenny was still alive, but is only slowly creating a history and meaning separate from those which he shared with her. Jesse has yet to wholly remake his aunt's place into his own.

In humanist geographic theory, "home is an exemplarily kind of place where people feel a sense of attachment and rootedness. Home, more than anything else, is seen as a center of meaning and a field of care" (Cresswell 2004, 24). In Jesse's case, this idea of home as a field of care grows out of his experience of his aunt's love. Michael A. Godkin (1980) suggests that, as a person struggling with addiction, the house at 9808 Margo Street would be particularly important to Jesse as a refuge, a safe place where Jesse "escapes an otherwise unhappy existence," and Jesse does indeed display a profound sense of belonging and attachment to this particular place (77). The fact that Jesse has not made any real attempt to modify the décor is evidence of a desire to remember Jenny, and to maintain his home as it was when she was alive, with all the existing associations of safety and security.

Will he or won't he, Jesse's new relationship with Walter White quickly forces significant changes to Jesse's home. Although Jesse seems to have been very careful to keep his meth-cooking activities well separated from his home, one of the first things to come out of Jesse's new partnership with Walt is the storage of equipment for meth manufacture in his garage. When Walt suggests that they cook at Jesse's house, Jesse reacts strongly, "No. We're not gonna cook here. 'Kay? This is my *house*. I don't shit where I eat" ("Pilot" 01/20/08). This fits in well with Cresswell's (2004) observation that home is a place of withdrawal and rest from the outside world where one has some degree of control over what happens. By the series' second episode "The Cat's in the Bag . . ." (01/27/08), Jesse's home has largely passed beyond his control, and rather than a place of rest it has become a place of increasing tension and danger.

The inevitable and increasing encroachment of Walt and Jesse's criminal activities into their personal and private lives is a major theme in *Breaking Bad*. This growing domination is often shown by the intrusion of Jesse and Walt's illegal adventures into their respective homes. In relating the arrangement of a house to the human psyche, the French philosopher Gaston Bachelard (1964) gives particular places within a house a psychological equivalent (17-20). The invasion and changing of Jesse's home by the darker, criminal elements of his life therefore becomes a reflection of his psychological state as he moves more deeply into that life. For Jesse, this psycho-spatial invasion begins immediately, for in Bachelard's theory of place, the basement is a kind of spatial manifestation of the subconscious, and of nightmares (1964, 18). Krazy-8's imprisonment and killing in Jesse's basement in the second and third episodes of season one ("The Cat's in the Bag . . ." 01/27/08) and ". . . And the Bag's in the River" (02/10/08), and the later use of the same place as a temporary lab to manufacture precursor in "A No-Rough-Stuff-Type Deal" (03/09/08) are events which signal the rapidly growing influence of the chaotic and immoral over Jesse's life—and his home.

Krazy-8's death, the disastrous attempt to dissolve the body of Jesse's ex-partner Emilio, and the strong, fish-like odor given off by methylamine as it is processed fundamentally change Jesse's home, and what started in the basement has moved into the main areas of the house. This most intimate of places is corrupted, and the taint cannot be contained within the basement/unconscious. The damage to the house, combined with lingering odors, make it unsalable, and leaves Jesse's home partially destroyed. The memories of his aunt and his life before Walt are being subsumed by these new events which drastically alter Jesse's experience of place in his own home.

These events cannot be erased, and become part of the history of Jesse's home. Indeed, the show reinforces these memories as the series progresses. In the season one finale "A No-Rough-Stuff-Type Deal" (03/09/08), the camera lingers on the sun-lit, empty, support-pole in Jesse's basement—the site of Krazy-8's death. Later, in season two's "Down" (03/09/09), Jesse's scooter is stolen, despite having been secured by the steel U-lock which he and Walt had placed around Krazy-8's neck. In each case the viewer is immediately reminded of what happened in Jesse's basement without need of any further exposition beyond the camera's focus. Moreover, the lab which Jesse and Walt set up in the basement is the immediate cause of Jesse's eviction by his parents in season two, when his mother discovers it. This reinforcement serves to keep the memory of these events in the basement alive, and to imbue the place itself with a history and meaning that go beyond the diegetic world of the series to become part of the audience's experiential history of that place, and a kind of social memory. Basements thus become a place of death and danger for both the characters and the viewer.

For Jesse, much of the history contained in his home, both that which occurred off-screen (Jesse and his aunt) and that which the viewer has witnessed (Krazy-8, Emilio, etc.) is partially concealed when Jesse's parents repossess his house and extensively remodel it for later sale in season two. By the time Jesse purchases the house through the efforts of his lawyer Saul Goodman, all traces of him, his aunt, and even his misadventures with Walt have been removed, including furniture, keepsakes, art, appliances, and countertops. Even the walls have been uniformly painted rental white. To everyone but Jesse (and perhaps Walt), the house on Margo Street is no longer a place, but an empty space.

Moving into these spaces, however, humans begin what Edward Relph (1976) calls "the largely unself-conscious intentionality that defines places as profound centers of human existence" (43). In the case of living spaces, even at the bare minimum we usually bring with us clothing and a toothbrush. These articles are generally viewed as private possessions, as being "ours," and in storing these belonging in a new space, the process of changing that space into a place, into *our* place, is begun. Jesse goes through this process twice in the course of the series. First, when he moves in to the duplex apartment next to Jane Margolis in season two, and again after Jane's death when he moves back into the house on Margo Street in season three. At first, Jesse's sole possessions are some clothes, a sleeping bag, and very little else. Later, some minimal furniture appears: a futon couch, a glass-topped coffee table, and a beanbag chair. Jesse is claiming the space, but is apparently resisting making it into a truly intimate place.

This is because, during season three, Jesse is largely out of place, and resistant to the idea of having a home, a place in the world where he belongs. Tim Cresswell (1996) links being "out of place" with having stepped out of accepted boundaries, crossing what is "often a geographical line and a socio-cultural one" (103). Taken in concert with Yi-Fu Tuan's (1991) view that "home, insofar as it is an intimately lived in place, is imbued with moral meaning," this helps to explain Jesse's seemingly indifferent attitude to his house in season three (105). In redefining himself as "the bad guy" ("No Mas" 03/21/10), Jesse believes he has crossed a socio-cultural line. By basically blackmailing his parents into selling him the house at a price well below its value, he has transgressed geographically. Most damning of all in Jesse's eyes is Jane's death, for which he holds himself responsible. This final transgression makes Jesse feel that he is unworthy of a home in Tuan's sense of a morally meaningful place.

Season three also marks a change in the way in which Jesse's home is portrayed in the series. In part this is due to the sale of the actual house used as the set for 9809 Margo Street in seasons one and two, necessitating its replacement by a carefully constructed studio set (Slovis 2012). This set includes only the living room, dividing wall, short hallway and the stairs leading up to the second floor. Viewed in terms of humanist geography, circumscribing the audience-visible narrative to this particular place is highly significant. Relph (1964) notes that traditionally, living rooms have been thought of as "deeply private place[s] . . . truly the center of both family and individual life" (36). In the modern United States, the living room can be read as a region of overlap for private, social, and public spaces. The living room is definitely an inside place, separated from the wider world outside, and remains the room in which many people spend the majority of their time at home. It is also a kind of liminal space and interface between the private and the social. When we have guests into our homes it is the living room which usually becomes the main social area. Certainly, this is true for Jesse in seasons one through five.

In Jesse's house, the primary passage from outside to inside, and vice versa, is the door separating his living room from the front porch. The living room thus becomes particularly vulnerable to incursions from the outside world, including an enraged and violent Hank Schrader in season three, who pushes into Jesse's living room as he beats him senseless. In season four, Jesse is rarely seen alone in his living room, and when he is, he is usually uncomfortable to the point of distress. Though by this point in the narrative he has managed to come to some kind of terms with Jane's death as nobody's fault, Jesse is inescapably and directly responsible for the murder of Gale Boetticher, a transgressive act that places him beyond all normal social and moral boundaries ("Fly" 05/23/ 10). His desperate psychological condition, racked by guilt and flashbacks to his murder of Gale, is clearly reflected in his home.

Unable to find refuge and comfort in his home as a private place, Jesse partially destroys the boundaries between outside and inside, public and private, by turning his living room into the site of a frenetic, ongoing, drug-fueled party where people come and go as they please and at all hours. As this cycle continues, Jesse's psychological state of being out of place, of having transgressed, is given physical expression as the walls of his living room become stained and are covered with graffiti. Left-over pizza crusts and fast-food wrappers mix with cigarette butts, blood, and discarded clothing as Jesse's house becomes polluted by the outside world, just as Jesse himself has been. This is especially disturbing to the viewer because of the place where it is happening—Jesse's home. This should be a private place, but this chaos is inherently anti-place, and Jesse's living room comes more and more to look like a place abandoned to the whims of whoever might pass through. No longer a center of memory and care, of moral meaning, Jesse's place, no matter how full of people, is again empty space. Yet in abandoning his place to outside forces Jesse is not turning away from the idea of home as a place of retreat and refuge. Indeed, Jesse is actually seeking refuge *by means of* the noise and constant activity. Alone, he has no choice but to face and dwell upon his recent actions and so Jesse turns his house into an unending party in order to create a place of retreat from himself by means of constant distraction.

As Jesse begins to recover from his downward spiral, his psychological state is again reflected in his efforts to recover his home from the forces he has invited in. The brilliant episode "Problem Dog" (08/28/11) opens with Jesse having begun to clean his house, and later in the same episode Jesse is seen carefully repainting the walls of his living-room. In a nice bit of symbolism, the graffiti still shows through the first coat of paint, a reminder that this passage too is now an indelible part of the history of this place. By literally getting his house in order Jesse is also restoring order within himself and in his life. In "Bug" (09/11/11) the climax of this process occurs with a violent confrontation in Jesse's living-room in which he brutally beats Walt and tells him to leave his house and never come back again. With this demand, Jesse's house has once again become a place where he controls access and which is clearly separated from the outside world. By the end of season four and into season five, Jesse has once again found his place, and for the first time since season one, his home has returned to a traditional state of being a place of respite and care. At least for now, Jesse has found his place in his home, and while none of his experiences there can be erased from history and memory, all are important parts of this place, and of Jesse's peace within it.

308 NEGRA ARROYO LANE: THE WHITE HOME

Walter White's home begins the series as a place shared with his family: his wife, Skyler; teenaged son, Walter Jr. and—by the end of season two—infant daughter Holly. The White house of season one presents a very traditional, middle-class, white depiction of home and of family. In the episode "Full Measure" (06/13/10), the viewer learns that the house at 308 Negra Arroyo Lane is the only home the White family has ever had, and two very effective scenes encapsulate the transformation of the place from empty house to family home. In the cold open to the episode, set some sixteen years prior to the main storyline, the camera reveals an empty space of unfurnished rooms that is so visually different from the place the audience has become used to seeing that it is only belatedly recognized as the White's future home. Later, in the opening to the fourth act, the same camera sequence is repeated exactly, revealing in this instance the more familiar, thoroughly lived-in, White home of the series' present. Superimposed on the empty floors and walls of the house seen earlier are all of the furnishings, decorations, and history both diegetic and beyond which make the house a home, and a familiar place to the viewer. The material artifacts of the family's life in this place are symbolic for the meaning they have created in this place. This sense of deep significance taps into the audience's own experience of home and place, where according to Gaston Bachelard (1964) "our house is our corner of the world . . . it is our first universe, a real cosmos in every sense of the word" (4). However, while the White home is very much a place of deep rootedness and care, it is also an example of the darker nature of place.

In season one, Walt is a man who, in the words of actor Bryan Cranston (Walter White), has "imploded into his life . . . [Walt] carries the weight of regret and lost opportunities" (Gilligan, et al., 2009). Walt's story in "Bit by a Dead Bee" (03/22/09), though told in order to escape the consequences of having disappeared for several days, reveals some essential truths about the pressures he faces with a pregnant wife, a son with cerebral palsy, a low-paying teaching job, and the shame of having all of his past colleagues pass him by in their successful careers. Walt feels trapped by and in his life, and apparently has for some time. His is an extreme example of what Edward Relph (1976) calls the drudgery of place, "a sense of being tied inevitably to *this* place, of being bound by the established scenes and symbols and routines" [emphasis in the original] (41). This mood of being trapped in his life is pervasive, beginning in the pilot episode as Walt is seen exercising in what was once his study and is now being remodeled into a nursery for a new baby. As he robotically moves up and down on a stair-step machine, Walt stares at a plaque on the wall celebrating his participation as leader of the crystallography project in research that was awarded the Nobel Prize in 1985 ("Pilot" 01/ 20/08).

Twenty-three years after receiving this award, Walt is a high school chemistry teacher forced to work a crappy second job just to get by. In large part, Walt's decision to break bad is a last, desperate attempt to escape this feeling of being entrapped by his own life, and in the place he once disdainfully referred to as a "starter-home" ("Full Measure" 06/13/ 10). A place of refuge for most, Walt's home has become something of an ever-constricting prison. Ironically, as the series progresses, Walt is re-vealed not as a failure, but as a man who has built a strong and loving family, a bond that extends to his brother and sister-in-law. Walt is much admired by his superiors, parents, and peers at the high school. He has enough friends to fill his house to overflowing, and his son comes close to worshipping the ground he walks on. Walt's prison is a life that many would both admire and envy, but Walt's tragic flaw may be that he is incapable of seeing what he already has. Instead, Walt only sees what he thinks he lacks.

As with Jesse and the house on Margo Street, basement space becomes important for Walt's home as well. In "Over" (05/10/09), during his first abortive attempt to stop cooking meth, Walt is drawn into the hidden places in his home, as represented by the closet-sized utility room which contains the leaky, barely functioning water heater for the house. After imposing order on this place by replacing the water-heater, Walt moves even deeper into the recesses of his home, going beneath the house and into the Bachelardian cellar place of the crawlspace beneath. It is while Walt is buying supplies to repair this space that he confronts the truth he has been trying to deny—he doesn't want to quit. In a chilling scene wherein he lays claim to his subconscious desires, Walt warns two wan-nabe cooks to leave his territory.[1] In Bachelard's (1964) terms, Walt's journey into the crawlspace, though ostensibly driven by the logic of home maintenance, takes place within "the *dark entity* of the house, the one that partakes of subterranean forces . . . in harmony with the irration-ality of the depths" [emphasis in the original] (18). Walt's desire to keep cooking, even after making enough crystal meth to secure the money he needs, and despite his cancer being in remission, is the psychological manifestation of that irrational depth, and of his own irrepressible id. Later, Skyler will use the crawlspace to hide the money from Walt's cooking she is unable to launder, emphasizing this as a place of secrets and illegality.

For both Walt and Skyler, the crawlspace mirrors their psychological condition as each separates life into the legal and the criminal, the known and the hidden. Though it is a part of their home, the crawlspace is separate from the rest of the place, and divorced from the existential meanings inherent in the upper places in the house. Where the upper rooms partake of the order and routine of the Whites' lives, the crawlspace is disordered and dirty, often shown festooned with cobwebs. It is only when outside forces have a profound effect on their lives that the crawlspace is entered, when its secrets are needed. It is a transgressive place where the usual boundaries are blurred. Outside and inside, order and chaos are mixed beneath the White house.

Walt will have to turn to the crawlspace several times during the series. In "Caballo sin Nombre" (03/28/10) he uses the crawlspace and trap-door he constructed during his renovations to break into the house after Skyler has kicked him out and changed the locks, a very prominent symbol of Walt's criminality rising up from the depths to invade his home, and quite literally a transgressive act in and of itself. Further, Walt's escape into the realm of lawlessness and the unrestrained primitive id is given physical substance as he twice attempts to use the crawlspace as a means of escape from his life. In "Crawl Space" (09/25/11), Walt dives under his house to access the money he needs to allow him and his family to escape the wrath of Gustavo Fring. Skyler, however, has given the money away, having earlier reached into this secret place to cover up her own criminal actions as Ted Beneke's bookkeeper. The episode ends with a brilliant crane shot of Walt laughing hysterically in the crawlspace surrounded by the trapdoor's frame. Trapped, that is, by secrets, and by his and Skyler's desires, and trapped in this transgressive place. Later, as Walt's battle with Fring escalates, he again uses the crawlspace and trap to enter and leave the house without alerting the hired killers who are watching the place ("End Times" 10/02/11). The crawlspace has become the means of covert entry and exit, the unconscious space of the home, bringing both secret knowledge and chaos.

Walt's home also undergoes a fundamental change of meaning for him personally, by changing from a place of care to a largely empty emotional space. Despite his feelings of entrapment associated with the house, as the series begins Walt still has very significant roots there. He has lived his marriage there, raised a son there, and performed all of the everyday routines that make up the majority of human life. The house on Negra Arroyo Lane is his *place*, and he belongs there. This idea of rootedness in a particular place is at the core of the sense of home. Relph (1964) states that "To have roots in a place is to have a secure point from which to look out on the world, a firm grasp of one's own position in the order of things, and a significant spiritual and psychological attachment to somewhere in particular" (38). After forcing his way back into the house against Skyler's wishes, however, Walt has made an enemy who will eventually uproot him.

With Skyler's affair in "I. F. T." (04/04/10), Walt begins to lose his home while still inhabiting his house. Although there are periods of seeming rapprochement between Walt and Skyler, even after he has voluntarily moved back out in "Mas" (04/18/10), Walt's sense of home at 308 Negra Arroyo Lane is progressively destroyed. As the truth of Walt's criminal activities is revealed and Skyler decides to make herself a part of the enterprise, Walt finds himself forced to negotiate for the privilege of access to his own home ("Half Measures" 06/06/10), and from this point on Walt no longer truly belongs in his house. It has become Skyler's place, and to a greater or lesser extent, Walt moves through it at her sufferance. This becomes strikingly apparent in season five when, despite having moved back in and apparently dominating Skyler, she nonetheless manages to remove their children from the house and to turn their home into a cold place of reheated take out and silent dinners. Walt may live there, but he no longer belongs. This may add impetus to Walt's much more complete assumption of his Heisenberg persona in season five. As Anne Buttimer (1980) notes, "people's sense of both personal and cultural identity is intimately bound up with place identity. Loss of home or 'losing one's place' my often trigger an identity crisis" (167). As will be shown, however, Walt has put down new roots elsewhere long before season five.

THE LABS

The truth of the matter may be that, at least during the series, the only places where Walt ever feels completely at home, completely secure, and completely self-confident are the series of meth labs he runs. From their first cook in the RV, Walt makes it clear that, in the lab, he is in charge, and Jesse is to obey his rules. The lab is fundamentally Walt's place, for he has mastered its mysteries to a greater depth than perhaps anyone in the country. Even the supremely talented Gale admits that he cannot match the purity of Walt's crystal meth, and when his life literally depends upon the quality of his cook, Jesse is able only to match Gale's best efforts, though that proves good enough. It is his labs to which Walt seems to devote the most attention, and the most care.

Walt's adamantine insistence on respect for the chemistry, for lab procedures, and for a precision bordering on obsession when it comes to cooking all demonstrate a deep concern for the chemistry lab as a very personal place, and for his own self-image as a professional scientist. This kind of fully invested care for a particular place is defined by Relph (1964) as "a real responsibility and respect for that place for itself and for what it is to yourself and to others. There is, in fact, a complete commitment to that place, a commitment that is as profound as any that a person can make" (38). In all of his life, the meth lab is the one place where Walt consistently excels, where he is "the *best* at something" ("Say My Name" 08/26/12). While he may be losing his wife and his children, his job, and everything else that was once important to him, in the lab Walter White remains in control and in charge.

Walt sets up the first lab himself, converting a 1986 Fleetwood Bounder recreational vehicle (RV) into a mobile meth lab. The RV has become perhaps the most iconic symbol of *Breaking Bad*, and for the first three seasons, takes on such a central role that it can be considered a character in its own right. In terms of place, the RV is a complicated study. According to Tuan (1977), "place is a pause in movement. . . . The pause makes it possible for a locality to become a center of felt value" (138). This is underlined by the uniquely human conception of home as a place where one can recover from illness, further developing the idea of home as a place of refuge from the outside world (Tuan 1977; Bachelard 1964). Further, Anne Buttimer (1980) links the dualities of stillness and movement to something essential in human experience: "The lived reciprocity of rest and movement, territory and range, security and adventure, housekeeping and husbandry, community building and social organizations—these experiences may be universal among the inhabitants of Planet Earth" (170). The RV, however, partakes of all of these reciprocal experiences, and is both a place of pause and of movement ("Madrigal" 07/22/12).

The RV is inherently mobile, yet it also includes essential elements of home and of permanence. Though moving through the outside world, it provides a sheltered, inside place for anyone within it. The vehicle is designed to allow for the performance of all of the most basic human life-experiences including sleeping, eating, eliminating, and socializing. Though a hotel room provides the same type of space, the RV is personal property, literally the owner's place, and often imbued with rooted memory by various personal possessions and the memories shared in it. This seeming paradox is humorously demonstrated by Hank's attempt to enter and search the RV in "Sunset" (04/25/10), which is frustrated by the convoluted legal question of the RV as both vehicle and domicile. For Walt and Jesse, the RV becomes a true place of meaning and care, where their personal relationship is formed and solidified. In "4 Days Out" (05/03/09), it becomes their temporary home, shelter from the desert's nighttime cold, and the setting for the deep intimacy of facing death and finding a way out of a dangerous situation together.

Jesse also finds the RV a refuge against his exploding life in "Down" (03/29/09), when, homeless, defeated, and covered in human waste, he collapses on the floor of the RV and cries himself to sleep in the one relatively secure place that remains to him. When an attempt is made to take even this away from him the next day, Jesse risks everything to take the RV and thus hold on to the last meaningful place in his life. The RV is a place of memory and meaning in a darker sense as well, becoming the place where Walt first takes a human life, an act with resounding repercussions for both Walt and Jesse. As with Jesse's basement, this history is emphasized after all traces of Emilio and Krazy-8's deaths have been removed by a lingering shot of the spotlessly clean floor of the RV in ". . . And the Bag's in the River" (02/10/08). Thus the RV is a sight of profound experiences for Walt, Jesse, and for the viewer as well.

The episode "Sunset" (04/25/10) is, in part, a love song to the RV and to its importance as a place for Walt and Jesse. Before the RV is destroyed, Walt takes a lingering moment to caress the equipment in the rear of the Crystal Ship, smiling slightly as he does so, while Jesse flies into an unthinking fury and rushes off to try and save the RV, inadvertently making its destruction all the more urgent. In a beautiful montage set to "He Venido" by Los Zafiros, Walt and Jesse watch as the RV is crushed into scrap metal, their faces and body language undeniably conveying a melancholy farewell (Neuman 2010). Indeed, this feeling of the RV as a place with deep meaning goes beyond the show's diegetic realm. Actor Aaron Paul (2011) (Jesse Pinkman) was deeply affected by the loss of the RV: "When we crushed the RV, it felt like losing a character on the show. I dug through the rubble and grabbed the key ignition—this very small, metal piece you stick the key into in the RV—so I have that." For Paul, and likely for Cranston as well, the RV had become a place of meaning beyond the storyline of *Breaking Bad*, as a place in which they had spent a significant amount of time and energy.

The second lab in the series, the 'Superlab' created by Gustavo Fring, appears at first to be a place of realized dreams for Walter, emphasized by the wonderful scene in "Mas" (04/18/10), where he explores the lab to the almost Disney-esque melody of Peder's "Timetakesthetimeittakes" (Neuman 2010). The candy-red floor, shining stainless steel equipment, and Walt's look of child-like wonder as he explores the place all combine to give the Superlab a dream-like aura. This perfection is reinforced in "Sunset" (04/25/10), when Walt meets Gale Boetticher, a chemist after Walt's own heart, and the kind of lab assistant that is usually *only* found in dreams. The problem with this wonderful space, at least for Walt, is that in the final analysis, it belongs to Gus.

Initially, the Superlab appears to be Walt's place, as Gus allows him a tremendous amount of leeway in terms of his hours, and even when it comes to replacing the incredibly over-qualified Gale with Jesse, despite the latter's history of addiction and erratic behavior. In the episode "Fly" (05/23/10), however, Walt's conception of the Superlab as his place begins to shift. Suffering from a kind of mini-psychic break exacerbated by sleep-deprivation, Walt becomes obsessed with destroying a single housefly which has made its way into the lab. Referring to the insect as a "contaminant," Walt desperately tries to remove the fly from the Superlab and to thus restore cleanliness and order to this place as the symbol of his life and ambition, both of which are now spiraling out of his control. The quest is ultimately successful as Jesse finally kills the fly, but in a larger sense, Walt's efforts are utterly futile for, when it comes to his own world, and his place in it, it is polluted. The Superlab has become a trap for Walt, a prison of his own making.

As first Jesse and then Walt himself flouts Gus' authority, and Walt kills two of Gus' street-level dealers, Walt's control over the Superlab is lost. Gale returns, bringing with him Gus' thugs to keep watch on Walt. After Gale's murder at the end of season three, and Jesse's co-option by Gus and Mike in season four, the Superlab can in no way be considered Walt's place any longer, and he is progressively out of place within it. In season four, the boundaries or the "spatial ordering" of the Superlab, which defines the acceptable practices and people within it, once defined by Walt, are now defined by Gus, Mike, and Jesse (Cresswell 1996). Walt's presence in the lab has become largely transgressive for he is inserting himself into the others' place, and is tolerated only because he remains of some minimal use to Gus. Further, Walt knows that, as Cresswell (1996) writes, "constant transgression is permanent chaos," a state of affairs that Gus will not tolerate indefinitely (166). By the final episode of season four, Jesse too has become a prisoner of the Superlab, and in one scene is literally chained to the place. Now unwilling actors in the Superlab, yet seemingly unable to escape it, Walt and Jesse find themselves in a position somewhat analogous to prisoners on death row.

This dungeon-like aspect of the Superlab further reveals the Bachelardian cellar elements of the place. The Superlab is the most prominent basement or cellar room in the series. Indeed, the Superlab's location is rich with symbolism. This lovely initial framing of the Superlab is subverted by its underground location, where the "dreamer knows that the walls of the cellar are buried walls . . . walls that have the entire earth behind them" (Bachelard 1964, 20). This is yet another deadly basement place, where hundreds of pounds of poison are made every week. Every day Walt, Jesse, and others must descend out of the light and into the windowless darkness of the Superlab to work secretly in a red-painted hell to produce pure chemical misery. The entrance to this morally unclean place is beneath an industrial washing machine which has been disabled, thus emphasizing that those who enter there are moving from the upper world of cleanliness, logic, and reason to the chthonian underworld where these virtues are changed into vices, and constrained to a deadly purpose.

In order to make his escape (and coincidentally Jesse's), Walt must eliminate both the man who ultimately creates the boundaries of the Superlab and has placed Walt outside of them, and the Superlab itself. Appropriately for a place that has increasingly become a kind of Hell for Walt, he and Jesse destroy the lab with a chemical fire ("Face-Off" 10/09/

11). Though the Superlab has become a place every bit as central to the story as the RV was, its destruction is very different, as neither Walt or Jesse show hesitation or regret, and the montage of the Superlab's fiery end takes place to the almost frenetic guitars of The Taalbi Brothers' "Freestyle," rather than to music which provokes feelings of loss and regret (Neuman 2012). This time Walt and Jesse are destroying a place which has taken on meanings that are wholly negative and they act to free themselves not only from Gus' domination, but from the sense of being out of place and out of control. In their next effort, Walt will make sure to maintain the maximum amount of control over his new lab and over who has a place in it.

In season five, Walt, still in the powerful grip of the belief that his skills as a meth cook give meaning to his life, and a notable place, however infamous, in the world, must find a new lab space, one that he can exercise full authority over. This time Walt *chooses* to be transgressive, using the cover of Vamanos Pest Control's house-covering fumigation tent to set up his meth lab within other people's homes. In a very real way, Walt and Jesse have now become home invaders who violate the most intimate places of people whom they have never even met. Security and secrecy is provided by setting up a tent within the house being treated for pests and mixing the toxic outflow of meth production with the venting pesticide used in the house after the cook.

The invasive nature of Walt and Jesse's new operation is clearly and chillingly emphasized by the noise of children playing nearby as the toxic gas from Walt and Jesse's first cook is released into the neighborhood and the gas is vented into a backyard full of children's toys and a swing set. This lab is not removed from the everyday places of the innocent. Walt and Jesse are not cooking in the desert anymore, or even underground, but right in the middle of residential neighborhoods. This transgression is not merely against personal place, but also against the larger social space of ordered life. The emphasis on the waste products of meth production tainting these places is important, for "often, when people, things and practices are seen as 'out-of-place' they are described as pollution and dirt" (Cresswell 2004, 103). Upper middle-class residential neighborhoods like the ones using Vamanos Pest Control's house fumigation services are places which are theoretically intended to keep out chaotic, criminal, and impure elements. This idea is even more central to the places in which the most intimate aspects of our lives take place. These inherently 'inside' places are in part constructs that keep danger and dirt away and 'outside.' By breaking these boundaries, Walt's new lab is not merely a place where poison is produced, it is poison itself.

Yet Walt seems immanently comfortable in this new lab and in his role as invader. When not actively involved in cooking, Walt, Jesse, and later Todd make themselves comfortable in whatever home they happen to be in at the time. Their breaks to rest, watch TV, and eat are transgressions into someone else's private spaces. In Walt's eyes, the lab is now truly his home, and the fact that it regularly changes location is irrelevant. Where ever the lab is, that place is home, *Walt's* home, and the actual owners of the place, and the meanings those people attach to it, are of no consequence. It is perhaps the ultimate act of spatial transgression—the theft of another's place.

THE DESERT

More than any other location in *Breaking Bad* it is the desert that evokes the idea of 'space': vast, amorphous, and strikingly devoid of memory. Indeed, the timelessness of the landscape *denies* memory. Even when littered with the debris of former human habitation the sense evoked is always of a place abandoned, left to revert to empty space, with no one to give meaning to the old tricycles, toys, farm equipment, bottles and rotting fences that remain. The desert, free of memory, is a place where anything can happen and everything is allowed. When a secure and private place is needed to cook meth, Walt and Jesse park their RV deep in the desert, far from prying eyes. When mortal threats must be made, Gus and Mike take Walt into the desert, which can swallow a new body as easily as it has all that have come before. When Tuco's cousins cross the Mexican-American border, they do so in the desert, and it is in the desert spaces that they worship at the shrine of Santa Muerte, the Saint of Death.

The desert, then, is the ultimate outside space for most of the characters in *Breaking Bad*. This sense of the desert's outsideness carries with it the idea of spaciousness. As portrayed in *Breaking Bad*, the New Mexico desert is truly vast, a feeling that is deliberately reinforced by cinematography which emphasizes the huge, open sky, and the smallness of human beings in this space.[2] Tuan (1977) notes that "spaciousness is closely associated with the sense of being free. Freedom implies space; it means having the power and enough room in which to act" (52). As mentioned above, Tuan (1977) also emphasizes the "threat of space" (6), as an integral part of this freedom. The Cousins coolly slaughter a truck full of illegal immigrants and their driver in the desert, and walk calmly away. Later it is at a house in the desert that they kill an old woman and slaughter a policeman with an axe. Tuco repeatedly fires a fully automatic weapon in the desert at any and every target he chooses, and it is in the desert that Gus promises to kill Walt's infant daughter ("Crawl Space," 09/25/11).

The deadly freedom and power found in the desert is a result of the space itself. Mostly uninhabited and uninhabitable, the desert is not a place of human experience, and thus cannot become a 'place' imbued with history, and a field of care. What happens there is quickly forgotten, and even the spaces where people live quickly fall into meaninglessness when they are abandoned. Yet as a space, the desert requires place to define it, and in *Breaking Bad* the desert very quickly becomes the place where death is done, and where murder goes unpunished and all but unnoticed (Tuan 1977). Soon, every scene filmed in the desert evokes unease in the viewer, and the show's characters are always noticeably nervous when they find themselves there. Because anything can happen in that place, in the desert, and be swallowed up forever within that vast and empty space. Even children at play.

CONCLUSION

Breaking Bad's continuing use of universal human experiences of place has created a narrative world in which the audience is fully invested. For five years the viewer has journeyed with Walter White and Jesse Pinkman through a succession of places, and shared their feelings of triumph, joy, grief, and terror in them all. In the episode "Live Free or Die," (07/15/12), the audience is confronted unexpectedly with a Walt who is living under a false name, and using faked identification, having apparently been driven away from his home, family, and everything which is familiar to both him and *Breaking Bad*'s loyal viewers. This Walt is wholly out of place, cut off from all fields of care, and every meaningful setting with which he has been familiar. After four seasons of Walt's desperate scrabbling for meaning and for his place in the world, he is now adrift. Homeless. Dangerous. What final place Walt will create for himself, and how he will carve it out of the world, remains to be seen. Whatever may happen, viewers around the world have become rooted in the diegetic world of *Breaking Bad*, and with the conclusion of the final season, that place will be sorely missed.

NOTES

1. Interestingly, the two men Walt confronts in the parking-lot have more than a passing resemblance to Walt and Jesse. One is goateed and bald, while the other wears a toboggan and loose, hip-hop inspired clothing. In addition, the two mean are travelling in a large van which is not too dissimilar to Walt and Jesse's RV.
2. For examples of this, see almost any of the RV cooking montages in seasons one through three and the montage of Jesse and Walt's walk out of the desert in "Seven Thirty-Seven" (03/08/09).

WORKS CITED

Bachelard, Gaston. *The Poetics of Space*. trans. Maria Jones. New York: The Orion Press, 1964.
Buttimer, Anne. "Home, Reach, and the Sense of Place," In *The Human Experience of Space and Place*, edited by Anne Buttimer and David Seamon. 73-85. New York: St. Martin's Press, 1980.

Cresswell, Tim. *In Place/Out of Place: Geography, Ideology, and Transgression.* Minneapolis: University of Minnesota Press, 1996.

———. *Place: A Short Introduction.* Oxford: Blackwell Publishing, 2004.

Gilligan, Vince, Bryan Cranston, Aaron Paul, Anna Gunn, Dean Norris, Betsy Brant, and R.J. Mitte. "Audio Commentary on Pilot Episode." *Breaking Bad: The Complete First Season.* DVD. Creator/E.P. Vince Gilligan. Culver City, CA: Sony Pictures Home Entertainment, Inc., 2009.

Godkin, Michael A. "Identity and Place: clinical Applications Based on Notions of Rootedness and Uprootedness." In *The Human Experience of Space and Place,* edited by Anne Buttimer and David Seamon. 73-85. New York: St. Martin's Press, 1980.

Neuman, Clayton. "Music from *Breaking Bad* Season 3." *AMCTV.com.* 2010. 10 October, 2012. http://blogs.amctv.com/breaking-bad/2010/03/season-3-music.php.

———. "Music from *Breaking Bad* Season 4." *AMCTV.com.* 10 October, 2012. http://blogs.amctv.com/breaking-bad/2011/06/season-4-music.php.

Paul, Aaron. "Q and A—Aaron Paul (Jesse Pinkman)." Interview by Eli Rosenberg. 2011. *AMCTV.com.* Accessed 1 November 2012. http://blogs.amctv.com/breaking-bad/2011/07/aaron-paul-interview.php.

Relph, Edward. *Place and Placelessness.* London: Pion Ltd., 1976.

Slovis, Michael. "Inside *Breaking Bad*: Jesse's House." *AMCTV.com.* 2012. 26 October, 2012. http://www.amctv.com/breaking-bad/videos/inside-breaking-bad-jesses-house.

Tuan, Yi-Fu. *Space and Place: The Perspective of Experience.* Minneapolis: University of Minnesota, 1977.

———. "A View of Geography." *Geographical Review* 81, no. 1 (January 1991): 99-107.

TEN

Mediating Fictional Crimes: Music, Morality, and Liquid Identification in *Breaking Bad*

Carlo Nardi

The population inhabiting the fictional world of *Breaking Bad* engages in a wide range of deviant activity: from the main protagonist, Walter White (a.k.a. Walt), to the villainous Gus Fring, his more or less reluctant partners in crime, Jesse Pinkman, Saul Goodman, and Skyler White, and his brother-in-law and adversary, Hank Schrader—every character is bound to transgress social norms, break the law, or both. In fact, a complex web of ethical concerns, desires, regrets, fears, bonds, and matters of honor, as well as problematic risk assessment and management, constitute the rationale fueling the narrative of this serial drama, calling us to witness the metamorphosis of its protagonist from a mild-mannered chemistry teacher into a fearsome drug lord. It is also true that Walt's illegal activity, presented as the inevitable consequence of circumstances, is excused to a certain extent. In particular, Walt finds himself in a state of chronic debt and isolation that is all too familiar to the show's public. Appropriately, Walt can be said to act within what Bauman (2000) describes as liquid modernity, that is, "an individualized, privatized version of modernity, with the burden of pattern-weaving and the responsibility for failure falling primarily on the individual's shoulders. It is the patterns of dependency and interaction whose turn to be liquefied has now come" (7-8). Far from clearing the way to ethical approval, the discomfort of helplessly watching unpleasant facets of Walt's personality and the catastrophic consequences of his actions might cause moral dissonance and problematize identification processes in the viewer.

173

According to disposition theories, character appreciation is linked to moral judgment. Raney (2004) writes,

> [W]hen viewing a drama, we come to like characters whose actions and motivations we judge as proper or morally correct while we dislike characters whose actions and motivations we judge as improper or morally incorrect. . . . This intertwining of affective dispositions and moral judgment permits and governs our emotional involvement in the drama." (350-51)

Raney suggests that affective evaluation can precede moral judgment, meaning that we expect that characters that we already like will be morally upright (356) and be motivated by goodness and justice (357). Character liking is established first and foremost through standard narrative patterns and directorial and production choices that condition viewers' perception of and hence identification with the characters. Predispositions, however, are not unconditional, in that "characters can lose their favored or unfavored status if their behaviors or motivations significantly violate associated expectations, based on initial disposition formation" (357). This is, I argue, precisely what happens in *Breaking Bad*, where a favorable predisposition toward Walt is systematically challenged, through a complex development of the character and his inexorable moral decline.

Walt's initiation into crime takes place when he decides to become a methamphetamine cook in order to leave a nest egg for his family after being diagnosed with terminal lung cancer. At that point, as he downplays his involvement in crime by overemphasizing the neutrality of his role as a skillful chemist, viewers can still recognize an altruistic, although distorted, goal in his choice. However, after a vicious spiral of related actions and reactions, including killing or failing to help a dying person, tampering with the DEA investigations, manipulating his former student Jesse into breaking the law, dodging taxes, and laundering money, his acquired status as a criminal becomes unequivocal. Unsurprisingly, he starts behaving like a rogue at home, too, by forcing his wife to have sex, and offering whiskey to his underage son. At the same time, we witness a series of events that reveal several other unpleasant traits of his character that, while not leading in themselves to outright illicit actions, complete his metamorphosis. They shed light on the uneasy transformation of a seemingly respectable man who, in order to conceal his disreputable second life, repeatedly lies to his family and shows little empathy to those around him, while still believing in his own probity.

In serial drama, it is also through identification with the protagonist's concerns that viewer loyalty is maintained. Since identification with an ambiguous, at times frankly irksome character like Walt can disorient the spectator, however, various narrative and production mechanisms mediate character disposition, alternatively stimulating positive identification, disengagement, and critical distancing in the viewer, thus paving the way for more or less rigorous moral scrutiny. It is worth noting that, even though the events depicted on screen are fictional, the moral codes that viewers bring into play while watching are, on the other hand, real—that is, viewers do not cease to be moral subjects while consuming entertainment. Whereas crime is a common ingredient of drama, allowing for vicarious enjoyment of the pleasures of transgression, fictional representations of crime may intersect with identification processes. As a result, the potential discovery that we have been rooting for the wrong guy may become a cause for concern.

Popular culture has regularly exploited the public's fascination with crime, often capitalizing on the fine line between reality and fiction. In this regard, Ferrell (1999) argues that popular culture and the media do not merely mirror actions and symbolic constructions of crime in the "real" world; rather, criminal acts and cultural representations of crime feed each other in a "hall of mirrors" (397). Consequently, not only is the fictional world of *Breaking Bad* similar to ours, thanks to its realistic depiction of places, characters, and incidents, but it also addresses us as moral subjects, inviting us to confront our understanding of crime and challenge our everyday morality.

To sum up, two opposing dynamics are at work, at the level of the text and the reading respectively: firstly, morally questionable actions challenge character-identification processes; secondly, the psychological dynamics of television spectatorship require some kind of character identification. Characterization is the result of a composite process of writing, direction, production, performance and postproduction, embracing narrative elements in their strict sense, such as events and dialogues, and features such as camera angles and the soundtrack that, while serving a representational function, impose interpretive criteria on the viewer. In particular, I shall explore how a compiled music score encourages or inhibits identification processes as it articulates representations of crime. Drawing on Bauman's concept of liquid modernity and by way of comparison, I shall define this gamut of processes as *liquid identification*: just as Walt finds himself in a "liquid-modern world of flexible norms and floating values" (Bauman 2008, 209), the viewers have to continually renegotiate their identification processes, accommodating the cognitive dissonance resulting from a dissociation of the desire for identification from their moral code.

THE COMPILED SCORE

It is only fairly recently that the use of preexisting music in films has received scholarly attention.[1] Television fiction, however, has specific features that merit a closer look. In fact, the benefit of creating synergies between television and the music industry is based on specific structural premises. In particular, the limited production time available for television series as compared to feature films requires that the time between production and airing be considerably shorter, thus making it possible to promote current popular songs. However, small budgets generally imply more constraints, so that reliance on preexisting music can effectively be a shortcut to lower costs while fulfilling production requirements. Nonetheless, clearance costs can be exceptionally high[2]; hence, the role of the music supervisor, as a mediator between production needs and administrative demands, is especially important.[3] In any case, in an attempt to cut expenses, television-series producers resort extensively to library music, which, as we shall see, can replicate the functions of either the scored or compiled soundtracks, or both.

Unlike the traditional Hollywood film score and its rules of "invisibility" and "inaudibility" (Gorbman 1987, 73), the use of previously recorded material in films is meant to call attention to itself, based on the assumption that its familiarity will draw on preexisting symbolic and emotional bonds to trigger expectations towards the product (Shumway 1999, 36-37). Similarly, Kassabian (2001) argues that, as a general rule, composed and compiled film scores track two different kinds of identification. More precisely, composed scores condition what she calls "assimilating identifications" by drawing the spectator into unfamiliar positions (2). In other words, unlikely identifications with situations or characters demand that the score remain "unheard," to leave narrative functions unaffected by critical reflection. On the other hand, compiled scores condition "affiliating identifications" insofar as they convey symbolic ties that the viewer has established before watching the film: "These ties depend on histories forged outside the film scene, and they allow for a fair bit of mobility within it. If offers of assimilating identifications try to narrow the psychic field, then offers of affiliating identifications open it wide" (3).

While Kassabian's theory has many advantages, in that it provides a simple and coherent model for interpreting film music, it also suffers from some limitations, especially when applied to television fiction. More precisely, close observation of television serials suggests that assimilating identifications are not confined to composed scores; likewise, compiled scores do not necessarily foster affiliating identifications. There are several reasons for this, some of which are shared with film music. Firstly, for compiled scores to work in the way Kassabian suggests, the viewer needs to know the songs beforehand. However, related issues like globalization, changing television technology, and audience diversification show that it is problematic to target specific songs at specific viewers. Secondly, not all the music used for the screen can be assigned to either of the aforementioned categories. I am referring in particular to library music, which cannot establish familiar ties with the audience in the same way that the compiled score can; nonetheless, although it has not been composed to accompany specific visuals, library music can have the same functional characteristics of scored music insofar as it is categorized according to parameters such as mood, tempo and instrumentation[4] (Nardi 2012). Thirdly, as I shall demonstrate, the effect of music on identification processes often relies primarily on factors other than the composed/compiled score dichotomy. Finally, and on a similar note, the compiled score also has narrative functions that can interfere with affiliating identifications. In short, Kassabian's model does not always work, because the distinction between composed and compiled scores is only one of many dimensions of music for the moving image, and not necessarily the most important.

I shall now examine five scenes from *Breaking Bad*, four of which feature a preexisting song and one features an original song that, as such, constitutes a hybrid between a compiled and a composed score. This will allow me to keep one variable (composed/compiled score) essentially constant in order to highlight how other relevant variables, while serving narrative functions, foster or inhibit identification. More precisely, I shall consider the music's source—whether it is heard or not by the characters—and its popularity. Moreover, I shall examine the role of the lyrics and the music, including sound editing and mixing, in relation to both representation and identification. On a detailed level, this theoretical framework will account for how music mediates paths of identification with deviant characters, and in particular with Walt. On a broader level, it will help clarify whether there is a common thread running through these different paths that supports a comprehensive model of identification that is peculiar to *Breaking Bad*—which I have previously defined as *liquid* identification.

SELECTIVE IDENTIFICATION, MORAL RISK, AND DISENGAGEMENT

In the episode "Over" (3/29/09), Skyler throws a party to celebrate the remission of Walt's cancer. As she publicly thanks Walt's former business partners Gretchen and Elliott Schwartz for having paid his medical bills, Walt appears visibly frustrated. He still has grievances with the Schwartzes, who have become billionaires while he has had to settle for a career as a schoolteacher. Moreover, having paid the bills himself through his illegal activity, he probably feels that his self-sufficiency should be acknowledged. Later on, we see Walt putting all his efforts into renovating the house, but this does not meet with his family's favor, either. At the end of the episode, he finally gets his moment, albeit in the underworld. While shopping at a building supply store, Walt bumps into another meth cook. Initially, he gives the young man some unsolicited advice;

however, while waiting in line at the counter, he has second thoughts: he abandons the cart and faces the cook and his sidekick in the parking lot, telling them to keep out of his territory. It is probably here that Walt accepts his criminal identity once and for all. Furthermore, he realizes (and we with him) that there is an element of excitement in crime, and that this excitement can be and end in itself. Indeed, Ferrell (1999) claims that crime subcultures involve "intense and often ritualized moments of pleasure and excitement" (404), so that Walt's activity can be understood as "edgework" (Ferrell, Milovanovic, and Lyng 2001), involving both highly specialized, albeit criminal, skills and the thrill of avoiding arrest.[5] Fiction allows these pleasures of crime to be transferred vicariously to the viewer, preserving the thrill while insulating from actual risk. However, I argue that risk involves not only apprehension but also moral sanctioning, which is as much a social as an interiorized process and as such cannot be completely suspended during television viewing. This does not necessarily mean that viewers judge fictional characters in the same way that they judge real people, nor that they lack a sense of reality, but rather that they remain moral subjects while watching serial dramas. Consequently, identification with media characters that are dissonant with the viewer's moral code can be problematic and can require some form of mediation. In this regard, moral disengagement (Bandura 2002) allows for a selective application of moral codes, "redefining harmful conduct as honorable by moral justification, exonerating social comparison, and sanitizing language" (102). Accordingly, viewers apply attitude-maintenance strategies in order to maintain cognitive harmony toward liked characters (Raney 2004, 360).

The song that accompanies this scene is "DLZ" by the American indie band TV on the Radio. Released as a track (not a single) on the album *Dear Science*, it reached No. 12 on the US Billboard chart and received a very positive critical response. Yet, "DLZ" in itself can hardly be considered a widely popular song. Here it is not so much the individual song but its genre and sound, mixing punk and electronica, that the viewer can link to other familiar cases. This suggests that, although "DLZ" can also work analogously to the compiled score, it most probably works in a hybrid way, fostering affiliating as well as assimilating identification. Other elements support this hypothesis, starting from the heavy editing on the song.[6] Specifically, only the lyrics adding interpretive depth to the story have been preserved: we have the entire first stanza, containing the verse "Congratulations on the mess you made of things" and the word "Oxidation," followed, as in the original, by a wordless refrain in which Walt says his line, and an edited collage of verses, including "Never you mind, death professor," "Your victim flies so high," and "It's crystallized, so am I." These images fit so well that it is almost surprising that "DLZ" was not composed specially for the series.[7] Moreover, the music, which is mixed exceptionally loud in the soundtrack, reaches a dynamic peak, first intensifying the tension of the confrontation and then granting release, as the antagonists surrender. In fact, the song, like dramatic scoring, involves the spectator in an emotional climax that is calculated to function as a means of empathizing with Walt's rancorous feelings and his overdue gratification.

There are also directorial and performance elements that emphasize Walt's line, like the low-angle shot on Walt while he faces his more threatening rivals, and Bryan Cranston's minimalist acting—a stiff walk, a subtle twist of his neck and a murmured utterance—reminiscent here of Clint Eastwood's classic macho characters. It is also this set of elements that fosters identification with the antihero. Nonetheless, I want to stress the role of music in mediating both Walt's desire for revenge and his newly acknowledged identity, while establishing a dual process of identification that is mainly rooted in what Kassabian (2001) calls "assimilating identification" but does not preclude affiliating identification as well: on one hand, the song, working as dramatic scoring, draws the viewers into "socially . . . unfamiliar positions" (2); on the other, it can enable those who know the song or are familiar with its genre to identify positively with the main character's feelings. Identification is also assisted by narrative development. On a moral level, Walt's recognized excellence as a meth cook and the trials and tribulations he has undergone to reach this status, may justify his territorial claim. At the same time, the shift in the viewer's attention from the wider frame of the drug business to a dispute between the central character and two thugs may favor moral disengagement by inhibiting moral sanctioning (Bandura 2002) of Walt's aggressive behavior, hence understating his role in causing harm.

The ambiguity of this process of identification has an advantage, in that it singles out any positive affinities with the fictional character while ignoring his most troubling features; the disadvantage is that viewers might "excuse" Walt "through music" (see MacRory 1999). In other words, as we are invited to step into Walt's shoes based on an emotional affiliation, reflecting on the moral propriety of his actions appears not only unimportant but also very challenging.

FROM SYMPATHY TO NOSTALGIA

Unlike *mood music*, which communicates emotions, and *identification music*, which communicates details about characters, period, or place, *commentary music* is used to contradict the visuals, challenge the narrative, or expose the means of representation. If "mood is more often associated with (unconscious) identification processes . . . commentary often requests reflective evaluation" (Kassabian 2001, 59). Commentary includes the use of music for comedic purposes, "one that comments on the situation depicted in a film either through its lyrical content or through an extramusical system of pop culture references"[8] (Smith 2001, 408). This effect is achieved not through preexisting emotional bonds but by means of musical and verbal intertextuality at the level of individual work, artist, period, music style, or genre. Intertextuality produces pleasure in many ways, first of all by engaging the spectator in a gratifying game of interpretation. Moreover, screen music can itself be a source of pleasure; hence, it is not necessarily subordinated to the story[9] or the visuals. This is especially true for music videos, which, rather than being "non-narrative" (Vernallis 2008), show "extraordinary degrees of repetition and stability at the aural level" (Goodwin 1993, 42), imposing a musical order on the visuals (38).

The two sequences that I shall consider display remarkable creativity and a conscious engagement with the aesthetics of music videos. Both sequences consist of a montage glued together by a theme and an extradiegetic song[10] that contrasts with that theme. More precisely, in both instances, a dramatic situation is ironically juxtaposed with a cheerful song that references, among other things, youth and hippie culture. The ironic effect is created by a formal conflict between the visual track, which has primacy at the level of realistic representation, and the sound track, which, by calling attention to itself rather than being "unheard" and by imposing its structure and rhythm on the visuals, allows music to act as a commentary on the visual track.[11] The resulting ambiguity, I argue, will demand either critical reflection or condition temporary disengagement, according not only to character liking and expectations but also to the capacity to tolerate cognitive dissonance and the willingness to invest energy in moral monitoring.

The first of the two sequences, from the episode "Full Measure" (6/13/10), uses the song "Windy" to play on the assonance with Wendy, the name of a secondary character, a drug addict and prostitute. Smith (2001) borrows from Arthur Koestler the concept of *bisociation* to indicate ". . . the movement between two associative chains of logic, each of which represents a distinct interpretive frame. According to Koestler, humor arises from the juxtaposition of these two associative chains to create two incongruous ways of seeing something, such as a person, sentence, or situation" (416). Similarly, "Windy" is at once congruous and incongruous with the visuals: by way of illustration, the verse "Who's bending down to give me a rainbow" is juxtaposed to images of Wendy bending down to give oral sex to her customers. On the other hand, it is clear that the song's character does not have the same tragic traits associated with Wendy. At the same time, any humor arising from this juxtaposition is challenged by the chance that viewers might sympathize with Wendy, especially after her courageous resolution to help Jesse take revenge on a young boy's killers. However, her secondary role and the nature of her character, including her being portrayed as a victim, complicate identification processes. Consequently, while this sequence can still be understood as a one-off spectacle to be enjoyed for its stylistic and thematic wit, irony might possibly trigger a critical reflection capable of tracking sentiments like sympathy or compassion.

In the second example, the song "Crystal Blue Persuasion," included in the episode "Gliding Over All" (9/2/12), accompanies a brilliant sequence showing the production and distribution chain of Walt's blue-meth business. Visually, the sequence displays an associational method of montage that avoids fades and uses cues and opposite movements of the camera, zooming in or out on similar objects, or panning continuously through different environments. The song, which like "Windy" was a hit in the late 1960s, expresses hope for peace and brotherhood, again acting as a commentary on the visuals.[12] Here, the bisociative element mainly comprises the words blue *and* crystal, which have different meanings in the song and in relation to Walt's activity.[13] There are other puns that play on double entendre: for example, during the verse "People are changing," we see drug trader and Madrigal attorney Lydia, indicating that Walt's business partners have changed; with the verse "Love, love is the answer," we see Skyler laundering money, as, by this time, viewers have acknowledged that her love for Walt has gone.

Irony blooms at the musical level, too, with the gravity of the meth business contrasted with a psychedelic pop song with a West Coast hippie feel and a Latin flair.[14] Here, again, music does not seem to track identification with the characters; rather, it contributes to a sense of estrangement that overshadows the fun of the puns. More precisely, "Crystal Blue Persuasion" brings in an element of nostalgia as if, for Walt and his associates, things have changed forever. Tincknell (2006) argues that recourse to the nostalgia effect in films will inevitably affect the meaning and value of the quoted text, "restructuring . . . the past at the level of style" (135).[15] This prompts us to ask if *Breaking Bad* actually constructs the drug business as style, employing a distancing mechanism not as a means to stimulate criticism but in order to refrain from a serious engagement with the most troubling issues about drugs. Insofar as stylization produces temporary moral disengagement, identification processes can be reestablished in subsequent scenes, allowing viewers to empathize with Walt once again on less troubling moral domains, when he deals with his financial concerns or faces ruthless gangsters.

To sum up, in both examples, a preexisting popular song is used to mediate and, partly, defy identification processes. In the first case, distancing is aimed at provoking a critical reflection on drug addiction; if the mechanism is successful, then we can expect the spectator to sympathize with Wendy. The second example is perhaps more ambiguous; here again, commentary generates detachment, but this is complemented by a skillful stylization of the main character's successful activity. Stylization might engender critical reflection and thus distancing or, instead, suspension of judgment, hence allowing for new positive identification with

Walt. However, needless to say, it is not possible to infer solely from a textual analysis which of the two responses will be favored, because an audience analysis would be required.

THE EXPANSION OF THE DIEGETIC SPACE

Diegetic music comes from a source within the fictional world, while nondiegetic or extradiegetic music is external to it. This distinction, borrowed from narratology, raises both conceptual and practical problems when translated to audiovisual media.[16] Supposing that we agree on a common definition of diegesis,[17] the diegetic/nondiegetic distinction neglects all those instances that do not fit in either of the two categories, and most of all, it "obscures music's role in producing the diegesis itself" (Kassabian 2001, 42).[18] This assumed, I shall now analyze two sequences in which, for reasons that I shall soon clarify, music not only constructs the fictional space but also conveys the idea that this construction goes beyond what can be heard and seen on screen. In other words, the viewer is invited to pay attention to what the music hints or omits, as much as to what it says, about the diegesis.

The episode "Negro Y Azul" (4/19/09) opens with a song in the *narcocorrido* style about Heisenberg, Walt's alias in the drug trafficking world.[19] As a music genre, the *narcocorrido* is a fairly recent development of the Mexican *corrido*, sharing with it, among other things, a ballad structure.[20] Although both deal with controversial themes involving lawbreaking and rebellion, narcocorridos appropriate subjects such as oppression, poverty, and national pride to praise peasants and drug traffickers, united in their fight against the common enemy embodied especially by transnational companies and the United States.

Narcocorridos circulate on the Internet, too, in the form of music videos marked by low-budget production values as well as by aesthetic and narrative choices, including standardized digital visual effects, the combination of original and television footage, and camera tricks, such as low-angle shots of the performers. "Negro Y Azul" draws on this imagery and mimics the style of narcocorrido songs and music videos to celebrate the quality of the blue meth and spread the aura of mystery surrounding Heisenberg, as it emerges that a Mexican drug cartel has sentenced him to death.

The sequence can be understood as a postmodern parody due to its use of quotations and intertextuality, its emphasis on stylistic features, and its puzzling mix of reality, fiction, and metafiction: in an ironic twist, it features a fictional narcocorrido about the metafictional alter ego of a fictional character, performed by a real band, Los Cuates de Sinaloa. Nevertheless, this reading might obscure the song's functions within the overall narrative. In particular, it is worth investigating how this sequence manages to open up the diegetic space at least in two ways. First of all, "Negro Y Azul" occupies an ambivalent position within the story: because no character reacts to it, we may tend to consider it a tongue-in-cheek aside. On the other hand, this does not rule out the possibility that we are actually receiving a confidential piece of information that is inaccessible to Walt: after all, the narcocorrido culture is as far from his everyday world as could be. But this sequence expands the diegesis in another different sense, too, in that its ambiguity and intertextual references call for the audience to join the dots. Consequently, it is perhaps not surprising that fans have been engaged in lively discussions as to whether the song belongs to the fictional world or not, and whether it anticipates future events in a similar way to the flash-forwards that open other episodes.[21] In any case, this sequence demands an aware engagement with the narrative construction. The sequence's metadiegetic status (neither fully diegetic nor completely extradiegetic) and the liminal status of the music video (both narrative and spectacular, realistic and nonrealistic) allow the music to transcend its functions of dramatic development or "myth" (Brown 1994) to engage the viewer in complicit identification with the authorial voice. In this sense, a distancing effect is achieved through what Fiske (2010) calls the producerly text:

> It draws attention to its own textuality, it does not produce a singular reading subject but one that is involved in the process of representation rather than a victim of it, it plays with the difference between the representation and the real . . . and it replaces the pleasures of identification and familiarity with more cognitive pleasures of participation and production. (95)

This grants viewers a perspective from which to take a more objective look at the consequences of Walt's actions.

The last sequence that I analyze consists of a succinct sketch of the private life of Gale Boetticher, Walt's chemist assistant and designated successor in Gus's meth laboratory, at the end of the episode "Full Measure," which I have discussed earlier. Gale is shown singing along to an old Italian swing song, "Crapapelada," while preparing tea and watering plants.[22] In the meantime, we see a view of his flat, which is full of books, memorabilia, a telescope, a hookah, a potato-powered clock, and rugs aplenty, in sharp and deliberate contrast with Walt's dull, spartan apartment. The thrilling effect of the scene arises because, even as we are getting acquainted with Gale's intriguing personality, we already know that Walt has sent Jesse to kill him.

In all likelihood, the song is unknown to the audience, so that it can hardly work to track affiliating identifications in the way that Kassabian suggests. On the other hand, there are many elements of Gale's characterization that could work in that direction. In fact, Gale, unlike the other characters, is not greedy or aggressive, and he has a keen interest in science, ethnic cultures, literature, and even social anarchism. He is not a passive consumer but has a refined and unconventional music taste that transcends the borders of American popular culture. Furthermore, not only does he choose his music, but he also knows it well enough to sing along. It may reasonably be argued that Gale has more in common with *Breaking Bad* viewers than does Walt, and he would therefore be an ideal target for positive identification processes. Nevertheless, identification with him would be problematic, firstly because we already know his fate, and secondly because he has become a rival to the protagonist, who, as such, is still a more likely target for identification. Again, the music works to defy identification processes, although in a different way than in the sequence with "Windy" during the same episode. At the same time, since the music is both "visible" and "audible" (Gorbman 1987, 73), it is unlikely that it works as dramatic scoring to track assimilating identification. It is indeed diegetic music, in that its source belongs to Gale's world, but its function is not merely descriptive or realistic. Rather, together with the other details of the mise-en-scene, the oddity of the song and Gale's somewhat surprising ability to master its intricate melody—unlike his own fate—manage to complicate the story further, ultimately inviting us to extend the diegetic space beyond the text.[23] Once again, as spectators, we are stuck between sympathy and bemusement before identification can take place.

But there is a further element that adds to the text's indeterminacy: at the end of the episode—the season's finale—Jesse faces Gale with a gun, we hear a gunshot, but we do not see Gale being hit. Interestingly, many viewers refused to accept that Jesse had actually killed Gale—an eventuality that producer Vince Gilligan had not anticipated.[24] The point is that identification with Walt and Jesse, whom viewers struggle to think of as cold-blooded killers, induced viewers to infer conclusions that, to paraphrase Bunia (2010), are not explicitly conveyed by a representation. What I argue is that the condition for this (mis)interpretation is not limited to Gale's implicit death but is also due to the role that music plays in enticing and puzzling viewers at the same time. That is, by implying that (fictional) reality is more complicated than it may appear at first sight (and at first listen), this sequence demands an interpretive effort that breaches the confines of the text to involve the viewer in the construction of an expanded diegesis. In this way, the producerly text becomes a platform for a selective application of moral codes in order to maintain cognitive consistency with character disposition or, alternatively, an opportunity for monitoring characters' moral behavior—a task that may require, once again, a significant expenditure of cognitive resources and the capacity to cope with cognitive dissonance. Moreover, the chance to discuss this expanded diegetic space with others can increase viewing pleasure, making the producerly text a collective rather than an individual endeavor.

CONCLUSION

Not only is music of central importance in *Breaking Bad,* it also plays multi-dimensional roles in the series, thus affecting character liking and mediating identification processes. The need to maintain bonding (especially, but not necessarily only) with Walt throughout the series, or, in other words, to keep viewers interested enough to watch each new episode—an essential feature of serial drama—is continuously challenged by his becoming involved in actions that viewers may well find morally repugnant. In fact, the dissonance between the viewer's moral code and Walt's troubling wrongdoings can impact negatively on identification processes. To obviate this, *Breaking Bad* employs various strategies that allow for temporary shifts in identification while also using more subtle techniques that simultaneously prompt identification and detachment, engaging the spectator in Walt's concerns through emotional affinities, while glossing over the consequences of his actions for society at large.

The ambivalence of identification processes in *Breaking Bad* implies that *liquidity* is not just an option but a condition that viewers have to negotiate throughout the series. This is because we realize that there is no higher morality justifying Walt's efforts to defend his drug empire, just as there is no grand narrative to make sense of his initial impasse. Instead, viewers are faced with the deterioration of social bonds as a structural condition of late modernity—viewers share this condition with Walt, who experiences it on screen, and around this similarity, identification, albeit unsteadily, is built.

NOTES

1. See, in particular, Vernallis (2008); Powrie and Stilwell (2006); Tincknell (2006); Lannin and Caley (2005); Wojcik and Knight (2001); Kassabian (2001); Mundy (1999); Smith (1998); Romney and Wootton (1995).

2. "The growing demand for popular recordings in film, television, and advertising," writes Smith (2001), "has driven up licensing revenues at a comparable rate. EMI-Capitol Music, for example, has seen its master licensing business nearly quintuple since 1989. Likewise . . . the costs of using a particular recording over a film's opening credits are now five to ten times higher than what they were ten years ago" (412).

3. Not surprisingly, *Breaking Bad* music supervisor Thomas Golubić has been a member of the crew throughout all five seasons.

4. This kind of hybrid scoring is predominant in relatively low-budget, quickly packaged—as compared to cinema—television series, and *Breaking Bad* is no exception.

5. See also Presdee (2000) on the ritualizing of transgression, and Katz (1988) on the seductions of crime.

6. This hybrid characteristic also arises because an existing song is recomposed to fit into the audiovisual text. This suggests, among other things, that the concept of musical scoring should be revised to include editing and mixing.

7. In an interview, Thomas Golubić describes the moment he found the song: "It was one of the key scenes in Walt's transformation from teacher to meth cook, and I found TV On The Radio's 'DLZ' at like 3 a.m. There was nobody to celebrate with but my cat who had no idea why I was so deliriously happy at that hour. I can't imagine another song in that scene, and thankfully we were able to beg, borrow, and steal to afford it" (Ray 2012).

8. As Smith (2001) continues, ". . . the use of popular music in such ironic modes has become an ever more important part of cinematic signification. In fact, within the film industry, music supervisors commonly refer to such locutions as 'joke cues', and they must be identified as such when requesting copyright clearance from the song's publisher or the recording artist's record label" (408).

9. Indeed, as Gorbman (1987) writes: "The organizing structure of [classical Hollywood] films . . . is, precisely, a classical narrative with its own demands for pacing, development, spatiotemporal structure, and so on. Music is subordinated to the narrative's demands" (2). The influence of Gorbman's theory—which referred explicitly to classical Hollywood films—on subsequent studies of screen music should not make us forget that music does not function in the same way in every audiovisual text, especially those in which music is supposed to be in the foreground.

10. I shall use the term extradiegetic for music that apparently does not issue from the fictional world inhabited by the characters. The term is somewhat misleading, however, as all the music helps to construct the diegesis. I shall return to this point later.

11. Neither scene has source sound; this choice can be understood not only as a means to lend continuity to the montage but also as a way to amplify the separation between the visual track (realism) and the sound track (commentary).

12. Unlike "DLZ," neither of the two songs has been edited, except for the fadeout at the end of "Windy," which in the series starts slightly earlier.

13. According to Tommy James, one of the song's authors, the color blue was meant to have religious connotations. Allegedly, some listeners believed instead it referred to drugs. On this regard, see the interview, "Tommy James," *Songfacts*, accessed 12 October 2012, http://www.songfacts.com/blog/interviews/tommy_james/.

14. Previously, there have been other montages showing meth manufacturing and dealing with the accompaniment of contrasting music. In passing, it is worth noting that all these sequences are set to Latin music, making this a good example of self-reflexivity.

15. Booker (2007) argues that nostalgia is a prevalent mode in postmodern film and television, where it is not necessarily linked to personal experience or historical truth: "Postmodern nostalgia is more mediated by culture than are earlier forms of nostalgia. ... By focusing on culture, postmodern representations of the past tend to be doubly mediated because they are representations of remembered representations" (51).

16. While the meaning of diegetic, nondiegetic and extradiegetic music is sometimes taken for granted in case studies, several authors have attempted to problematize it. For a comprehensive summary, see Winters (2010).

17. Bunia (2010) contends that the term "diegesis," notwithstanding its widespread use, lacks a coherent definition. More precisely, when it is used to identify the narrated world, the related concept of extradiegesis tends to break down. Accordingly, he suggests a narrower definition of diegesis as information explicitly conveyed by a representation. I shall later show how this definition is also not without problems.

18. Music, Winter (2010) argues, occupies the same space of the events directly represented: "Trying to imagine the opening idol-stealing scenes of *Raiders of the Lost Ark* ... without John Williams's music is, I would suggest, an unnerving experience" (230).

19. The song, also entitled "Negro Y Azul," has been written by Mexican performer, composer and artist promoter Pepe Garza, who adapted Vince Gilligan's lyrics in Spanish and into a *narcocorrido* structure.

20. In the past decade there has been a growing interest in *narcocorridos*; see in particular, Ramírez-Pimienta (2011; 2004); Villalobos and Ramírez-Pimienta (2004); Valenzuela Arce (2002); Wald (2001); Simonett (2001).

21. I have found these comments on YouTube discussions and online forums, such as "Negro Y Azul," *A.V. Club*, accessed 12 October 2012, http://www.avclub.com/articles/negro-y-azul,26858/ and "Episode 7: Negro Y Azul," *AMC*, accessed 12 October 2012, http://www.amctv.com/shows/breaking-bad/episodes/season-2/negro-y-azul.

22. The song "Crapapelada" was composed by Gorni Kramer (music) and Tata Giacobetti (lyrics) in 1936, therefore during the fascist regime, while the version used in the series was recorded in 1945 some months after the Liberation. The title of the song is the equivalent for "bald head" in Milanese dialect and allegedly was a way to make fun of Mussolini while avoiding censorship. Interestingly, some fans interpret the song as a riddle and discuss on YouTube and in other forums whether it is a reference to Walt's shaved head.

23. This sequence, surely supported by David Costabile's remarkable performance (he is a trained classical singer) as Gale, leaves us with the impression that this character would have many more surprises in store for us, were he given more fictional time to live. In fact, in a later episode ("Bullet Points"), Gale reappears while performing in a Thai karaoke booth (we can recognize it from the Thai subtitles). His passionate performance of Peter Schilling's English version of "Major Tom" and the exotic setting add further mystery to this character. The scene with this video, recorded on a DVD that has been sized as body of evidence in Gale's flat after his murder, allows us to compare Hank's sarcastic reaction at "Albuquerque's public enemy number one," to Walt's enigmatic concern, which is left to the viewer to interpret: does he feel guilty that he has killed such a friendly and positive person? Or is he just worried for himself, as he foresees clues that may lead to his identification? Or rather, is he outraged that this bizarre guy, passing for Heisenberg, is taking all the credit for the purest blue meth that has been such a big hit?

24. "Gilligan's intention with the scene was to have Jesse hit his target. But viewers found it so hard to believe that Paul's sensitive, soulful character could commit cold-blooded murder—debates raged in fan forums—that Gilligan reconsidered, opening the season-four writers' room 'with a long and spirited discussion of whether we should actually have Aaron go through with it.' Paul's performance was that powerful" (Romano 2011, par. 19).

WORKS CITED

Bandura, Albert. "Selective Moral Disengagement in the Exercise of Moral Agency." *Journal of Moral Education*. 31(2) (2002): 101-119.

Bauman, Zygmunt. *Liquid Modernity*. Cambridge and Malden, MA: Polity Press, 2000.

———. *Does Ethics Have a Chance in a World of Consumers?* Cambridge and London: Harvard University Press, 2008.

Booker, M. Keith. *Postmodern Hollywood: What's New in Film and Why It Makes Us Feel So Strange*. Westport and London: Praeger Publishers, 2007.

Brown, Royal S. *Overtones and Undertones: Reading Film Music*. Berkeley: University of California Press, 1994.

Bunia, Remigius. "Diegesis and Representation: Beyond the Fictional World, on the Margins of Story and Narrative." *Poetics Today*. 31:4. (2010): 679-720.

Ferrell, Jeff. *Crimes of Style: Urban Graffiti and the Politics of Criminality*. Boston: Northeastern University Press, 1996.

———. "Cultural criminology." *Annual Review of Sociology*. 25. (1999): 395-418.

Ferrell, Jeff, Dragan Milovanovic and Stephen Lyng. "Edgework, Media Practices, and the Elongation of Meaning." *Theoretical Criminology*. 5:2. (2001): 177-202.

Fiske, John. *Television Culture*. 2nd ed. Abingdon and New York: Routledge, 2010.

Goodwin, Andrew. "Fatal Distractions: MTV Meets Postmodern Theory." In *Sound and Vision: The Music Video Reader*, edited by Simon Frith, Andrew Goodwin and Lawrence Grossberg. 37-56. London: Routledge, 1993.

Gorbman, Claudia. *Unheard Melodies: Narrative Film Music*. Bloomington and Indianapolis: Indiana University Press, 1987.

Kassabian, Anahid. *Hearing Film: Tracking Identifications in Contemporary Hollywood Film Music*. New York and London: Routledge, 2001.

Katz, Jack. *Seductions of Crime*. New York: Basic Books, 1988.

Lannin, Steve and Matthew Caley, eds. *Pop Fiction: The Song in Cinema*. Bristol and Portland: Intellect, 2005.

MacRory, Pauline. "Excusing the Violence of Hollywood Women: Music in *Nikita* and *Point of No Return*." *Screen*. 40:1. (1999): 51-65.

Mundy, John. *Popular Music on Screen: From Hollywood Musical to Music Video*. Manchester: Manchester University Press, 1999.

Nardi, Carlo. "Library Music: Technology, Copyright and Authorship." In *Issues in Music Research: Copyright, Power And Transnational Musical Processes*, edited by Salwa El-Shawan Castelo-Branco et al., 73-83. Lisbon: SIBE, 2012.

Powrie, Phil and Robynn Stilwell, eds. *Changing Tunes: The Use of Pre-existing Music in Film*. Aldershot and Burlington: Ashgate, 2006.

Presdee, Mike. *Cultural Criminology and the Carnival of Crime*. London and New York: Routledge, 2000.

Quartetto Cetra. "Crapapelada." B-side of "Peppone il calciatore." Cetra. AA 421. Vinyl Single Record. 1945.

Ramírez-Pimienta, Juan Carlos. "Del Corrido de Narcotráfico al Narcocorrido: Orígenes y Desarrollo del Canto a los Traficantes." *Studies in Latin American Popular Culture*. XXIII. (2004): 21-41.

———. *Cantar a Los Narcos: Voces y Versos del Narcocorrido*. Mexico City: Editorial Planeta, 2011.

Raney, Arthur A. "Expanding Disposition Theory: Reconsidering Character Liking, Moral Evaluations, and Enjoyment." *Communication Theory*. 14:4. (2004): 348-369.

Ray, Austin L. "The Chemistry Behind the Music in 'Breaking Bad'." *MTV Hive*. 16 July 2012. http://www.mtvhive.com/2012/07/16/breaking-bad-music/.

Romano, Andrew. "The Most Dangerous Show on Television." *Newsweek*. 158:2. 4 July, 2011. 58-63.

Romney, Jonathan and Adrian Wootton, eds. *Celluloid Jukebox: Popular Music and the Movies since the 50 s*. London: BFI, 1995.

Shumway, David R. "Rock 'n' Roll Sound Tracks and the Production of Nostalgia." *Cinema Journal*. 38:2. (1999): 36-51.

Simonett, Helena. "Narcocorridos: An Emerging Micromusic of Nuevo L.A." *Ethnomusicology*. 45:2. (2001): 315-337.

Smith, James. "Popular Songs and Comic Allusion in Contemporary Cinema." In *Soundtrack Available: Essays on Film and Popular Music*, edited by Pamela Robertson Wojcik and Arthur Knight. 407-430. Durham and London: Duke University Press, 2001.

Smith, Jeff. *The Sounds of Commerce: Marketing Popular Film Music*. New York: Columbia University Press, 1998.

The Association. "Windy." Warner Brothers, 1967. 7041. Vinyl Single Record.

Tincknell, Estella. "The Soundtrack Movie, Nostalgia and Consumption." In *Film's Musical Moments*, edited by Ian Conrich and Estella Tincknell. 132-145. Edinburgh: Edinburgh University Press, 2006.

Tommy James and The Shondells. "Crystal Blue Persuasion." Roulette. R 7050. Vinyl Single Record, 1969.

TV On The Radio. "DLZ." On *Dear Science*. Interscope. 2008. CAD2821CD. CD.

Valenzuela Arce, José Manuel. 2002. *Jefe de Jefes: Corridos y Narcocultura en México*. Mexico City: Plaza y Janés.

Vernallis, Carol. "Music Video, Songs, Sound: Experience, Technique and Emotion in *Eternal Sunshine of the Spotless Mind*." *Screen*. 49:3. (2008): 277-197.

Villalobos, José Pablo and Juan Carlos Ramírez-Pimienta. "'Corridos' and 'la Pura Verdad': Myths and Realities of the Mexican Ballad." *South Central Review*. 21. (Fall 2004): 129-149.

Wald, Elijah. *Narcocorrido: A Journey Into the Music of Drugs, Guns, and Guerrillas*. New York: HarperCollins, 2001.

Winters, Ben. "The Non-diegetic Fallacy: Film, Music, and Narrative Space." *Music and Letters*. 91:2. (2010): 224-244.

Wojcik, Pamela Robertson and Arthur Knight, Eds. *Soundtrack Available: Essays on Film and Popular Music*. Durham and London: Duke University Press, 2001.

ELEVEN

Feeling Bad: Emotions and Narrativity in *Breaking Bad*

E. Deidre Pribram

In an interview that took place in January 1984, five months before his death, Michel Foucault relates an anecdote to illustrate what he means by 'relations of power':

> For example, the fact that I may be older than you, and that you may initially have been intimidated, may be turned around during the course of our conversation, and I may end up being intimidated before someone precisely because he is younger than I am. (292)

His is a simple, almost offhand anecdote but one that has lingered in my mind precisely because of the inadequate means we possess to explain what occurs during this modest encounter and exchange.

In the interview, Foucault (1987) seeks to describe what he means by coercive power or states of domination versus strategies or relations of power. His interviewers remain more concerned with notions of dominance while Foucault repeatedly returns to relations of power that, for him, are both necessary to human society and quite ordinary. He acknowledges that states of domination do exist, in which power relations "are perpetually asymmetrical and allow an extremely limited margin of freedom" or strategy (292). In such situations, although the power differential cannot be reversed, certain strategies of resistance remain possible. Still, even a severely limited field of resistance constitutes the deployment of power relations.

Foucault (1987) is taking exception to the belief that his work is associated with a lack of freedom or agency, that "because power is everywhere, there is no freedom" (292). Quite the contrary, he insists, "if there are relations of power in every social field, this is because there is freedom everywhere" (291-292). Foucault is arguing that relations of power are linked with freedom and resistance, not static dominance or social paralysis. Instead, "in human relations, whether they involve verbal communication...or amorous, institutional, or economic relationships, power is always present" (291-292). Further, "these power relations are mobile, they can be modified, they are not fixed once and for all" (292). Power relations can only exist to the degree in which subjects are free and capable of some form of resistance. Without some measure to act, there would be no power relations, only powerlessness: stasis and solidification in social relations, rather than mobility and mutability.

And because such power relations appear everywhere in the social field, often occurring in minute and ordinary ways, he selects a suitably mundane anecdote as his example. His anecdote constitutes an instance of what he designates as "verbal communication" rather than amorous, institutional, or economic relations. At the outset the older participant possesses the ability to intimidate the younger. By the end, however, some modification has occurred so that the younger now intimidates the elder. In this minor event, the kind that transpires multiple times a day in every person's life, the recalibration of a power differential, however small, has taken place.

Perhaps initially age is associated with wisdom and the older party is treated with, and expects, the power to intimidate that attaches to respect or veneration. Then, in the process of conversation, alternative implications of age are taken up. Age may emerge as the sign of generational change in which the involved parties either wish to or are forced to recognize the passing of expertise from one generation to the next. Intimidation by a younger other may be precipitated through being made aware of one's own dwindling intellectual powers or influence. The meaning of 'age' modulates over the course of the conversation. Initially, the power to intimidate through age belongs to the older individual but during their discussion alternate meanings are produced and negotiated, with the result that the advantage of age—in the sense of being able to intimidate— shifts to the younger individual.

However, what Foucault fails to specify about his anecdote is that the relations of power he describes are enabled and enacted through emotions. Emotional dynamics render possible the negotiation and exchange of altered relations, in this instance whether through fear, awe, respect, sadness over diminished vigor, or other feelings entirely. Further, the emotions engaged and exchanged are quite likely different for each of the participating parties. Yet, regardless of the specific emotions put into play, they function as strategies in the circulation of power relations.

Foucault describes transactions of power relations as the ongoing set of circumstances "in which one person tries to control the conduct of the other" (292). I am suggesting a somewhat different understanding, in which such power relations refer to situations in which one person attempts to *affect* the conduct of others. In Foucault's example, age is saturated with emotional meanings that become realized once they are *felt*. Emotions fluctuate, meanings are transmitted and accepted, rejected, or amended with the result that power differentials, however slight, become altered. The interrelationality of emotions, meaning, and power enables such routine, unceasing transactions. Emotions are strategies that allow such moves and counter-moves, negotiations and exchanges to occur. In order to elaborate on power relations as emotional strategies, I now turn from Foucault's simple anecdote to the more complex narrative of AMC's *Breaking Bad*.

EMOTIONAL ACTION

I have argued elsewhere that emotional action—usually described as 'talk' or character interaction—constitutes a form of narrative action as significant as physical or bodily endeavor (Pribram 2011). Yet acts of physicality are normally what we refer to when we speak of filmic or televisual action.

However, emotional action, like bodily activity, shapes and propels a narrative. If we understand action as that which impels and, ultimately, resolves the narrative problems posed, then narrativity is more accurately understood as a dialectic relationship between emotional action and physical action. In these terms, a narrative becomes the accumulated effects of both forms of action. In contrast, film and television studies largely have established an erroneous dichotomy based either on emotional talk or physical action, rather than tracing the crucial relationship between them as equally productive modes of action in popular narrative forms.[1]

The relationship between emotional and physical action is made evident in the initial episodes of the series, *Breaking Bad*, because the usual trajectory of developing characters through dialogue and interaction with other characters, which then builds to resolution through physical confrontation, becomes reversed. In the most familiar analysis of narrative structure, character development through the establishment of social and emotional stakes exists in order to 'set-up' some later climactic physical confrontation. In this configuration, physical acts are viewed as that which generates the resolution of the social and emotional stakes earlier placed in jeopardy.

In contrast, the first episodes in season one of *Breaking Bad* sustain a series of fast-paced, exciting events culminating in the talking sequence or "verbal communication" between Walter White (Bryan Cranston) and Krazy-8 (Max Arciniega) in the third episode, ". . . And the Bag's in the River" (2/10/08). The normal narrative sequence is inverted so that physical action serves as establishing activity that leads to an emotional dramatic payoff.

Focusing only on the scenes that involve Walter, the pilot episode of season one (1/20/08) begins with a mysterious pair of pants falling from air to ground in slow motion, followed by shots of an RV driving frantically. In the front, sit a pantless Walter and an unconscious Jesse Pinkman (Aaron Paul), both wearing gas masks. In the back, we spot two male bodies on the floor—either unconscious or dead. They slide around uncontrollably in response to the frenetic movements of the RV. Presented as a series of quick cuts and rapid changes of camera angles, Walter then accidentally runs the RV off the road as, in the distance, we hear police sirens. Walter grabs a gun from one of the male bodies and exits the RV, where he videotapes a farewell message for his family. He then raises the gun, aiming it at what we assume are the oncoming police. We then cut to the events leading up to this moment beginning, as a title tells us, "Three Weeks Earlier."

In swift succession, we see Walter turn fifty, teach a high school chemistry class, work a humiliating second job at a car wash for the sorely needed money, suddenly pass out and get taken to the hospital by ambulance, and learn he has inoperable lung cancer. Later, he goes for a ride-along with his DEA brother-in-law, Hank (Dean Norris), to the take down of a meth lab. Here he encounters his former student, Jesse, who has managed to escape the drug raid. Cornering Jesse later, Walter threatens to turn him into the DEA if Jesse refuses to partner with him in making and selling methamphetamine. Having no choice but to agree, Jesse purchases an RV in which to cook the meth, which the two do in the desert beyond Albuquerque.

Jesse takes the pure-grade crystal meth to Krazy-8 to sell. However, he is forced by Krazy-8 and Emilio (John Koyama) at gunpoint to lead them to the RV in the desert to show them where he obtained the drugs. In order to save his and Jesse's lives, Walter agrees to show Krazy-8 and Emilio how to make the pure meth. Instead, he concocts a mixture that causes an explosion, rendering Krazy-8 and Emilio unconscious and presumably dead or dying, while he and Jesse escape by donning gas masks.

Walter frantically drives off with Krazy-8's and Emilio's bodies rolling around in the back of the RV. Walter's pants, which he has taken off in order to preserve his 'good' clothes while he cooks, fly off the RV and into the air. We then return to the opening of the episode with Walter now turning the gun on himself, preparing to commit suicide before being apprehended by the approaching police whom, he believes, are coming for them. Instead, fire engines pass him by, hurrying to put out a fire started by their activities at the RV's original location. Later that night, Walter returns home and has what we are led to believe is unusually passionate sex with his wife (Skyler: "Walt, is that you?"), at which point the pilot episode ends.

The second episode, "The Cat's in the Bag . . ." (1/27/08), is more comedic in tone than the pilot, centering on sometimes gruesome, black humor as Walter and Jesse attempt to "clean up the mess" they have created in the pilot. But in both episodes much ground is covered through short scenes and a continually forward-moving series of events. "The Cat's in the Bag . . ." chronicles a succession of mishaps as Walter and Jesse attempt to dispose of Emilio's body and kill the badly wounded but still alive Krazy-8. Through the flip of a coin, Jesse is charged with dissolving Emilio's body in acid while Walter becomes responsible for killing Krazy-8 whom, in the meantime, they have shackled to a column in Jesse's basement with a rigid, motorcycle U-lock around his neck, rendering him immobile. Walter, however, cannot bring himself to murder Krazy-8. Instead, he provides the shackled Krazy-8 with water, a bologna and cheese sandwich, a waste bucket, toilet paper, and hand sanitizer, as if preparing him for a prolonged stay. Walter's inability to act heightens the suspense as we wait for the inevitable encounter between him and Krazy-8.

The pace and tone of the third episode, ". . . And the Bag's in the River," vary from the initial two. It is slower and more contemplative, including a flashback to Walter's past. Character development and character interaction play a more prominent role, and do so in an especially noteworthy manner between Walter and Krazy-8. The first time we see the two together in ". . . And the Bag's in the River," Krazy-8 insists that Walter look at him, complaining that the lock around his neck is degrading. Walter apologizes, indicating his susceptibility to feeling guilty for the inhumane way he is treating Krazy-8. Krazy-8 then exerts additional emotional pressure by challenging Walter to either kill him or let him go. Krazy-8 has sized Walter up, telling him that he isn't suited for "this line of work"—the drug business. Again increasing the pressure and playing to Walter's vulnerabilities, Krazy-8 emphasizes that Walter's choices are either to let him go or to commit cold-blooded murder. In their initial to-and-fro, Krazy-8 extends a challenge to Walter, based on the guilt and fear the prisoner has accurately identified as his captor's emotional 'weaknesses.'

For his part, Walter has just learned that Krazy-8 knows who he is and where to find him if released. Walter attempts to make his decision on whether to commit cold-blooded murder through rational means, in a situation and over a choice that is wholly unreasonable within the terms of Walter's existence heretofore. Nonetheless, he draws up a pro and con list over whether to kill Krazy-8 but finds that next to six 'cons' he can only come up with one 'pro:' "He'll kill your entire family if you let him go."[2] As the subsequent sequence between them makes clear, Walter must act by making a decision based on emotions—his 'gut' feelings—with which he is not particularly comfortable or adept at, rather than relying on his accustomed, 'calm,' 'scientific,' powers of reasoning. Thus begins an intricate emotional encounter between the two, in which they each attempt to gauge the other's feelings and influence the other's emotions over life and death stakes.

Walter again makes Krazy-8 a bologna and cheese sandwich, this time cutting off the bread crusts, having previously noticed that Krazy-8 does not like them. This seems an odd gesture of thoughtfulness in view of the situation facing the two men, but one that Walter strategically hopes will help 'seduce' Krazy-8 to engage with him. Walter places the sandwich on a yellow Fiestaware plate and heads down to the basement. Before he reaches Krazy-8, Walter suffers another coughing fit and passes out.[3] When he comes to, Krazy-8 informs him that he has been unconscious for ten to fifteen minutes. Then, in a startling admission given the context, in which Walter must decide whether to kill Krazy-8 or not while Krazy-8 knows full well this is the decision Walter must make, Walter confides in Krazy-8 that he has lung cancer. The two men share similarity of circumstances, both facing the threat of impending death that creates a certain bond between them. And, as we are beginning to understand, Walter is attempting to entice Krazy-8 to his side in order to escape having to kill him. Here, though, it is the captor who is trying to humanize himself to the prisoner.

Walter returns to the kitchen to make Krazy-8 another sandwich, throwing the pieces of broken plate in the garbage, and returning to the basement. This marks the beginning of a remarkable set-piece, lasting twelve minutes—a full quarter of the episode's running time—establishing an emotional intimacy between the two that belies the reality of the circumstances, and in which Walter's decision whether to kill Krazy-8 becomes a mutual determination.

The two now sit down, taking up more casual, less confrontational bodily positions. Walter rolls a can of beer to Krazy-8 from the six-pack he has brought with him to the basement, then asks Krazy-8 what his given name is: Domingo. Walter next questions Krazy-8 about his background. Instead of answering, Krazy-8 counters that getting to know him will not make it easier for Walter to kill him (nor, narratively, for the audience to witness). Krazy-8's frankness in warning Walter about the dangers of 'personalizing' him serves as a strategic move on Krazy-8's part, singling out his sincerity and capacity for truth telling because he does not immediately jump at the chance of humanizing himself to the clearly uncertain Walter. Rather than opting to establish the familiarity that is in Krazy-8's best interests for survival, he appears to consider the predicament from Walter's position as well. Krazy-8's ability to appreciate Walter's circumstances is critical to the encounter, as we will see. Further, Krazy-8 is being honest in that he is genuinely resentful of the situation, finding himself in a position of emasculating humiliation after having been outsmarted by a neophyte in the drug business, in which he perceives himself as having attained a certain status of prominence and toughness.

In a surprisingly honest—or desperate—countermove, Walter tells Krazy-8 that he is searching for a good reason to not kill him and Krazy-8 should tell him one. Here, Walter admits to what motivates his apparent gestures of kindness. Again, Krazy-8 returns the volley with a mixture of pride and defiance, telling Walter he could promise not to go after him if released, but that doing so is pointless because Walter will never know if he's telling the truth or not. Thus, Krazy-8 initially rejects Walter's efforts to establish a sympathetic connection between the two. He refuses to beg, grovel, or be submissive, even with his life at risk. Krazy-8's courage must strike Walter as admirable, especially in light of his own failure of nerve. Both men have clearly staked out their positions in this encounter that is simultaneously a battle of wills and an intimate exchange.

Concluding that Krazy-8 is not willing to respond to his questions, Walter moves to leave the basement, spurring Krazy-8 to begin talking about himself, his educational background, his family. Krazy-8's father owns a furniture store with which Walter is familiar. He explains that he knows who Krazy-8's father is from the store's TV commercials. His prisoner's concession in responding to Walter provides the latter with a sense of victory, a moment in which Walter has exerted his power over the physically constrained and trapped Krazy-8. Effectively using the asymmetrical power relations between them, at this point Walter has prevailed.

Walter builds commonality on the basis of Krazy-8's divulgences, telling his captive that he bought his son's crib at the family's furniture store, infusing a current of innocence into what, at its core, is a vicious encounter. His anecdote connects the two through their parallel relations as father or son, in a conversation in which the theme of family is woven throughout. Walter hands Krazy-8 another can of beer and the two sit in what appears to be or, at any rate, mimics comfortable familiarity. Walter is trying to prove that he is not a threat, even as he threatens Krazy-8, in order to convince Krazy-8 to view Walter in similar terms.

Krazy-8's next comment signals a pivotal turning point in their emotional engagement, his apparent acceptance of Walter's desired arrangement. Krazy-8 asks Walter if Jesse or Walter's family know he has cancer. Walter acknowledges that Krazy-8 is the only person in whom he has confided because it's not a conversation he is ready to have with his family. This is a crucial moment in their encounter because it signals that Krazy-8 understands Walter and what he is going through. He recognizes what Walter is experiencing emotionally and how important his admission of illness has been. This is a moment in which Krazy-8 extends awareness and empathy by acknowledging what Walter is unable to speak, an act of recognition that does much to constitute the scene's strange tone of intimacy. Krazy-8 further affirms his empathic understanding by recognizing that Walter is cooking meth in order to take care of his family after his death. Krazy-8 thus validates that which Walter most wants acknowledged or, perhaps, to himself believe: that his illegal activities, up to and including murder, are undertaken out of his deep love for and commitment to his family and that, therefore, his actions are justified and his motives acceptable in terms of this perceived greater good. It is at this point that Walter decides not to kill Krazy-8. More accurately, the two reach the decision together. Walter returns to the kitchen to retrieve the key for the U-lock so that he can let Krazy-8 go. His eye is drawn to the pieces of broken plate in the garbage. He hastily begins reassembling the pieces, discovering that a large shard is missing. Krazy-8 had managed to reach it and conceal it while Walter was passed out.

Walter returns to the basement and grips the U-lock. But instead of unlocking it, he pulls it as tightly as he can against the concrete column, choking Krazy-8 to death. This is a prolonged act that requires his full strength, as Krazy-8 desperately tries to resist. Walter has fulfilled the act of "cold-blooded murder" that Krazy-8 predicted.

For Walter, their interaction has been about desperation: he has asked Krazy-8, almost pleaded with him, for another way out. But, for Walter, the encounter has also been about trust. He must come to believe, or be convinced, that he can trust Krazy-8, as unreasonable a proposition as that may sound. On Krazy-8's part, also acting out of desperation to save his own life, he must convey honesty and sincerity in order to assure Walter that he is neither lying to nor manipulating his warder. This is why his frankness and defiance in refusing to promise he will not go after Walter is effective.

However, all of these emotional transactions, negotiated and exchanged, are undermined by the piece of broken shard in Krazy-8's pocket. The fragment of broken plate becomes the marker of his broken word, extinguishing Walter's unreasonable but heartfelt desire to trust Krazy-8. Ultimately, it is the breaking of trust—not the threat to Walter or his family—that, in contrast to his previous days of lethargy and procrastination, imbues him with the angry energy required to kill Krazy-8.

The set piece between Walter and Krazy-8 is action as transaction, constructed from moves and counter-moves: a strategic maneuver deployed, its effects sized-up, a corresponding response awaited, then delivered. Theirs is an ongoing series of thrusts and parries, all in terms of emotional, not physical, action. Their engagement takes shape as a negotiation, an exchange that moves forward, building to an inevitable but not initially predetermined outcome. This is the freedom or agency described by Foucault in the ability to either exert or resist power in ongoing transactions of social mobility.

And ultimately, it is Walter's encounter with Krazy-8 that enables him to go home and entrust his wife with the news of his illness—if not of his drug-related, violent activities. The man Walter kills is the first person in whom he confides, making it possible to admit his own impending mortality to others, to his wife, and perhaps to himself. Although Walter's and Krazy-8's relations end in a brutal act of murder, the impact of their startling sequence together rests not solely in that final event but in the process taken to arrive at that point and in the unveiling of Walter's motivations as he comes to believe that he must commit such an act. Their encounter stands as emblematic of the development of Walter's character over the entire course of *Breaking Bad*, in which suspense and fascination are engendered by Walter's process of determining what actions to take and the feelings, more than the reasons, he uses to justify his choices. The impact of the series does not derive solely from the audaciousness of Walter's actions but, also, through the emotional process by which he comes to believe he must commit those acts and how he justifies them to himself and others. The physical action of the series' opening two episodes serves to establish the emotional payoff of "... And the Bag's in the River," located in the drama, strategy, desperation and, ultimately, poignancy of the lengthy encounter between Walter and Krazy-8 that, in turn, renders the finale to their time together all the more ruthless.

RELATIONS OF POWER

The relationship between Walter and Krazy-8 in the third episode is based on a disequilibrium or asymmetry of power, in Foucault's terms, because Krazy-8 is held captive in the basement while Walter is charged with ending his life. In contrast, Walter's relationship with his wife, Skyler, over the course of his increasing involvement in drugs and her increasing awareness of his involvement, more closely resembles the way Foucault defines relations of power in purer form.

For instance, Walter's dealings with Gus Fring (Giancarlo Esposito) are dominantly situated within the framework of coercive power through Gus' very overt threats of violence or death to Walter's person or to members of his family. In turn, these threats demand the response of similar acts of coercive power: physical actions such as executing Gale (David Costabile), Walter's former lab assistant and, ultimately, killing Gus (although it is worth noting that in both instances Walter finds someone else to commit the actual act of murder).

In contrast, relations of power based in emotional strategies dominate Walter's relationship with Jesse. The two draw the line at engaging in coercive power—acts of physical harm beyond the fist fights they have with each other—nor will they allow others to do so, on occasion each having committed murder to rescue or protect his partner. However, emotional strategies of power between the two are fair game and, to Walter's mind, do not have to be played fairly.[4]

None of this is to suggest that emotions are absent from coercive acts of power. Between Walter and Gus pride, anger, frustration, and the desire to prove oneself superior all figure as motivations in their engagement. And certainly, coercive power enacted through physical deeds clearly is possible in domestic relations, for instance, through physical abuse, economic deprivation, and so on. In the case of Walter and Skyler, however, these do not predominate. Instead, acts between them principally are committed for their emotional value and impact.

At the beginning of season three, having realized that her husband is involved in illegal activities, Skyler demands that Walter move out of the family home and starts divorce proceedings. Skyler threatens to turn Walter into the authorities if he does not stay away from the house and their two children, whom she believes Walter has placed at risk as a result of his involvement in the drug business. Skyler's leverage, then, is constituted in her ability to give Walter up to legal forces which, if put into effect, would comprise a coercive act. Simultaneously, however, she repeatedly refuses to explain to her teenage son, Walter Jr. (R.J. Mitte), or to her sister Marie (Betsy Brandt) and brother-in-law Hank, "what Walter did," despite their frequent demands or requests to know.

Skyler's refusal to allow Walter to see his own children seems especially harsh and punitive to Walter Jr., Marie, and Hank. However, she cannot explain the situation to Marie or Hank, the DEA agent, because doing so, in fact, would be to turn Walter in. Further, as Skyler explains to her lawyer, she does not want her son to find out that the father he so admires is a criminal. As a result, she bears the opprobrium for the marital separation and Walter's estrangement from his children, the negative perceptions of which she does nothing to refute or clarify to others. The blame she incurs from her teenage son is particularly cruel; he either rails at her with fierce anger, for example, calling her a "bitch," or ignores her, refusing to speak to her or otherwise interact.

For his part, Walter denies the gravity of the situation, insisting their separation is temporary. He believes Skyler will alter her stance once he has explained to her that everything he has done has been unselfish because he has acted in what he believes is the best interests of the family. Referring to the great sacrifices he made for the family, Walter fails to listen to Skyler or respect her wishes. Perhaps most disconcertingly, he allows—even encourages—his son and other family members to believe the marital separation and his banishment from the children are the result of Skyler's inexplicable, unreasonable impulsiveness. He does so, in part, because Walter cannot bear to be perceived as a bad guy and so permits that characterization to fall to Skyler. Additionally, he believes he can use her apparent status as guilty party in order to exert more emotional pressure on Skyler to relent, due to the pain her son's anger is causing her.

While Skyler takes responsibility for what is not her doing in order to protect others, Walter refuses to be held responsible for that which he is indeed culpable. Further, as Skyler continues to spurn his attempts at reconciliation or to accept the justifications he makes for his actions, Walter grows increasingly frustrated and angry. His lawyer, Saul (Bob Odenkirk), assures Walter that Skyler will not make good on her threat to give him up to the authorities due to the ensuing repercussions. These include professional embarrassment and potential job loss for her DEA brother-in-law, trauma to her children because their father is a drug dealer and their mother turned him in to the police, and the risk of having her home confiscated as the proceeds of drug sales. Following this conversation, Walter unilaterally moves back in by breaking into the house in order to circumvent the locks Skyler has had changed.

When Skyler returns home, she finds Walter there refusing to leave and, thereby, forcing his presence upon her:

> Walter: It's my house too, Skyler. I'm staying. End of story.

Instead of departing as she repeatedly demands, he openly challenges her to turn him in. Skyler does call the police but, perhaps for all the reasons Saul has outlined, cannot bring herself to provide them with the full story. She tells the police only that Walter is there "against my will." When the officer explains they need legal grounds to remove him and pointedly asks Skyler if Walter has broken any laws, we see her struggle over whether to speak. At this moment, the other officer asks Walter Jr. his impression of events.

> Walter Jr.: It's my mom's fault. She won't even say what my dad did. . . . I don't know why she's being this way. My dad, he is a great guy.

Rather than react to the unfair accusations being made against her, Skyler is silenced by the feelings her son has for his father. She cannot bring herself to disillusion him. This marks the moment of Skyler's defeat and Walter's victory over her.[5] The threat to surrender Walter to the authorities has been Skyler's only power over him. Her inability to make good on Walter's dare has undermined what little power she has within the family. Power now reverts to Walter. Skyler becomes his emotional captive, just as Krazy-8 previously was his physical prisoner, as Walter forcibly reclaims what he perceives as his rightful place in the home and with the family.

This complex series of events, occurring in the first three episodes of season three ("No Mas," 3/21/10; "Caballo Sin Nombre," 3/28/10; and "I. F. T.," 4/4/10), serve to narratively position the couple in emotional terms. Their relationship plays out in the form of increasingly escalating emotional maneuvers between the two characters, fought over the meaning of marriage and what each partner owes or does not owe the other.

Following Skyler's failed appeal to the police, she feels trapped in her own home, miserable and deeply resentful of the constraints imposed upon her by her husband. She spends most of the time locked in her bedroom with her infant daughter, Holly, while Walter continues 'playing house,' by performing a simulation of happy family, established primarily through the domestic tasks of cooking and child care. Dressed for work in the morning, Skyler waits until she hears a door shut elsewhere in the house, hoping to sneak out of the bedroom without having to encounter Walter. Instead, when she unlocks the bedroom door, she finds an open bag of money waiting for her on the hallway floor: Walter's black duffel containing half a million dollars. Walter itemizes the expenses for which the money is intended after his death (college tuition, health insurance, groceries, gas, the mortgage). When Skyler attempts to respond, he cuts her off, refusing to let her speak. Instead, he continues by explaining that he didn't steal the money; rather, he *earned* it. Walter explains that he must live with the guilt of what he did to earn the money. But, he insists, all that will have been for nothing if Skyler refuses to accept the money he has earned.

Walter's persistence that Skyler accept the money derives from several motivations. First, it would make him feel better, providing him with some measure of absolution for the bad things he did to earn it. Additionally, her acceptance of the money would draw her into his illegal activities, also making her guilty because she is aware of the money's origins. In effect, her acquiescence would render her 'moll' to his illegal ventures. But most relevant for this discussion, he stakes his claim for her to accept the money on the basis of an economic argument, located in his role as primary breadwinner for the family. For this reason, he earmarks the money for family expenses, for mortgage, groceries, health insurance, and the children's college tuition. Similarly, this accounts for why he repeatedly emphasizes that he has *earned* the money.

Walter's belief that he is fulfilling—even excelling at—his marital and familial role as economic provider constitutes his side of the story, which he earlier chastises Skyler that she has not yet heard. Indeed, he is convinced that his motivation is so reasonable, so evidently laudable, he fully expects she too will be won over by the dutiful selflessness he has exhibited for the sake of the family. At a certain level, Walter does not believe—cannot imagine—Skyler will fail to see events in his terms: not only acceptable but admirable because he carries out his role as husband and father, understood primarily as breadwinner. Yet clearly, Skyler does not accede to the situation within the framework Walter has established.

We may conjecture that she opposes Walter because he has acted in ways that affect the entire family without having consulted her and, as such, unilaterally has altered the family's fundamental operations, practices, beliefs, and values. We can suppose that she does not approve of Walter's drug involvement on moral grounds, as well as because they are illegal. And certainly we can surmise that Skyler is in conflict with Walter's choices because they endanger not solely himself but the entire family, for example, as Gus' threats of physical harm or Saul's explanation of the economic risk make evident.

Ultimately, Skyler manages to recoup some power later in the episode "I. F. T.," if only temporarily. The turning point occurs when, at work, she resolves to have sex with her boss, Ted (Christopher Cousins). Approaching Ted in the photocopy room, she kisses him, then asks the divorced Ted if his children are at home with him. This scene then immediately cuts to Skyler returning home later that night. None of the sexual encounter between Skyler and Ted is shown. For, the point of her 'extramarital' affair, in a situation in which the couple disputes whether their marriage remains intact or not, does not rest with the act of having sex with Ted. Therefore, their sexual encounter is treated in a narratively expedient manner, implied not visualized. Rather, the significance of the event resides in the emotional impact it has on Walter when Skyler tells him. The motivation for and importance of Skyler's affair with her boss lies not in the physical action but in her ability to *affect* her husband.

Thus, she returns home that evening to find Walter reveling in his domesticity, cooking a family dinner for the waiting Walter Jr. and his friend Louis (Caleb Jones). Wearing an apron, Walter calls Skyler into the kitchen where, while preparing a salad, he pretends family normality as he asks Skyler how her day was and chatters away about inviting Walter Jr.'s friend to stay for dinner. He also tells her that he feels better about their talk that morning—although she was not given the opportunity to speak—concerning the drug money and his motivations for earning it.

Skyler remains silent, simply staring at Walter from the doorway as he cheerily prattles away until, finally, she approaches him, picks up the finished salad, looks him directly in the eye, and utters a mere three words: "I fucked Ted," the I. F. T. of the episode's title. Now their positions are reversed as Skyler takes the salad into the dining room and calls the two teenagers in to dinner, her turn to chat in a normal family manner while Walter remains stunned and speechless in the kitchen, leaving him as the spouse who feels alienated in his claimed home, as the episode ends.

Skyler's hard-won victory provides her with some measure of feeling she retains control over her own life, however fleeting that sensibility. Walter has prevented Skyler from voicing her own position or has failed to actually listen to her when she does. By having sex with Ted, Skyler has managed to command Walter's attention, making her presence *felt*. Initially, her act of having sex with Ted may seem disconnected from the core of the couple's conflict, concerning Walter's drug-related activities. On further reflection, however, we can see that Skyler also stakes her claim on the rights and responsibilities involved in marriage and family.

Walter conceives of Skyler's objections as existing *only* in the means he has taken to reach his end goal—providing financially for the family. He cannot comprehend that she could object to the end he has achieved. For this reason, Walter remains firmly convinced that his wife will accept his behavior once she has heard his viewpoint, constituting *why* he has done what he has done. Yet Walter's end goal, in addition to his means, is precisely that to which Skyler takes exception. For, the couple contest different meanings of what it is to 'protect' or 'take care' of the family; indeed, of what 'loving' one's family means. Walter situates his role in taking care of the family in financial terms. In contrast, Skyler prioritizes guaranteeing the family's safely from physical harm and, in addition, from emotional harm or pain, as events involving her son make clear.

On the one hand, Walter's and Skyler's characters are intended to represent role-reversal or gender neutrality, exemplified by his participation and delight in domestic tasks and her strength and independence as woman, wife, and mother. On the other hand, to the degree that Walter asserts his economic role as breadwinner while Skyler fights for the physical and emotional safety of her family from her position as nurturing mother, the two take up traditional gender stances.

Skyler and Walter are arguing their divergent views of 'marriage' and 'family,' given that Skyler's sexual act addresses expectations between the couple—from Walter's perspective regarding marital sexual fidelity. Her action is not intended simply to grab his attention but is intimately connected to the contestation they are engaged in over the emotional values and ethical meanings of marriage and family. Walter pauses in his headlong rush to justify his actions to Skyler only once he believes she has betrayed him, in terms of the rules and expectations of their marriage.

Yet, from Skyler's perspective, Walter as spousal partner has betrayed her by failing to listen to her "side" of the story, in refusing to consult her over drastic changes in the way the family operates, by taking unilateral actions that affect the entire family and, perhaps most of all, in failing to preserve the family from physical danger or emotional harm. Skyler, then, attempts to convey the marital betrayal she feels through an act she recognizes Walter will perceive as the breaking of a marital trust. The emotions negotiated and exchanged between Walter and Skyler are effective precisely to the degree that they link closely to the meanings of marriage and family because, in light of recent changes to the ways they have previously functioned as spousal partners and as a familial unit, the meanings and feelings each holds now differ sharply. At stake are their expectations, rights, and responsibilities as spouses, contested over their divergent meanings of marriage and family, and enacted through their respective emotional feelings and expressions, that is to say, performed via their affective positions. *Breaking Bad*, then, recognizes and frames marriage as an emotional institution as well as an economic and legal one.

Skyler's sexual act has proven effective—and dramatic from the audience's perspective—because she has rightly gauged Walter's emotional response. He receives her sexual 'infidelity' as an act that destroys the sanctity of their marriage, even as he fails completely to see that his own actions have undermined the trust between the marital partners, from Skyler's point of view. Although Walter proves incapable of grasping the points that Skyler strives to express, arguably the audience does.

In order for her sexual act to prove effective, Skyler must recognize and operate upon the basis of Walter's system of values that, in turn, determines his emotional susceptibilities. Her familiarity with and correct assessment of his emotional makeup enables her to act on that which resonates for Walter in feeling terms. Indeed, the entire storyline of their relationship is dependent upon their mutual capacity to recognize and act upon the other's emotions, although usually in the negative sense of making the other 'feel bad.' The most significant point here, however, is that theirs are not 'private' or merely personal sets of feeling but, rather, a high stakes struggle, involving repeated acts of emotional contestation, to determine who holds power in the family and over the family.

FEELING BAD

The narrative line of Walter's and Skyler's relationship follows a complex and exponentially expanding range of characters' feelings, of emotional expressions and actions in response to the other's feelings, of attempts to make his or her counterpart feel certain ways, and of blaming the other for the way one feels. Such emotional action is not limited to Walter's and Skyler's relationship but permeates the series. Arguably, it is not solely Walter's physical actions (although certainly these too) that render the series such compelling drama. Equally, *Breaking Bad's* heightened sense of excitement and suspense are created by the rationalizations and motivations for Walter's actions, the basis upon which he decides it is necessary, or even his right, to commit the actions he undertakes.

It may well be that relations of power conducted through emotional strategy are more visible in instances of characters 'feeling bad' and, reciprocally, working to make other characters feel bad. However, emotions that we may perceive as more positive—cases of 'feeling good—also involve relations of power. For example, in Foucault's list of social circumstances in which relations of power are present, he includes "amorous" as well as "institutional" and "economic" relationships. To love another or to be loved involves ongoing emotional transactions, working to 'make' another feel certain ways.

Such efforts expended to 'make' others feel in specific ways are intended to *affect* others. As I argued at the beginning of this chapter, working to 'affect' others may be a more useful way of understanding the productivity of power relations in contrast to Foucault's vocabulary of attempting to "control" the conduct of others, precisely because so many ongoing, mundane acts of sociality are not accomplished through coercion but through emotionality. For social relations to exist, emotions must be transmitted and received, whether they are accepted, rejected, or amended. Such emotional negotiation and exchange produces the constant play of and modification in power relations.

In this reading of *Breaking Bad*, I have rather artificially distinguished between emotional action and physical action, although they are interconnected narrative processes, normally operating in tandem. I have made this distinction in order to examine the centrality of the representation of emotions to narrativity as a whole. Substantial value exists in bringing a more developed understanding of the functions of emotions into the critical analysis of narrative, from which they largely have been absent. Considering narratives within the framework of both emotional and physical action opens them up to new interpretations. The more typical approach of psychological readings based on characters' motivations and feelings tend to locate emotions as, and limit them to, internalized experience.

In contrast, thinking in terms of emotional action works to externalize characters' emotional feelings, expressions, and behaviors, rendering them eminently social. Through the intimate interaction of emotions, meaning, and power, ongoing social transactions of negotiation and exchange occur at all levels of the social spectrum, from the most routine to the grandest. Finally, I began with Foucault's anecdote about age and intimidation not because of something he explicitly states but, rather, due to that which he leaves out: the vital role of emotions in relations of power, that is, in all human relations.

NOTES

1. For example, see D'Acci (1994) on the television series, *Cagney and Lacey*, which I discuss in Pribram, 2011, 12-16.

2. Walter's reasons on the "Let Him Live" side of the page include: "It's the moral thing to do"; "Won't be able to live with yourself"; and "Murder is wrong!"

3. The fact that both Walter and Krazy-8 cough continuously serves as another link between them.

4. This indicates that emotional strategies come equipped with their own rules and procedures regarding what are acceptable versus abusive means to an end. Thus, when Walter poisons Brock (Ian Posada), the young son of Jesse's girlfriend, in order to get Jesse to agree with him on a certain course of action, Walter is understood to have gone too far. Yet, for most of the series Walter draws the line at directly endangering Jesse's life by, for instance, poisoning him in order to coerce agreement.

5. Skyler explains to her lawyer, the only person she ever confides in, that instead of having her family pay all the material and emotional repercussions for Walter's illegal activities, her plan is to wait until her husband's lung cancer 'resolves' the situation for them.

WORKS CITED

D'Acci, Julie. *Defining Women: Television and the Case of Cagney and Lacey.* Chapel Hill: University of North Carolina, 1994.

Foucault, Michel. "The Ethics of the Concern for Self as a Practice of Freedom." In *Ethics: Subjectivity and Truth, Volume One,* edited by Paul Rabinow, translated by Robert Hurley. 281-301. New York: New Press, 1987.

Pribram, E. Deidre. *Emotions, Genre, Justice in Film and Television: Detecting Feeling.* New York: Routledge, 2011.

Breaking Bad: Main Cast, Production History, and Episode Guide

Main Cast	Production History
Walter White - Bryan Cranston	Original broadcast channel - AMC Network
Skyler White - Anna Gunn	Original run - January 20, 2008 - September 29, 2013
Jesse Pinkman - Aaron Paul	Series creator - Vince Gilligan
Walter White, Jr. - R.J. Mitte	Executive producers - Vince Gilligan, Mark Johnson, Michelle MacLaren
Hank Schrader - Dean Norris	Producer - Various Producers
Marie Schrader - Betsy Brandt	Cinematographers - Michael Slovis, Reynaldo Villalobos, Peter Reiners, Nelson Cragg
Saul Goodman - Bob Odenkirk	Editors - Kelley Dixon, Skip MacDonald, Lynne Willingham
Mike Ehrmantraut - Jonathan Banks	Series original music - Dave Porter
Gustavo Fring - Giancarlo Esposito	
Steven Gomez - Steven Michael Quezada	

Season One

Episode 1: Pilot
Writer - Vince Gilligan
Director - Vince Gilligan
Krazy-8 - Max Arciniega
Emilio - John Koyama

Episode 2: "Cat's in the Bag . . ."
Writer - Vince Gilligan
Director - Adam Bernstein
Ben - Jason Byrd
Emilio - John Koyama
Ob-Gyn - Shane Marinson
Backhoe Operator - Anthony Wamego

Episode 3: ". . . And the Bag's in the River
Writer - Vince Gilligan
Director - Adam Bernstein
Krazy-8 - Max Arciniega
Emilio - John Koyama

Episode 4: "Cancer Man"
Writer - Vince Gilligan
Director - Adam Bernstein
Mrs. Pinkman - Tess Harper
Mr. Pinkman - Michael Bofshever
Ken Wins - Kyle Bornheimer

Episode 5: "Gray Matter"
Writer - Patty Lin
Director - Tricia Brock
Elliot Schwartz - Adam Godley
Gretchen Schwartz - Jessica Hecht

Episode 6: "Crazy Handful of Nothin"
Writer - George Mastras
Director - Bronwen Hughes
Skinny Pete - Charles Baker
Hugo - Pierre Barrera
Tuco - Raymond Cruz
Mrs. Pope - Vivian Nesbit
Office Manager - Judith Rane
Carmen - Carmen Serano

Episode 7: "A No-Rough-Stuff-Type Deal"
Writer - Peter Gould
Director - Tim Hunter
Tuco - Raymond Cruz
Realtor - Beth Bailey
Gonzo - Cesar Garcia

Season Two

Episode 8: "Seven Thirty-Seven"
Writer - J. Roberts
Director - Bryan Cranston
Tuco - Raymond Cruz
Gonzo - Cesar Garcia
No-Doze - Jesus Payan

Episode 15: "Better Call Saul"
Writer - Peter Gould
Director - Terry McDonough
Jimmy In-'N-Out - Jimmy Daniels
Getz - DJ Qualls
Jane - Krysten Ritter

Episode 9: "Grilled"

Writer - George Mastras

Director - Charles Haid

Tuco - Raymond Cruz

Sgt. Tim Roberts - Nigel Gibbs

Mrs. Pinkman - Tess Harper

Episode 10: "Bit by a Dead Bee"

Writer - Peter Gould

Director - Terry McDonough

Dr. Chavez - Harry Groener

Dr. Delcavoli - David House

Badger - Matt L. Jones

Episode 11: "Down"

Writer - Sam Catlin

Director - John Dahl

Mr. Pinkman - Michael Bofshever

Mr. Gardiner - Dan Desmond

Mrs. Pinkman - Tess Harper

Louis - Caleb Jones

Episode 12: "Breakage"

Writer - Moira Walley-Beckett

Director - Johan Renck

Skinny Pete - Charles Baker

Jane - Krysten Ritter

Episode 13: "Peekaboo"

Writer - J. Roberts and Vince Gilligan

Director - Peter Medak

Skinny Pete - Charles Baker

Spooge's Woman - Dale Dickey

Spooge - David Ury

Gretchen Schwartz - Jessica Hecht

Episode 16: "4 Days Out"

Writer - Sam Catlin

Director - Terry McDonough

Dr. Delcavoli - David House

Jane - Krysten Ritter

Clovis - Tom Kiesche

Episode 17: "Over"

Writer - Moira Walley-Beckett

Director - Phil Abraham

Ted Beneke - Christopher Cousins

Jane - Krysten Ritter

Carmen - Carmen Serano

Episode 18: "Mandala"

Writer - George Mastras

Director - Adam Bernstein

Skinny Pete - Charles Baker

Ted Beneke - Christopher Cousins

Donald Margolis - John De Lancie

Jane - Krysten Ritter

Episode 19: "Phoenix"

Writer - John Shiban

Director - Colin Bucksey

Ted Beneke - Christopher Cousins

Donald Margolis - John De Lancie

Episode 20: "ABQ"

Writer - Vince Gilligan

Director - Adam Bernstein

Donald Margolis - John De Lancie

Dr. Delcavoli - David House

Dr. Victor Bravenek - Sam McMurray

Jane - Krysten Ritter

Episode 14: "Negro Y Azul"

Writer - John Shiban

Director - Felix Alcala

Ted Beneke - Christopher Cousins

Badger - Matt L. Jones

Jane - Krysten Ritter

Dr. Victor Bravenek - Sam McMurray

Combo - Rodney Rush

Season Three

Episode 21: "No Mas"

Writer - Vince Gilligan

Director - Bryan Cranston

Group Leader - Jere Burns

Donald Margolis - John De Lancie

Pamela - Julie Dretzen

Episode 22: "Caballo Sin Nombre"

Writer - Peter Gould

Director - Adam Bernstein

Victor - Jeremiah Bitsui

Mr. Pinkman - Michael Bofshever

Mrs. Pinkman - Tess Harper

Episode 23: "I.F.T."

Writer - George Mastras

Director - Michelle MacLaren

Ted Beneke - Christopher Cousins

Pamela - Julie Dretzen

Juan Bolsa - Javier Grajeda

Louis - Caleb Jones

Episode 24: "Green Light"

Writer - Sam Catlin

Director - Scott Winant

Victor - Jeremiah Bitsui

Episode 27: "One Minute"

Writer - Thomas Schnauz

Director - Michelle MacLaren

Gale - David Costabile

Tio - Mark Margolis

The Cousin 2 - Daniel Moncada

The Cousin 1 - Luis Moncada

Trucker - Nate Mooney

Episode 28: "I See You"

Writer - Gennifer Hutchinson

Director - Colin Bucksey

Skinny Pete - Charles Baker

Victor - Jeremiah Bitsui

Gale - David Constabile

Juan Bolsa - Javier Grajeda

The Cousin 2 - Daniel Moncada

Episode 29 - "Kafkaesque"

Writer - Peter Gould and George Mastras

Director - Michael Slovis

Skinny Pete - Charles Baker

Group Leader - Jere Burns

Ted Beneke - Christopher Cousins

Badger - Matt L. Jones

Ted Beneke - Christopher Cousins

Cashier Girl - Jolene Purdy

Carmen - Carmen Serano

Episode 25: "Mas"

Writer - Moira Walley-Beckett

Director - Johan Renck

Skinny Pete - Charles Baker

Ted Beneke - Christopher Cousins

Pamela - Julie Dretzen

Janice - Mary Sue Ellen

Mrs. Ortega - Carole Gutierrez

Episode 26: "Sunset"

Writer - John Shiban

Director - John Shiban

Deputy Kee - Jose Avila

Skinny Pete - Charles Baker

Gale - David Costabile

Old Joe - Larry Hankin

Clovis - Tom Kiesche

Episode 30: "Fly"

Writer - Sam Catlin and Moira Walley-Beckett

Director - Rian Johnson

Episode 31: "Abiquiu"

Writer - Thomas Schnauz and John Shiban

Director - Michelle MacLaren

Skinny Pete - Charles Baker

Group Leader - Jere Burns

Badger - Matt L. Jones

Tomas - Angelo Martinez

Jane - Krysten Ritter

Episode 32: "Half Measures"

Writer - Sam Catlin and Peter Gould

Director - Adam Bernstein

Victor - Jeremiah Bitsui

Rival Dealer 1 - Antonio Leyba

Tomas - Angelo Martinez

Brock - Ian Posada

Episode 33: "Full Measure"

Writer - Vince Gilligan

Director - Vince Gilligan

Granddaughter - Kaija Bales

Chinese Secretary - Tiley Chao

Gale - David Costabile

Season Four

Episode 34: "Box Cutter"

Writer - Vince Gilligan

Director - Adam Bernstein

Victor - Jeremiah Bitsui

Gale - David Costabile

Episode 40: "Problem Dog"

Writer - Peter Gould

Director - Peter Gould

Jere - Jere Burns

Gaff - Maurice Compte

Huell - Lavell Crawford

Locksmith - John Lawler

Episode 35: "Thirty-Eight Snub"

Writer - George Mastras

Director - Michelle MacLaren

Lawson - Jim Beaver

Skinny Pete - Charles Baker

Tyrus Kitt - Ray Campbell

Andrea - Emily Rios

Episode 36: "Open House"

Writer - Sam Catlin

Director - David Slade

First Realtor - Ralph Alderman

Hard Hat Guy - Bill Burr

Tyrus Kitt - Ray Campbell

Huell - Lavell Crawford

Tim Roberts - Nigel Grubbs

Second Realtor - Jennifer Hasty

Episode 37: "Bullet Points"

Writer - Moria Walley-Beckett

Director - Colin Bucksey

Interested Dude - Frank Andrade

Tyrus Kitt - Ray Campbell

Gale - David Costabile

Sketchy - Jeremy Howard

Speaker - Paul Neis

Episode 38: "Shotgun"

Writer - Tom Schnauz

Director - Michelle MacLaren

Tyrus Kitt - Ray Campbell

Episode 41: "Hermanos"

Writer - Sam Catlin and George Mastras

Director - Johan Renck

Don Eladio - Steven Bauer

Huell - Lavell Crawford

Tim Roberts - Nigel Gibbs

Juan Bolsa - Javier Grajeda

Episode 42: "Bug"

Writer - Moira Walley-Beckett and Tom Schnauz

Director - Terry McDonough

CID Special Agent - Rob Brownstein

Tyrus Kitt - Ray Campbell

Ted Beneke - Christopher Cousins

Episode 43: "Salud"

Writer - Gennifer Hutchinson and Peter Gould

Tyrus Kitt - Ray Campbell

Gaff - Maurice Compte

Ted Beneke - Christopher Cousins

Francesca - Tina Parker

Lead Chemist - Carlo Rota

Episode 44: "Crawl Space"

Writer - Sam Catlin and George Mastras

Director - Scott Winant

Doctor - JB Blanc

Kuby - Bill Burr

Tyrus Kitt - Ray Campbell

Ted Beneke - Christopher Cousins

Episode 45: "End Times"

Writer - Tom Schnauz and Moira Walley-Beckett

Mortgage Realtor - Rutherford Cravens

Tim Roberts - Nigel Gibbs

Pollos Manager - Ashley Kajiki

Episode 39: "Cornered"

Writer - Gennifer Hutchinson

Director - Michael Slovis

Tucker - Berris Blake

Tyrus Kitt - Ray Campbell

Gaff - Maurice Compte

Scary Skell - Damon Herriman

Henchman - Luis Pimber

Bogdan - Maruis Stan

Director - Vince Gilligan

DEA Agent - Matt Berlin

Tyrus Kitt - Ray Campbell

Huell - Lavell Crawford

Brock - Ian Posada

Episode 46: "Face Off"

Writer - Vince Gilligan

Director - Vince Gilligan

DEA Agent - Matt Berlin

Tyrus Kitt - Ray Campbell

Munn - Jason Douglas

Tio - Mark Margolis

Season Five

Episode 47: "Live Free or Die"

Writer - Vince Gilligan

Director - Michael Slovis

Lawson - Jim Beaver

Doctor - JB Blanc

Waitress - Monique Candelaria

Ted Beneke - Christopher Cousins

Old Joe - Larry Hankin

Nurse - Gail Starr

Episode 48: "Madrigal"

Writer - Vince Gilligan

Director - Michelle MacLaren

Kaylee - Kaija Roze Bales

Detective - Brennan Foster

Lydia - Laura Fisher

Corporate Lawyer - Mathias Kaesebier

Chris - Christopher King

Herr Herzog - Wolf Muser

Herr Schuler - Norbert Weisser

Episode 52: "Buyout"

Writer - Gennifer Hutchinson

Director - Colin Bucksey

Kaylee - Kaija Roze Bales

Declan's Driver - Morse Bicknell

DEA Agent - Phil Duran

Declan - Louis Ferreira

Todd - Jesse Plemons

Boy - Samuel Webb

Episode 53: "Say My Name"

Writer - Thomas Schnauz

Director - Thomas Schnauz

Kaylee - Kaija Roze Bales

Declan's Driver - Morse Bicknell

Dorothy Yobs - Kathleen Brady

Declan - Louis Ferreira

Dan Wachsberger - Chris Freihofer

Agent - Philip Hart

Todd - Jesse Plemons

Episode 49: "Hazard Pay"

Writer - Peter Gould

Director - Adam Bernstein

Skinny Pete - Charles Baker

Dennis - Mike Batayeh

Huell - Lavall Crawford

Defense Attorney - Chris Freihofer

Sandor - Joshua Gomez

Fernado - Miguel Martinez

Episode 50: "Fifty-One"

Writer - Sam Catlin

Director - Rian Johnson

Mechanic - John Ashton

Ron - Russ Dillen

Lydia - Laura Fisher

Lydia's Secretary - Melissa McCurley

SAC Ramey - Todd Terry

Episode 51: "Dead Freight"

Writer - George Mastras

Director - George Mastras

Good Samaritan - Ryan Begay

Kuby - Bill Burr

Janice - Mary Sue Evans

Lydia - Laura Fisher

Sandor - Joshua Gomez

Todd - Jesse Plemons

Boy - Samuel Webb

Episode 54: "Gliding Over All"

Writer - Moira Walley-Beckett

Director - Michelle MacLaren

Dennis - Mike Batayeh

Jack - Michael Bowen

Ron - Russ Dillen

Lydia - Laura Fraser

Dan Wachsberger - Chris Freihofer

Kenny - Kevin Rankin

NOTE

The information on the series' production history, its main cast, and episodes is derived from AMC Network's website for the *Breaking Bad*. Some of the cast information for each episode has been condensed in the episode guide. For more information on the series, please consult AMC Network's website for *Breaking Bad* at http://www.amctv.com/shows/breaking-bad/about. Information was accessed on 7 May 2013.

About the Contributors

ABOUT THE EDITOR

David P. Pierson is associate professor of media studies and chair of the Department of Communication and Media Studies at the University of Southern Maine. His research interests are the aesthetic and discursive dimensions of cable and broadcast network programming, and the relationship between American television and history. He has published book chapters and articles in the *Journal of Communication Inquiry, Journal of Popular Culture* and *Film & History* on *C.S.I.: Crime Scene Investigation, Combat!, Mad Men, Seinfeld,* The Discovery Channel, and Turner Network Television made-for-TV westerns. He has recently published a monograph on the 1960s TV series *The Fugitive*.

ABOUT THE CONTRIBUTORS

Jami L. Anderson is associate professor of philosophy in the Philosophy Department at the University of Michigan-Flint and co-director of The Center for Cognition and Neuroethics. Her early research interests concerned retributivism; lately they have focused on race, gender, and disability studies. She recently co-edited *The Philosophy of Autism*.

Rossend Sanchez-Baro is a PhD candidate at Universitat Pompeu Fabra in Barcelona, Spain. His research interests focus on television authorship, serial narrative and fan cultures. He has written on contemporary television in *Media Commons: In Media Res*.

Pierre Barrette holds a PhD in semiotics. He is professor at Université du Québec à Montréal (École des médias), where he teaches courses in television and film studies. He publishes extensively in the field of semiotics and media analysis. From 2003 to 2008, he participated in the preparation of *Les Cahiers du Gerse*, a scholarly journal in film and communication studies published by the Presses de l'Université du Québec. He was a member of the editorial board of the film journal *24 Images* for 12 years and is now head of the Media and Society section in the online journal *Hors Champ*, in which he has published more than 300 articles about film and television.

Alberto Brodesco earned his PhD in Audiovisual Studies of Cinema, Music, and Communication from the University of Udine. He currently works at the Department of Sociology and Social Research at the University of Trento. He has published a book and a number of papers on the representation of technoscience in film and television. His other research interest relates to the triad of film, body and violence. His bibliography and some open access articles are available at http://unitn.academia.edu/AlbertoBrodesco.

Brian Faucette teaches English and film courses at a community college. He holds a doctorate in Film and Media studies from the University of Kansas. His research focuses on the representation of American masculinities in classical and contemporary American film and television. His publications consist of numerous journal articles and book chapters, including one on alternative masculinities in *Valentino* in *Ken Russell: Re-Viewing Britain's Last Mannerist*.

Dustin Freeley has been lecturer in the English Departments of Hunter College and Berkeley College, where he taught various courses in literature, composition, research writing, critical analysis, speech, and persuasive communication. He is a contributing writer to NextProjection.com and a co-founder, writer, and editor of MoviesAboutGladiators.com. He is also a member of the Online Film Critics Society and has an essay titled "Reflections on Genocide in Stanley Kubrick's *The Shining*" being published in late 2013.

Ensley F. Guffey is a non-traditional graduate student in American history at the University of North Carolina at Greensboro. He has presented papers at regional, national, and international academic conferences on topics ranging from the American industrialist Samuel Colt to the television show *Breaking Bad*, and he has published peer-reviewed scholarly articles on the television shows *Buffy the Vampire Slayer* and *Farscape*. He and his wife, K. Dale Koontz, are currently co-authoring *Wanna Cook? The Unofficial Guide to Breaking Bad*.

Andrew Howe is associate professor of history at La Sierra University, where he teaches courses in American history, popular culture, and film studies. Particular areas of interest include science fiction, cultural views of nature, and the films of Alfred Hitchcock. Recent articles published or accepted for publication include a book chapter on race and racism in *Star Wars* (*Sex, Politics, and Religion in* Star Wars), a book chapter on *Avatar* as a post-9/11 Mohican narrative (*The Post-9/11 Western*), and innovative pedagogical techniques for teaching film clips in history courses

(*International Journal of the Humanities*). He is currently working on a book-length project on how communities react to biological invasions.

Carlo Nardi is associate lecturer at the University of Northampton. He has published numerous journal articles and book chapters. His work has focused on the use of technology from a sensory perspective, authorship in relation to technological change, coercive music practices, the organization of labor in music-making and Indian film music. In 2011, he was elected General Secretary of IASPM, the International Association for the Study of Popular Music.

Yves Picard is professor at Cégep André-Laurendeau in Montreal, Canada. He has been teaching for more than thirty years. Recently, he published a book on *Quebec TV: Quand le petit écran devient grand*. This work is the first draft of his doctoral thesis (Université de Montréal): De la télé-oralité à la télé-visualité (2013). That same year, he co-directed an issue of CiNéMAS, «Fiction télévisuelle: approches esthétiques» and an international colloquium on La télévision des premiers temps.

E. Diedre Pribram is associate professor and chairperson in the Communication Department at Molloy College, New York. She has published numerous journal articles and book chapters examining the way emotions are depicted in film and television, female spectatorship, and screenwriting. Her recent publications include *Emotions, Genre, Justice in Film and Television* and co-editor with Jennifer Harding of *Emotions: A Cultural Studies Reader*.

Index

221